"As in the original edition, Professor Gaillardetz provides a powerful antidote to a Catholic version of dogmatic fundamentalism by addressing the origin, development, and context of the church's formulation of its beliefs and the authority by which it teaches them. After an exploration of the nature of authority itself, he carefully distinguishes the basic gradations of authoritative teaching in the church and the important dynamic of the articulation and reception of that teaching. Inspired by Pope Francis's approach to the exercise and structure of authority in the church, the revised version freshly looks at the role of the *sensus fidei* in a more deliberately synodal church that depends on discernment and dialogue to articulate the faith in the present context.

> — Bishop John Stowe, OFM Conv
> Diocese of Lexington, Kentucky

"This new and expanded edition of Richard R. Gaillardetz's invaluable primer *By What Authority?* displays his characteristic thoroughness and nuanced approach to questions of the interpretation of dogma and doctrine. In particular, Gaillardetz's inclusion of disputed questions in each chapter retrieves ancient Christian methodologies that model constructive dialogue for our increasingly polarized world. Ecclesiologists, historians, and theologians in general will all benefit (as will their students) from this magisterial work."

> — Natalia Imperatori-Lee
> Manhattan College

"Richard Gaillardetz offers a reliable, balanced, and systematic guide to understanding key questions of authority in the Catholic Church. Historically grounded and pastorally oriented, *By What Authority?* demonstrates how the church has often sifted through competing and conflicting interpretations in order to arrive closer to a vision of church ministry and teaching that allows the gospel message to flourish around the world in diverse circumstances.

"Of special merit is the Disputed Questions feature that challenges us to wrestle with matters not yet firmly settled. These Disputed Questions invite readers and classroom students into the creative process of discernment, learning, and teaching that must involve all members of the church at every level and in every place."

> — Christopher M. Bellitto
> Kean University

"Richard Gaillardetz is the premiere authority on the multiple voices of ecclesial authority. He writes with clarity and grace. His new book with three additional chapters is an expanded version of one published 15 years ago, updated in light of Pope Francis's efforts to reclaim Vatican II's vision. It will be a basic text on authority for graduate students, seminarians, and pastoral ministers."

— Thomas P. Rausch, SJ
Loyola Marymount University

"Richard R. Gaillardetz's *By What Authority?* is a sound guide and a comprehensive introduction to the complex and often misunderstood world of Catholic belief and teaching. Beginning from a clearheaded discussion of the dynamics of power and authority, it moves from a consideration of Vatican II's personalist, Trinitarian understanding of revelation, to the canonicity, inspiration, and normative role of Scripture; the meaning of tradition; the understanding of 'magisterium'; and the various forms for the exercise of the pastoral teaching office by bishops and popes. The strength of his presentation is its description of the interdependence and constant interaction of the pastoral teaching office with the 'sense' of all the baptized faithful, including the community of theologians, as the whole church, guided by the Spirit, seeks to discern the meaning and the demands of the gospel. Particularly helpful is the sensible discussion of disagreement in the life of the Church. An excellent resource, this book should be required reading for anyone seeking to understand Catholic tradition and ecclesial life."

— Catherine E. Clifford
Saint Paul University

"It is hard to imagine that Gaillardetz could improve on his original masterpiece but he has done just that in this revised and expanded edition of his compelling work. Looking through the lens of Scripture, the magisterium, and the sense of the faithful, Gaillardetz offers valuable insight into the many ways that God, 'the only ultimate spiritual authority in our lives' chooses to manifest that authority through the sacred and yet quite human instrumentality of the Church. This new edition gives the reader a deeper appreciation for the Church which is at once the recipient and mediator of divine authority."

— Most Reverend John C. Wester
Archbishop of the Archdiocese of Santa Fe

BY WHAT AUTHORITY?

*Foundations for Understanding
Authority in the Church*

REVISED AND EXPANDED EDITION

Richard R. Gaillardetz

**LITURGICAL PRESS
ACADEMIC**

Collegeville, Minnesota
www.litpress.org

Cover design by Ann Blattner. Icon written by Isaac Fanous and courtesy of St. Peter and Paul Coptic Orthodox Church, Santa Monica, California.

Excerpts from documents of the Second Vatican Council are from *Vatican Council II: Constitutions, Decrees, Declarations; The Basic Sixteen Documents*, edited by Austin Flannery, OP, © 1996. Used with permission of Liturgical Press, Collegeville, Minnesota.

Scripture texts in this work are taken from the *New Revised Standard Version Bible*, © 1989, Division of Christian Education of the National Council of the Churches of Christ in the United States of America. Used by permission. All rights reserved.

2	3	4	5	6	7	8	9

Library of Congress Control Number: 2017954114

ISBN 978-0-8146-8788-8   ISBN 978-0-8146-8789-5 (e-book)

*To the Sisters of St. Benedict's Monastery, St. Joseph, Minnesota,
in gratitude for their inspiration and gracious hospitality.*

CONTENTS

═══════════════ PART ONE ═══════════════
FUNDAMENTAL THEMES

═══════════════ PART TWO ═══════════════
THE AUTHORITY OF SCRIPTURE AND TRADITION

═══════════════ PART THREE ═══════════════
THE AUTHORITY OF THE MAGISTERIUM

=============== PART FOUR ===============
THE AUTHORITY OF THE BELIEVING COMMUNITY

ABBREVIATIONS

Second Vatican Council

LG   Dogmatic Constitution on the Church (*Lumen Gentium*)

GS   Pastoral Constitutuion on the Church in the Modern World (*Gaudium et Spes*)

DV   Dogmatic Constitution on Divine Revelation (*Dei Verbum*)

SC   Constitution on the Sacred Liturgy (*Sacrosanctum Concilium*)

UR   Decree on Ecumenism (*Unitatis Redintegratio*)

CD   Decree on the Pastoral Office of the Bishop (*Christus Dominus*)

AG   Decree on the Church's Missionary Activity (*Ad Gentes*)

DH   Declaration on Religious Liberty (*Dignitatis Humanae*)

NA   Declaration on the Relation of the Church to Non-Christian Religions (*Nostra Aetate*)

AA   Decree on the Apostolate of Lay People (*Apostolicam Actuositatem*)

PO   Decree on the Ministry and Life of Priests (*Presbyterorum Ordinis*)

Pope Paul VI

ES   Encyclical on the Church (*Ecclesiam Suam*)

Pope St. John Paul II

UUS   Encyclical on Ecumenism (*Ut Unum Sint*)

Pope Benedict XVI

VD   Post-Synodal Apostolic Exhortation on the Word of God in the Life and Mission of the Church (*Verbum Domini*)

Pope Francis

EG   Apostolic Exhortation on the Joy of the Gospel (*Evangelii Gaudium*)

AL   Apostolic Exhortation on Love in the Family (*Amoris Laetitia*)

LS   Encyclical on Care for Our Common Home (*Laudato Sí*)

International Theological Commission

SF   "The *Sensus Fidei* in the Life of the Church"

PREFACE TO THE
REVISED EDITION

"By what authority do you do these things?" It was a question posed to Jesus by his critics on several occasions. He never gave them a direct answer. The question itself speaks to the very meaning of authority. In effect, what was being asked was this: "Who is the true *author* of your actions?" Jesus' entire life and ministry offered the only answer possible. God was the true Author of Jesus' life. His authority was grounded in his relationship to the one he dared address as "Abba." The church lives to proclaim the message of Jesus Christ, the Word of God. It too depends for its authority on God, the Author of life.

This book is about the church's exercise of that authority. Our focus will be on the exercise of authority primarily as it is oriented toward Christian belief, that is, the authoritative relationships concerned with the Bible, tradition, popes and bishops, creeds and doctrine, theologians and all the faithful. Except in a more general way in chapters 1 and 6, it will not be possible to attend to those aspects of church authority concerned more directly with church governance or the sacramental and liturgical life of the church.

Many of the sad divisions in Christianity have occurred because of disagreements about both the appropriate sources of Christian authority and its proper exercise. Often the authority of Scripture has been played off against the authority of tradition, or the authority of church office (e.g., pope and bishops) against the authority of theologians or ordinary believers. A healthy Catholic view of authority will try to avoid these oppositions and instead demonstrate how these various kinds of authorities interrelate and inform one another.

The fundamental reference point for our consideration of authority in the church will be the teaching of the Second Vatican Council. Held between 1962 and 1965, the Second Vatican Council effected a seismic shift in Catholic consciousness, unlike anything encountered since the sixteenth century.[1] The impact of the council lay not only in the sixteen documents that the bishops promulgated but also in the new frame of reference the council offered for considering Catholic faith today. This new framework benefited from a series of new relationships being forged where antagonisms had predominated. Once the rise of modern science and critical historical scholarship had been met with suspicion; now the council called for a new respect for science and an unprecedented openness to the fruit of historical scholarship. Where clergy and laity were seen as two "ranks" in which the sole responsibility of the laity was to obey the clergy, the council called for their cooperation and affirmed the shared identity of all believers as the *Christifideles*, "the Christian faithful." Where the work of theologians had been limited to defending the faith and explaining church teaching to the laity, now bishops and theologians were placed in common service to the Word of God. Where the world was seen as dangerous, now the council stressed the universality of God's grace and promoted a respectful dialogue with the world.

This new framework for understanding Catholicism did not repudiate the past in favor of novelty or relevance. It was the product of two principal forces at work in the council. The first was the determination to "bring the church up-to-date" in areas where its faith and practice were no longer intelligible to the modern world. Pope St. John XXIII used the Italian term *aggiornamento* to give expression to this impulse. The second was the desire to "return to the sources" of Christianity in order to rediscover biblical, liturgical, and theological insights from the early church that had been neglected in modern Catholicism. Many speak of this impulse by appealing to the French term, *ressourcement*.

This book has been written in "the spirit of Vatican II." This expression has sometimes been employed pejoratively, as if those who appeal to the "spirit" of the council are conveniently ignoring the text itself. This is not my intention. The documents of the council are a necessary and normative foundation for contemporary Catholicism. But those documents, like other normative elements in our great tradition, can

---

[1] For a fuller consideration of the ways in which Vatican II transformed modern Catholicism, see Richard R. Gaillardetz, *An Unfinished Council: Vatican II, Pope Francis, and the Renewal of Catholicism* (Collegeville, MN: Liturgical Press, 2015), esp. chaps. 1–3.

be interpreted adequately only by attending to both the context in which they emerged and their ongoing reception in the life of the church. Thus, we should not look to the council as if its documents were a kind of answer book for all the pressing questions of our time. As the council bishops themselves admitted:

> The church is guardian of the deposit of God's word and draws religious and moral principles from it, but it does not always have a ready answer to every question. Still, it is eager to associate the light of revelation with the experience of humanity in trying to clarify the course upon which it has recently entered. (GS 33)

Every council sets itself about the task of responding to the questions of the time but, inevitably, in doing so it raises new questions. Councils represent, in a sense, both an end and a beginning. Thus, to say that the teaching of Vatican II is normative for the life of the church does not mean that it represents the final word. Such an assertion would represent the denial of tradition as an ongoing and developing reality. In considering the teaching of the council as our primary reference point, we must also consider how that teaching has been received in the life of the church. That will include its reception in postconciliar church documents, in the work of theologians, and in the practice of the faith by ordinary believers.

When the first edition of this book was published in 2003, the church was in the final years of the long and remarkable pontificate of the first non-Italian pope in 450 years, St. John Paul II. His pontificate drew richly from the council documents, even if some of his interpetations of conciliar teaching were matters of some dispute. In his apostolic letter celebrating the jubilee year 2000 he wrote: "The best preparation for the new millennium, therefore, can only be expressed in a renewed commitment *to apply*, as faithfully as possible, *the teachings of Vatican II to the life of every individual and of the whole Church.*"[2]

Since the first edition of this text appeared, John Paul II was succeeded by his close adviser, Cardinal Joseph Ratzinger, who, as prefect for the Congregation for the Doctrine of the Faith for over two decades, helped articulate and shape John Paul II's interpretation and implementation of the council's teaching. Taking the name of Benedict XVI, he

---

[2] Pope St. John Paul II, *Tertio Millennio Adveniente*, 20. Emphasis is mine. Accessed online at https://w2.vatican.va/content/john-paul-ii/en/apost_letters/1994/documents/hf_jp-ii_apl_19941110_tertio-millennio-adveniente.html.

would continue to advance the teaching of the council in accord with his own particular theological commitments. Indeed, both John Paul II and Benedict XVI would play a considerable role in determining the institutional shape and practice of ecclesial authority that proceeded from the council.

Although Popes Paul VI, John Paul II, and Benedict XVI all carried forward key elements of the council's teaching, Pope Francis has offered a distinctive re-reception of conciliar teaching and is already enacting a bold reimagination of the exercise and structures of authority in the church. This is one of the reasons why the publisher and I agreed that, fifteen years later, the time was ripe for a new edition of this volume, one that would reflect important new developments in our understanding of church authority.

The first edition was divided into three sections. This new edition has added a fourth section, addressing more fundamental themes. As part of this expansion, two completely new chapters have been added (chapters 1 and 6) and virtually every chapter has been significantly expanded and updated. Part 1 considers fundamental themes that provide a necessary background for the consideration of the various topics that will follow. We will begin with a theological consideration of the basic concepts of power and authority in chapter 1, followed by a chapter that introduces the reader to a theology of divine revelation (a shorter version of this appeared as the introduction in the earlier edition). Part 2 considers the authority of Scripture and tradition within Roman Catholicism. Catholics give Scripture a central place in the life of the church, but many are confused about the authority of Scripture. We begin with a consideration of the Bible as a whole, what is generally referred to as the "canon" of the Bible. How exactly did this biblical canon, this definitive list of sacred texts, come into existence in the first place? What is the nature of its authority, as canon? Questions such as these will be explored in chapter 3. This will lead, in chapter 4, to a consideration of various theories of biblical inspiration and the difficult question of whether there can be errors in the Bible. In the fifth chapter we reflect on some contemporary Catholic perspectives on the necessity and authority of tradition, its relationship to Scripture, and the possibility of change and development within that tradition.

Part 3 shifts to a consideration of the magisterium, the distinctive doctrinal teaching of the college of bishops under the headship of the Bishop of Rome. There we address the history of the magisterium (chapter 6), key ecclesiological principles for appreciating the role and function of the magisterium today (chapter 7), and consideration of the different modalities by which the magisterium is exercised in the church today (chapter 8). Chapter 9 considers the object of formal magisterial teaching, namely, church doctrine. Since not all church teachings bear the same authoritative weight, this chapter will also consider the basic gradations in the authority of church doctrine.

Finally, part 4 attends to a topic that, before Vatican II, had been much neglected in official church documents, namely, the distinctive authority that ordinary believers and the entire believing community exercise by virtue of their baptism. Chapter 10 considers the teaching of the Second Vatican Council on the vital role of the *sensus fidelium*, the "sense of the faithful." There we will reflect on how the whole Christian community discerns the meaning and significance of the Word of God for today. Pope Francis has given this conciliar teaching much greater prominence. This, in turn, will lead us to a very sensitive topic in chapter 11: given that church doctrine does not carry the same degree of authority, is it possible to remain a Catholic in good standing and disagree with church teaching? The goal here will be to find a *via media* that avoids the twin dangers of dogmatic fundamentalism and consumer Catholicism. In chapter 12 we will conclude with a consideration of the proper relationship between theologians, the magisterium, and the sense of the faithful.

In the original edition, the book's subtitle referred to it as a *primer*, that is, an elementary or introductory textbook. The book has been expanded considerably in this new edition yet it remains, in many ways, a primer. By that I mean it is intended as a basic introduction to the various modalities of authority in the church. My hope is that it will prove useful as a text in undergraduate and graduate theology courses as well as in lay ministry, diaconate, and seminary formation programs. It may also be a useful resource for journalists and theologians who have not done extensive work in fundamental theology and ecclesiology and want to have an accessible reference. Each chapter offers a sample of mostly English-language works for further reading. Some are fairly basic while others would doubtless challenge those without a formal theological education. As will be evident in the pages that follow, I have borrowed considerably from the work of fellow theologians. My goal in this volume was not to provide an original and constructive theology of authority as much as to synthesize and present in an accessible manner the important foundational work that has been accomplished in the decades since Vatican II.

The main body of each chapter offers a straightforward theological perspective well within the parameters of accepted Catholic belief. However, each chapter concludes with a consideration of "disputed questions." The tradition of attending to *quaestiones disputatae* is an ancient one in Catholic theology. It emerged in the medieval university with the recognition that the careful reading (*lectio*) of an authoritative text often gave rise to lively disagreement regarding a text's adequate interpretation. Thus the *lectio* gave way to the *disputatio* so that a diversity of interpretations could be given a fair hearing in the *studium*. The great historian and expert on the thought of Thomas Aquinas, M.-D. Chenu, describes well the distinctive character of the disputation in medieval education:

> From this starting point, the pro and con are brought into play, not with the intention of finding an immediate answer, but in order that under the action of *dubitatio* [doubt], research be pushed to its limit. A satisfactory explanation will be given only on the condition that one continue the search to the discovery of what caused the doubt.[3]

This kind of lively discussion is essential for the vitality of the theological enterprise. Although they cannot be treated in any depth in a book such as this, readers should have some sense of the debates that are being engaged in academic and ecclesiastical circles. Some of the positions summarized in this section concern significant disagreements over issues viewed as open questions within mainstream Catholicism. Other views represent more marginal perspectives. My hope is that when used as a text, instructors might use these "disputed questions" as an opportunity to draw students into a deeper and more sophisticated exploration of the issues that are briefly outlined there. Readers wishing to explore some of the disputed questions will make a good start of it by consulting each chapter's reading list.

I want to thank Liturgical Press, especially Hans Christoffersen and Peter Dwyer, for supporting my proposal to produce a revised and expanded version of the original book. I am grateful for the work of my two research assistants, Peter Folan, who helped identify sections in the

---

[3] M.-D. Chenu, *Toward Understanding Saint Thomas* (Chicago: Henry Regency, 1964), 48.

original text that required updating, and Nicholas Hayes, who assisted with copyediting and indexing the final manuscript. I am extraordinarily fortunate to be able to work at Boston College and among an exceptional group of scholars who daily challenge me by their example to be a better theologian. I am grateful to the many colleagues whose work has had such a significant influence on me. Deserving pride of place are two senior Jesuit theologians whose work on a theology of revelation and the role of the magisterium has been, well, magisterial: Gerald O'Collins and Francis Sullivan. So that readers might have some sense of the theological currents within which I have been swimming over the last several decades, theologians whose work has further informed my thought on these topics include John Burkhard, Catherine Clifford, Paul Crowley, Peter De Mey, Dennis Doyle, Orlando Espin, Bradford Hinze, Natalia Imperatori-Lee, Joseph Komonchak, Paul Lakeland, Nicholas Lash, Richard Lennan, Gerard Mannion, Paul Murray, Thomas Rausch, Gilles Routhier, Christopher Ruddy, Ormond Rush, Sandra Schneiders, and John Thiel.

For the completion of this revised and expanded edition I owe a special debt of gratitude to St. Benedict's Monastery in St. Joseph, Minnesota. Much of the writing and revisions for this new edition were done during my participation in the Benedictine sisters' Studium program, ably facilitated by Sr. Ann Marie Biermaier and Sr. Theresa Schumacher. For six weeks this remarkable monastic community provided me with a room and office while also extending to me their distinctive Benedictine hospitality. My participation in their daily prayer and meals during much of the summer of 2017 was a marvelous and unexpected gift. This is an extraordinary community of women, whose commitment to the monastic life and love of Christ and his church was matched by their joyful spirit. How appropriate that, working on a book on church authority, I was witness to the humble, loving, and relational exercise of authority called for in the Benedictine Rule.

It now seems merely *pro forma* for an author to acknowledge his spouse and children in a preface such as this. I fear the reader will fail to appreciate the true depth and sincerity of my gratitude for my wife Diana as we now approach three grace-filled decades of marriage. You cannot live authentically with another person for that long and not have your most basic convictions tested and shaped by the engagement with your partner. Her patience and encouragement have long sustained me in my theological vocation. When I wrote the first edition of this text,

my four sons (Greg, Brian, Andrew, and David) were young boys rang-
ing from eight to thirteen. They are now adults and their many questions
over the years, often regarding the challenges and dysfunctions of ecclesial authority, have deeply shaped my approach to this book's topic.
I am not only a better theologian but a better person for having them
in my life.

PART ONE

FUNDAMENTAL THEMES

WHAT IS THE ROLE OF POWER AND AUTHORITY IN THE CHURCH?

In this volume we will be giving most of our attention to the various forms of authority in the church directly concerned with Christian belief. Consequently, we will be considering the authority of Scripture and tradition, the magisterium and doctrine, the Christian faithful and theologians. But of course, church authority is not only concerned with matters of Christian belief; it is also concerned with Christian practice. Questions of church authority come into play not only with regard to teaching, but also with governing, that is, pastoral leadership, and the exercise of authority as it relates to pastoral care and the sacramental/liturgical life of the church. It will be helpful, therefore, to offer at least some general reflections on the exercise of ecclesial authority in its diverse forms.

Moreover, we cannot properly grasp the nature and exercise of authority until we have also dealt with a theological understanding of power. This is all the more necessary since both power and authority have become controversial topics in the church today.[1] Sadly, for far too many Catholics these terms bring to mind not the enabling of authentic Christian freedom but tragic instances of abuse. I will argue in this chapter, however, that while the church has too often succumbed to

---

[1] The material in this chapter has been adapted from Richard R. Gaillardetz, "Power and Authority in the Church: Emerging Issues," in *A Church with Open Doors: Catholic Ecclesiology for the Third Millennium*, ed. Richard R. Gaillardetz and Edward P. Hahnenberg (Collegeville, MN: Liturgical Press, 2015), 87–110.

unhelpful and even damaging exercises of power and authority, in fact, both are necessary for the flourishing of the church and, indeed, for all human communities.

So, let's begin with some basic definitions. For our purposes, we may think of "power" simply as *the capacity for effective action* and ecclesial power, when it is exercised authentically, as *the capacity to engage in effective action in service of the church's life and mission.* "Authority," in turn, can be understood as *the legitimate, trustworthy, and accountable exercise of power.* Note also that you can have power without authority, but you can't have authority without power. A tyrant can exercise power without having legitimate authority. Yet a person cannot have genuine authority if they don't have real power (i.e., the ability to engage in effective action). As we will see, although it is common for us to use both terms, power and authority, as if they pertained to certain entities (e.g., the Bible) or persons (e.g., the pope), both terms are more properly concerned with a set of relationships. Although these two terms overlap considerably, it might help to consider each term on its own.

THE CHRISTIAN TRANSFORMATION OF POWER

In our common use of the term, we tend to think of power as a quantity, a kind of "fuel" for human action, something that one can have more or less of. This popular view presumes what we might think of as a zero-sum understanding of power such that, within any given community, some have power and others do not. Thus, in the arena of US politics, when we say that the Republicans are "in power," our assumption is that the Democrats are not. Power is conceived as a finite quantity. As our example suggests, this conception of power generally comes from the realm of politics and law. Power in this sense is often perceived as dominating and even coercive. For many, the most apt example of such dominating power is the bully on the playground. This dominating view of power has led many people to believe that Christians must repudiate claims to power altogether. We often speak of the need for prophets to "speak truth to power," a phrase, interestingly, that comes not from the Bible but from the Quaker tradition of nonviolent resistance. In this view, the Christian is called to repudiate dominating power in imitation of the powerlessness of Christ. Yet this line of thought identifies power only with its negative, coercive, and dominating forms. James Davison Hunter rightly challenges the assumption that the way of Christ is the way of powerlessness: "Only by narrowing an understanding of power to political or economic power can one imagine giving up power and becoming 'powerless.'"[2] Christians should not yield so easily to this narrow, dominating understanding of power. In truth, any form of authentic human existence will require the exercise of power in relation to others, and this is no less true within the church.

The human exercise of power has certainly been distorted by sin, hence Lord Acton's famous dictum, "Power tends to corrupt, absolute power corrupts absolutely."[3] Our God-given power to sustain life-giving relations with others can indeed devolve into a submission to the "powers and principalities" about which St. Paul warned (Eph 6:12).[4] This is power in its abusive form, a power that feeds on the distortion of human desire and is bent on domination, manipulation, and control. Jesus understood his own ministry as one of combating the "powers" of this world. His ministry, however, represented not the renunciation of power but its radical transformation.

Jesus exercised power as a manifestation of the love of God (the key Greek terms here are *dynamis* and *exousia*, which are often translated as "power" and "authority," respectively). His exercise of power was vulnerable and liberating. Jesus healed the sick and forgave sinners, embodying in his ministry the profligate mercy of God (Matt 9:20-22; Mark 2:1-12). The life and teaching of Jesus subverted the habits of worldly power and domination in favor of power exercised as humble service (Mark 10:42-45). That distinctive form of power was evident in Jesus' washing the feet of his disciples and his command that they do likewise (John 13).

Jesus promised his followers that they too would receive a power that comes from the Holy Spirit (Acts 1:8). Christians, then, are both recipients and agents of God's reconciling power. St. Paul reminds us that God "who reconciled us to himself through Christ . . . has given us the ministry of reconciliation" (2 Cor 5:18). The work of reconciliation accomplished in Jesus of Nazareth, through the power of the Spirit,

---

[2] James Davison Hunter, *To Change the World: The Irony, Tragedy and Possibility of Christianity in the Late Modern World* (New York: Oxford University Press, 2010), 181; italics in the original.

[3] Lord Acton to Bishop Mandell Creighton, 5 April 1887, in *Historical Essays and Studies*, ed. J. N. Figgis and R. V. Laurance (London: Macmillan, 1907).

[4] All biblical quotations are taken from the *New Revised Standard Version*, Catholic Edition.

is to continue in the mission of the church. In service of this mission, the church must become a school of discipleship in which dominating power and a preoccupation with control are transformed into the power of reconciliation. In that school, we acquire the habits of power appropriate to followers of Jesus.

What we are moving toward here is an understanding of power, not as a quantity or fuel that some have and some don't, but as a dimension of all human relationships. Power is not something that is acquired, seized, or shared, something that one holds on to or allows to slip away. Even the so-called powerless—think of those in prison or the poor—can find ways to exercise power through protest or resistance. Gandhi and Martin Luther King Jr. both witnessed to the power that can be exercised by the oppressed.

In the Catholic Church, we sometimes rely on a too exclusively juridical or legal understanding of power, the kind regulated by canon law. This kind of power does exist and indeed is necessary for any community to function, but it shouldn't be our primary understanding of power. In Catholicism, without ignoring the role of juridical power, we must recover that more comprehensive dimension of ecclesial power that comes from baptism and is animated by the Spirit. In a classic work, the great French Dominican theologian, Yves Congar, drew on biblical insights in reflections on Christian conceptions of power:

> We must get back to the true vision of the Gospel: posts of authority in the Church do indeed exist; a real jurisdictional power does exist, which the shepherds of God's people receive from Christ in conformity with the order which Christ willed and instituted (at least in its essential lines). But this power exists only within the structure of the fundamental religious relationship of the Gospel, as an organizational element within the life given to men by Christ, the one Lord and the one Head of his Body, for which each is accountable to all the rest according to the place and measure granted to him. So there is never simply a relationship of subordination or superiority, as in secular society, but always a loving obedience to Christ, shaping the life of each with all and for all, according to the position which the Lord has given him in the Body.[5]

For Congar, the witness of the early church did not undermine the need for institutional church structures, but it did challenge the way in which power was too often exercised in and through these structures.

---

[5] Yves Congar, *Power and Poverty in the Church* (London: Geoffrey Chapman, 1964), 98.

Feminist theologians have reflected on the situation of so many women in the church, across the centuries, who have had painful experiences of exclusion on the basis of their gender. Consequently, these theologians have given considerable thought to the question of power in the church and have helped us recognize where unhealthy power relations have been in play. The unhealthy manifestations of power often take the form of a "power over," that is, a relationship that calls for domination-submission.[6] The Protestant theologian Pamela Cooper-White nicely sums up much reflection on the topic and advocates for a different conception of power, one that eschews domination in favor of mutuality. Mutuality, she insists, should not be reduced to sameness: "Mutuality involves empowering each other to find and express what each can truly know and do, each one's unique contributions, not the dulling uniformity of the lowest common denominator."[7] This approach to power emerges out of a deep intuition regarding the interconnectedness of life. The result is an affirmation of "power-within," as that power that proceeds from one's own spiritual resources—one's wisdom and insight—and "power-with," which is "the power of an individual to reach out in a manner that negates neither self nor other. It prizes mutuality over control and operates by negotiation and consensus."[8] Feminist Christian theologians are inviting the church to recover more Gospel-inspired conceptions of power that empower and enable God's people for the life of discipleship.

Cooper-White admits that one of the principal difficulties with the typical feminist view of dominating power is that "there has been very little successful work on constructing an actual workable alternative. More often than not, feminists have tended to shy away from the exercise of any explicit sort of authoritative power in women's organizations, experimenting instead with models that are largely collective and leaderless."[9] For example, she admits that the "power-within" and "power-with" language offers no panacea. "Power-within" can lead to a kind of solipsism that absolutizes one's own voice, and "power-with" can sometimes suppress conflict in favor of harmony and become bogged down

---

[6] Pamela Cooper-White provides a helpful synthesis of this feminist analysis in *The Cry of Tamar: Violence against Women and the Church's Response* (Minneapolis: Fortress Press, 1995). Much of my treatment here draws from her work.

[7] Ibid., 35.

[8] Ibid., 33.

[9] Ibid., 34.

in decision-making processes. She even wonders whether feminist thought may need to revisit "power-over" to consider whether there are leadership exercises where such an authority can be legitimate and nondominating. This leads her to turn to yet another power modality, what she refers to as "power-in-community." This broader framework affirms the legitimacy of each of the three other modalities ("power-over," "power-within," "power-with"). Any and all exercises of power can only be intelligible and fruitful when they are realized within an adequate account of community.

A Catholic feminist theologian and biblical scholar, Sandra Schneiders, has also made helpful contributions to a Catholic reflection on power. She defines power simply as the capacity to move or influence oneself or others "either physically or spiritually."[10] Schneiders sees power as essentially neutral. It can be exercised coercively ("power over") or in a way that empowers and enables others ("power for"). Schneiders defines authority as "persuasive power."

If the church is a school of Christian discipleship, in this school we learn of the transformation of power in the light of the Gospel and in service of God's kingdom. This transformation of power can occur in many ways. In the celebration of the Eucharist, for example, we are drawn into the subversive power of God's self-giving love. In the family, we exercise a radically different form of power in the daily practices of forgiveness, generosity, and hospitality that constitute the household as a "domestic church."[11] Communities for consecrated life can accomplish something similar in their intentional common life. Parishes can transform power in their support of communal practices of solidarity with the poor and vulnerable and in their sacramental and nonsacramental ministries of reconciliation. In the opening weeks of his pontificate, Pope Francis provided a dramatic example of the transformation of power when he celebrated an ancient Holy Thursday ritual, not by

---

[10] Sandra Schneiders, *Buying the Field: Catholic Religious Life in Mission to the World*, Religious Life in a New Millennium, vol. 3 (New York: Paulist Press, 2013), 435.

[11] Richard R. Gaillardetz, "The Christian Household as School of Discipleship: Reflections on the Ecclesial Contributions of the Christian Household to the Larger Church," in *The Household of God and Local Households: Revisiting the Domestic Church*, ed. Thomas Knieps-Port Le Roi, Gerard Mannion, and Peter De Mey, Bibliotheca Ephemeridum Theologicarum Lovaniensium Series (Leuven: Peeters, 2013), 111–21.

washing the feet of twelve males as liturgical law had dictated at the time, but by visiting a juvenile prison and washing the feet of troubled youth, including women and Muslims.[12]

CHRISTIAN UNDERSTANDINGS OF AUTHORITY

We shift now from a consideration of ecclesial power to reflection on the various authority relationships within which authentic ecclesial power is exercised. As we saw in our consideration of the exercise of power, our modern age has experienced a widespread suspicion of authority as inherently dominating, coercive, and opposed to the exercise of human freedom. What is needed is an account of legitimate authority that supports and enables human freedom.

Authority in Service of Human Flourishing and the Common Good

David Stagaman has criticized our modern tendency to speak of authority as if it were the property of persons or things. Although we may speak of the Bible as *an* authority, that authority actually resides in the relationship established between the Bible and those who acknowledge it as a source of revelation.[13] The Bible has authority only for those who recognize it as a testimony to God's revelation. As a consequence, for the atheist, a Bible will hold no authority. This is just as true when speaking of the authority of a teacher or the authority of a pope. A teacher has genuine authority only to the extent that the students grant it to her. If they do not recognize her authority, they may still respond to her dictates and classroom requirements for fear of a failing grade (that is, they will respond to her exercise of power), but they will not allow her to actually teach them. Healthy authoritative relationships do not exist as an abstraction; they are exercised concretely and cooperatively in the life of a community.

According to Victor Lee Austin, "Authority is built into what it means to be human, and we never will escape from needing it for our

---

[12] Pope Francis would later revise the church's liturgical law regarding this ritual.

[13] David Stagaman, *Authority in the Church* (Collegeville, MN: Liturgical Press, 1999), 24–28. Joseph Komonchak also considers authority as a particular kind of social relationship in his "Authority and Magisterium," in *Vatican Authority and American Catholic Dissent*, ed. William May (New York: Crossroad, 1987), 103–4.

flourishing."[14] Austin provides a helpful distinction between *substitutionary* and *non-substitutionary* forms of authority. The former is evident in parental exercises of authority inasmuch as the parent's authority is filling in for (*substitutes* for) some lack of maturity or experience in the child. The parent tells a young child not to cross a street because the child is incapable of making such a judgment for himself. Substitutionary authority compensates for a fundamental lack in the person subject to that authority. It also functions as a corrective against some defect in the other. The authority exercised by law enforcement is often substitutionary in character to the extent that it responds to the social defects of criminals. One hopes that, as a person matures and develops, the exercise of substitutionary authority would diminish correspondingly.

The more mature exercise of authority, Austin contends, is non-substitutionary and functions so as to coordinate individual human activity for the sake of a community's common action. Non-substitutionary authority creates the conditions for individuals and groups to make the most of their gifts and abilities. Here, authority is enabling more than constraining. Austin uses the example of the authority of the symphony conductor who exercises her authority to maximize the individual gifts of the musicians so as to produce a coordinated human activity.

Austin's depiction of non-substitutionary authority draws on the work of the late French Thomist and political theorist Yves Simon.[15] Simon distinguishes between *materially* and *formally* willing the common good. Every member of a community is obligated to formally will the common good of the community. So, the members of an orchestra should all be concerned about the orchestra's performance of a particular piece of music. They are *formally* concerned with the overall performance. *Materially*, however, they must be concerned with their specific duty to perform those parts of the composition assigned to their particular instrument. The conductor, however, is both formally *and* materially concerned with the overall performance of the work. To offer another example, as a faculty member of a Catholic Jesuit university,

---

[14] Victor Lee Austin, *Up with Authority: Why We Need Authority to Flourish as Human Beings* (New York: Continuum, 2010), 2. Much of what follows is drawn from Austin's helpful study.

[15] Yves Simon, *A General Theory of Authority* (Notre Dame, IN: University of Notre Dame Press, 1962).

I am *formally* committed to serving the university's mission. At the same time, I accomplish this *materially* by dedicating myself to the practice of theology and the initiation and formation of our students into that practice. It is for those directly responsible for the leadership of the university, not only formally but also materially, to will the achievement of the university's mission.

The point that Austin and Simon are making is that these exercises of authority are concerned not with domination but with acting in such a way as to best bring about, materially, the common good. They do this through the empowerment and coordination of those in the community who are working to achieve a vast array of particular goods. This argument offers insight into the authentic exercise of governing authority, or pastoral leadership, in the church.

One of the principal contributions of Vatican II was its recovery of the role of the Holy Spirit in general and the recovery of the biblical understanding of charism in particular. The council taught that the Spirit "guides the church in the way of all truth (see Jn 16:13) and, uniting it in fellowship and ministry, bestows upon it different hierarchic and charismatic gifts, and in this way directs it and adorns it with his fruits" (LG 4). In this passage, the phrase "hierarchic gifts" refers to stable church office (e.g., ordained ministry) while "charismatic gifts" refers to those many charisms or gifts the Spirit distributes among all the faithful (which includes both the laity and the clergy). In council teaching, charism and office are not opposed to one another since both have the Spirit as their origin. This means that ordained pastoral leadership need not compete with the exercise of the many gifts of the faithful. Each requires the other. According to the council's teaching, those ordained to pastoral leadership are not to absorb into their own ministry all the tasks proper to building up the church. Rather, the distinctive authority exercised by the church's pastors must be directed toward recognizing, empowering, and ordering the gifts of all God's people. Those who have charge over the church "should judge the genuineness and orderly use of these gifts, and it is especially their office not indeed to extinguish the Spirit, but to test all things and hold fast to what is good" (LG 12; see also AA 3; PO 9).

The council situated ordained pastoral ministry within the Christian community. The ordained minister is responsible, among other things, for the discernment and coordination of the charisms and ministries of all the baptized. To transpose the council's teaching into Simon's account, we might say that ordinary believers are *formally* concerned with the common good of the whole community, but *materially*, they will pursue that by the exercise of their particular charisms. Church leaders will not only be *formally* concerned with the common good but will make this their *material* concern, directing the exercise of particular charisms in ways that will build up the church in the pursuit of its mission. Thus, the pastor and other church leaders will pursue the common good of the community by identifying, empowering, and ordering the exercise of individual charisms toward the church's larger mission.

Authority, Trust, and Accountability

The sociologist, Max Weber, contended that authority was simply *legitimate power* and that this power could be legitimated in three distinct ways.[16] (1) *Traditional authority* was legitimated by way of past precedents for determining present action. This authority finds warrants in customs, founding myths, and so on. In the life of the church, appeal to this kind of authority usually takes the form of "as the Bible says . . ." or "according to the teaching of the Catechism. . . ." According to Weber, such exercises of authority are largely resistant to change. (2) *Legal-rational authority* depends on accepted rules and conventions that are associated with a bureaucratic entity of one kind or another. Here too we can see an ecclesial example in the highly bureaucratized activity of the Roman Curia and the application of canon law at all levels of ecclesial life. (3) *Charismatic authority* is legitimated by the distinctive gifts of an individual or group of individuals that make them heroic or exemplary in some way and thereby elicit allegiance or adherence. In the life of the church we might think of the authority of a figure like St. Francis of Assisi or any leader whose authority is associated with their charismatic personality.

Weber's analysis is helpful, but it does not go far enough in describing the demands of authentic authority in the life of the church. For Weber, authority is legitimate only to the extent that people consent to it. In our contemporary ecclesial context, however, the nature of this consent requires more attention. Joseph Komonchak characterizes au-

---

[16] Max Weber, *Economy and Society*, ed. Günther Roth and Claus Wittich (Berkeley: University of California Press, 1978), 1:215–45.

thority not just as legitimate power but as "trustworthy power."[17] This trustworthiness can be established in multiple ways. First, we must assume the goodwill of those who exercise authority. Those who consent to another's authority must be able to trust that the subject of a particular authoritative relationship is acting out of good intentions and a commitment to act in support of the common good. If I suspect that a person in authority is concerned not with my well-being but with their own career advancement or the preservation of their reputation, for example, their authority will be fatally compromised. Second, the trustworthiness of one in authority requires competency. When I visit my doctor to complain of shortness of breath, I do so presupposing her competence as a physician and the consequent trustworthiness of her diagnosis. That trust in her competence allows me to accept her quite reasonable diagnosis that I need to lose some weight. However, the presumption of competence that I grant her is not absolute. Should she suggest to me that my shortness of breath is the direct consequence of my failure to trim my toenails, I might call her competence—and therefore her authority—into question! In the long run, authority cannot function in any meaningful way when competency is lacking. This too has implications for the exercise of ecclesial authority; we cannot simply assume that a cleric, for example, has the requisite competency simply by virtue of his ordination. The sacrament of holy orders does *not* confer competency on the ordinand!

Standard accounts of the exercise of authority generally distinguish between those who are *in authority* (exercising authority by virtue of office) and those who are *an authority* by virtue of some specialized knowledge, charisma, wisdom, competence, or aptitude.[18] When a police officer pulls behind me on the highway and hits his lights, I pull over, not because of the officer's knowledge or charism, but because of the authority of the office.

Yet this distinction can be overdrawn. The authority of office, after all, generally presupposes that the officeholder is in some sense *an authority*, that is, a person who has a specialized knowledge, wisdom, charism, experience, competence, or aptitude for a set of tasks. It is

---

[17] Komonchak, "Authority and Magisterium," 107.

[18] Richard E. Flathman gives detailed consideration to this distinction in his *The Practice of Political Authority: Authority and the Authoritative* (Chicago: University of Chicago Press, 1980).

possible, of course, and in fact rather common, that one would assent to the exercise of authority by an officeholder who lacks the requisite knowledge, experience, competence, or aptitude in the short run. This does not mean, however, that such an exercise of authority is likely to be effective in the long run. Over time, the exercise of authority by those who, in spite of their office, do not possess any of these things is bound to damage the life of the community. The fact that one may assent to the actions of one *in authority* who lacks the requisite personal knowledge, experience, charism, competence, or aptitude in the short run does not mean that this exercise of authority is likely to be effective in the long run. Any society would suffer in the long run, and no less the church, when those who are *in* authority fail to demonstrate that they are in some meaningful way also *an* authority on matters related to their exercise of leadership.

Finally, we can say that legitimate authority must be not only trustworthy but also accountable. Paul Lakeland insists that where the exercise of authority is concerned, "credibility is directly proportional to the level of practice of accountability."[19] Unfortunately, discussion of accountability in the church has been handicapped because of the term's association with the political and business sectors. The then-bishop of Pittsburgh, Donald Wuerl (now the cardinal archbishop of Washington) made a helpful contribution to a volume on governance and accountability in the church. Wuerl was frank in his admission that Catholic Church leadership needed to be more transparent in its exercise of authority, but he also cautioned that "when we address accountability in the church, we must be careful not to use a political model for a reality that transcends human political institutions."[20] Ecclesial accountability, he insisted, differs from its political analogue because the authority of the apostolic tradition and the divine origins of the apostolic office bind the church in a unique way. Wuerl defined ecclesial accountability as requiring an openness and transparency sufficient to allow one to assess whether church leaders are acting in fidelity to their divine mandate.

---

[19] Paul Lakeland, "Accountability, Credibility, and Authority," *New Theology Review* 19, no. 1 (2006): 8.

[20] Donald W. Wuerl, "Reflections on Governance and Accountability in the Church," in *Governance, Accountability, and the Future of the Catholic Church*, ed. Francis Oakley and Bruce Russett (New York: Continuum, 2004), 18.

Wuerl's views are shared by many in the church. Many bishops are willing to admit that "mistakes have been made" by those in authority, and they will often affirm the need for a more transparent and collaborative style of leadership. There seems to be a default assumption, however, that the divine origins of the church and its apostolic office preclude the bishops from being accountable to the baptized. Church leaders, they insist, are accountable only to their hierarchical superiors and ultimately to God. As John Beal has pointed out, this attitude toward ecclesial accountability is enshrined in canon law:

> Since all lines of accountability point upward in canon law, only hierarchical superiors are competent to judge whether their subordinates have adequately fulfilled the obligations of their offices or abused their powers. Bishops, pastors, and other officeholders are accountable for their stewardship to those who appointed them, not to those they serve. The faithful may express disgruntlement about the shoddy performance, nonfeasance, and malfeasance of their pastors and even bishops to their hierarchical superiors, but superiors are free to give these complaints as much or as little weight as their discretion dictates when deciding whether to retain, remove, or discipline their subordinates.[21]

According to this logic, any other form of ecclesial accountability would reflect at best an unacceptable Protestantizing and at worst a capitulation to the secular culture.

This view suffers from an inadequate appreciation for the trinitarian foundations of the church. Accountability to Christ must not be separated from accountability to the Spirit alive in the church today. As Yves Congar reminded us, "The Spirit did not come simply in order to animate an institution that was already fully determined in all its structures." In fact, the Spirit "is really the co-instituting principle" of the church.[22] Accountability to Christ and his Spirit requires both a fidelity to the apostolic tradition and openness to the witness of the Spirit in the church today, including the Spirit-breathed witness of all God's people. Faithful obedience to Christ will be manifested in practices of communal discernment that listen for the voice of the Spirit speaking

---

[21] John P. Beal, "Something There Is That Doesn't Love a Law: Canon Law and Its Discontents," in *The Crisis of Authority in Catholic Modernity*, ed. Michael J. Lacey and Francis Oakley (New York: Oxford University Press, 2011), 150.

[22] Yves Congar, "The Church Is Made by the Spirit," in *I Believe in the Holy Spirit* (New York: Crossroad, 1997), 2:9.

through a faith-filled people. When all in the church come to discover the dignity and demands of their baptism and the concrete shape of discipleship in service of the Spirit's promptings, "accountability" becomes simply another word for *koinonia*, our "shared communion" in Christ.

First the Protestant Reformation and then the Enlightenment encouraged what has been a long-standing suspicion regarding the role of power and authority in the church. The Catholic Church reacted to this suspicion with a heavy-handed reassertion of its authority, an authority that too often devolved into authoritarianism and clericalism. The Second Vatican Council called for a more balanced view. The Holy Spirit animates the church, working through a wide range of offices, charisms, institutions, and relationships that together empower the church and its members for the fulfillment of its mission. The task of the church today, as a school of discipleship, is to cultivate habits of power and authoritative relationships that are in keeping with the One who came not to be served but to serve.

DISPUTED QUESTIONS

(1) One of the principal disputes regarding a theology of power concerns the legitimacy of coercive power, or "power over," in the life of the church. Such power is often manifested in the form of disciplinary action within the community, including excommunication. Canon lawyers would insist that excommunications are intended to be "medicinal" rather than punitive and that they should always be accompanied by pastoral efforts to restore that canonical communion. Nevertheless, many theologians contend that such coercive power is never appropriate for a community seeking to follow the way of Jesus of Nazareth. Others argue that the need to regulate the life of faith requires binding laws that may require "coercive power" to preserve the good order of the community. As we saw, even some feminist theologians who have been most critical of dominating power admit that, at least as a last resort, some coercive power may need to be exercised.

(2) The relationship between being *in* authority and being *an* authority plays out in the life of the church with regard to how the community calls forth candidates for ordained leadership in the

church. Consider the situation in the church's process of calling forth and forming candidates for ordination to the diocesan priesthood. Our current process is frequently dominated by a theology of vocation that sees vocations as the private possession of an individual. When a man presents himself to a vocation director with the claim that he might have a vocation to the priesthood, there will eventually be an investigation into whether there are canonical impediments to his ordination. There will be, one hopes, some assessment of the candidate's sanctity and basic mental health. If no obstacles present themselves, the candidate will likely be accepted into the seminary. Now let us presume that over the course of his period of formation he passes all of his courses, dutifully attends daily Mass, sees his spiritual director regularly, does not manifest heretical views in his academic work, preaching, pastoral counseling, or field education. Even if this candidate manifests no aptitude for genuine pastoral leadership, is there not still considerable pressure to ordain this candidate? Our reflections on authority suggest the need for the church to consider more thoroughly its current processes for vocational discernment and formation.

FOR FURTHER READING

Austin, Victor Lee. *Up with Authority: Why We Need Authority to Flourish as Human Beings.* New York: Continuum, 2010.

Carroll, Anthony J., Martha Kerwijk, Michael Kirwan, and James Sweeney, eds. *Towards a Kenotic Vision of Authority in the Catholic Church.* Washington, DC: Council for Research in Values and Philosophy, 2015.

Congar, Yves. *Power and Poverty in the Church.* Baltimore: Helicon, 1964.

Hinze, Christine. *Comprehending Power in Christian Social Ethics.* Atlanta: Scholars Press, 1995.

Hoose, Bernard, ed. *Authority in the Roman Catholic Church: Theory and Practice.* Burlington, VT: Ashgate, 2002.

Komonchak, Joseph. "Authority and Conversion or: The Limits of Authority." *Cristanesimo nella storia* 21 (2000): 207–29.

Loomer, Bernard. "Two Conceptions of Power." *Process Studies* 6, no. 1 (Spring 1976): 5–32.

Mannion, Gerard, Richard R. Gaillardetz, Jan Kerkhofs, and Kenneth Wilson, eds. *Readings in Church Authority: Gifts and Challenges for Contemporary Catholicism*. London: Ashgate, 2003.

Oakley, Francis, and Bruce Russett, eds. *Governance, Accountability, and the Future of the Catholic Church*. New York: Continuum, 2004.

Oakley, Francis, and Michael J. Lacey, eds. *The Crisis of Authority in Catholic Modernity*. New York: Oxford University Press, 2011.

Stagaman, David. *Authority in the Church*. Collegeville, MN: Liturgical Press, 1999.

TWO

WHAT IS DIVINE REVELATION?

I taught at a state university for ten years. During my tenure there, a colleague of mine in the philosophy department complained that some of the students in her classes were uncritically quoting the Bible in papers they were submitting to her. After trying to voice her irritation tactfully, she finally blurted out in exasperation: "The problem with you Christians is that it always comes down to faith, and then critical thinking goes out the window!" I reassured her that the Christian tradition in general, and Roman Catholicism in particular, could not be reduced to blind faith and that there was considerable reflection within Christianity on the necessary role of human reason. Nevertheless, her comment does raise an important question for Christianity because there is a sense, of course, in which she is right. Christianity is ultimately premised on faith. But faith does not come out of nowhere. For Christians, faith is a graced response to something that comes prior to faith. Faith is a response to God's initiative. Christians believe that faith is possible only because God has first come to us in love and has "revealed" God's self to us. We are not left searching the world for an absent God; God comes to us in the wonder of creation, in the sublime beauty of art, in the initial stirrings of the human soul for the "beyond in our midst." The Judeo-Christian tradition claims to have been addressed by God in the history of Israel. Finally, Christians believe, God has spoken an unsurpassable "Word" of love in the person of Jesus of Nazareth. This revelation of divine love carries its own authority, the authority of God who is the Author of life. In this chapter we will consider the distinctive authority and character of divine revelation in the Catholic tradition.

Let us begin with two snapshots. The first is of early Christianity around 100 CE. Christianity was less than seventy years old and was in the process of shifting from a religious movement to a more structured community of believers. Christians believed that, in the person of Jesus Christ, they had encountered the very revelation of God. They did not, however, think of revelation as a distinct body of supernatural knowledge separate from "natural knowledge." Revelation was understood in relation to the person of Jesus of Nazareth who was for them the bearer of God's saving offer. The good news of Jesus Christ was fearlessly proclaimed by believers. A fluid collection of written texts composed by influential figures like St. Paul of Tarsus, or originating from churches renowned for their apostolic origins, would soon take on a privileged status in Christianity. Many of these texts, along with texts from the Hebrew Scriptures, would be read before the community when Christians gathered for weekly worship. Indeed, the worship of the church was the privileged context for both the creation of the biblical canon and for its interpretation. In some churches, individual leaders were emerging who were acknowledged to have a special responsibility for the authentic proclamation of the Christian message. By the year 100, however, there was as yet no Bible as we know it today, no developed creeds, no catechisms, no universally recognized episcopal structures.

The second snapshot comes 1,850 years later. The year 1950 offered a very different view of how Catholic Christians encountered God's revelation. Christianity had long since come to accept the uniquely authoritative role of the Bible. How it was to be interpreted and who had ultimate responsibility for that interpretation had become, more than four centuries earlier, a matter of dispute. Within Catholicism, the authority of the Bible was now accompanied by the authority of church traditions, though the relationship between the two was also in dispute. A stable church office with special responsibility for teaching the faith, the episcopate, was now commonly accepted by Catholics and, in varying degrees, by other Christian traditions as well. Divine revelation was still believed to be rooted in Christ, but there was a much greater emphasis on the way in which this revelation could be expressed in objective statements known as dogma. According to Ghislain Lafont, this theology assumed "a quasi-identity of revealed truth and the formulas expressing the truth."[1] Revelation was commonly thought to be a body of supernatural knowledge quite distinct from "natural" knowledge. Since not all of the dogmatic propositions offered by the church as divinely revealed could easily be found in Scripture, some theologians contended that Scripture and tradition were two distinct sources of divine revelation. In this view, while certain propositional truths were explicitly articulated in Scripture, others could be found only in tradition.

At the practical level, a sense of the then-dominant notion of revelation was reflected in the process by which an adult was invited into the Roman Catholic Church. In 1950 it was common for someone desiring admission into the Catholic Church to receive "instructions" from the parish priest. In these instructions divine revelation was often presented as a collection of discrete truths or doctrines. The assumption was that assent to these truths was equivalent to assent to the Catholic faith. If the inquirer could assent to these teachings, they could be admitted into the church. Revelation equaled doctrine. Many scholars refer to this as a *propositional* view of divine revelation since revelation was conceived as a collection of discrete propositional truths. Revelation was comprehended according to the analogy of verbal communication in which God literally "spoke" to the biblical prophets and apostles. The Bible was a record of this verbal communication. In like manner, church teaching was often viewed according to the model of human speech. Dogmatic propositions were treated like "divine utterances." Revelation was often referred to as the "deposit of the faith," which suggested a discrete collection of "truths of the faith." To learn "the faith" meant mastering these "truths."

The strength of this approach was its confidence that God was not some abstract Super Being; the God of the Christian faith could be known and the Bible and church teaching provided a concrete way to encounter that God. It affirmed that revelation was not just a vague feeling or experience but an objective reality that could be apprehended by the human intellect. The danger was that such a stress on revelation as a collection of objective truths, if taken to extremes, could lead to various forms of fundamentalism, biblical or ecclesiastical.

During the first session of Vatican II the bishops were presented with a draft document on divine revelation that presupposed much of

---

[1] Ghislain Lafont, *Imagining the Catholic Church: Structured Communion in the Spirit* (Collegeville, MN: Liturgical Press, 2000), 39.

this propositional model. In fact, it was titled "On the Sources of Revelation." It proposed problematic understandings of the inspiration of the biblical authors and the nature of the assistance of the Holy Spirit given to the church hierarchy. In considerations of biblical authorship, for example, the draft text downplayed the human element and considered the biblical authors as little more than passive conduits of divine truth. Fortunately, that draft was withdrawn and a new commission was created to propose a more adequate text on revelation, what would ultimately become the Dogmatic Constitution on Divine Revelation, *Dei Verbum*.

VATICAN II'S THEOLOGY OF REVELATION

Vatican II's treatment of divine revelation is a good example of the council's determination to "return to the sources." Its theology was indebted to the work of influential theologians like Karl Rahner, Joseph Ratzinger, and Yves Congar. We also see the influence, even if only indirect, of several Protestant theologians. *Dei Verbum* offered a biblically informed presentation of divine revelation grounded in the trinitarian grammar of God's self-giving love. It is in this sense that we might properly speak, not of divine words about God, but of a divine "Word"— the perfect self-expression of God. God's Word, God's personal self-disclosure, comes to humankind in history in the form of an address. As such, it is an "eventing" of God.

The origins of this dynamic theology of revelation can be found in the Hebrew Bible's use of the word *dābar* ("word"). We find testimony to the dynamism and effectiveness of God's "word" in the book of Isaiah:

> For as the rain and the snow come down from heaven,
> and do not return there until they have watered the earth,
> making it bring forth and sprout,
> giving seed to the sower and bread to the eater,
> so shall my word be that goes out from my mouth;
> it shall not return to me empty,
> but it shall accomplish that which I purpose,
> and succeed in the thing for which I sent it. (Isa 55:10-11)

For the biblical author, to speak of God's "word" was to speak of God's effective action in history. According to the New Testament, "in the fullness of time" God's self-communication becomes not just *a* word from God but the definitive Word, the *Logos* of God, Jesus the Christ. At the beginning of the Gospel of John we find this poetic prologue:

In the beginning was the Word,
and the Word was with God, and the Word was God.
He was in the beginning with God.
All things came into being through him,
and without him not one thing came into being.
What has come into being in him was life,
and the life was the light of all people. . . .
And the Word became flesh and lived among us,
and we have seen his glory,
the glory as of a father's only son,
full of grace and truth. (John 1:1-4, 14)

This passage expresses the conviction that the same Word of God, active in creation and present in the Law and Prophets, has entered definitively and completely into the world as one of us. Henceforward, in the New Testament, the expression "Word of God" will mean God's creative and saving Word Incarnate in Jesus of Nazareth.

In Jesus of Nazareth divine revelation takes the form not of information, facts, or even doctrines—revelation comes to the world as a person. The communication of God's Word to humankind in Jesus is God's definitive gift of self to the world. According to Christian belief, in Jesus, the Word Incarnate, we are given a share in the very life of God. This is reflected in the opening of the First Letter of John:

We declare to you what was from the beginning,
what we have heard,
what we have seen with our eyes,
what we have looked at and touched with our hands,
concerning the word of life—
this life was revealed,
and we have seen it and testify to it,
and declare to you the eternal life
that was with the Father and was revealed to us—
we declare to you what we have seen and heard
so that you also may have fellowship with us;
and truly our fellowship is with the Father
and with his Son Jesus Christ.
We are writing these things so that our joy may be complete.
    (1 John 1:1-4)

This passage conveys to us the remarkable truth that in Christ, God's Word Incarnate, we are able to have fellowship with God; the Word inaugurates and sustains our relationship with God. This theology of revelation informed the teaching of the bishops at Vatican II.

The Second Vatican Council affirmed the confidence that Christians ought to possess in the possibility of knowing God, in Christ, by the power of the Holy Spirit. It insisted on the primacy of Scripture and the necessity of church doctrine in the life of the church. At the same time, the council recognized that for many, revelation had been reduced to a body of information *about* God rather than a living encounter *with* God. Consequently, in *Dei Verbum* we find the recovery of a more ancient theology of divine revelation, one that offers a trinitarian account of God revealing God's self to us in Christ by the power of the Holy Spirit:

> It pleased God, in his goodness and wisdom, to reveal himself and to make known the mystery of his will, which was that people can draw near to the Father, through Christ, the Word made flesh, in the holy Spirit, and thus become sharers in the divine nature. (DV 2)

The bishops affirmed that revelation begins with Christ and God's desire that we enter into a communion of divine friendship through Christ and in the Spirit. "By this revelation, then, the invisible God, from the fullness of his love, addresses men and women as his friends, and lives among them, in order to invite and receive them into his own company" (DV 2). All revelation, the council wrote, is summed up in the person of Jesus Christ. The centrality of Christ in the council's teaching is all the more striking if you compare this to the teaching of Vatican I, where theological consideration of divine revelation was centered less on Christ than on the church.

The emphasis on a dynamic theology of the Word of God suggests the influence of the great Protestant theologian, Karl Barth. Yet articles 3 and 4 of *Dei Verbum*, which turn to the ways in which God's revelation is manifest in salvation history, are more indebted, at least indirectly, to the contributions of another Protestant theologian, Oscar Cullmann.

In article 3 the council taught that God's plan of salvation was made manifest "by deeds and words having an inner unity." No longer would it suffice to equate revelation only with words, whether the words of Scripture or of doctrine; revelation also includes God's saving *action* in history, culminating in the death and resurrection of Christ. The Bible, the liturgy, creeds, doctrinal pronouncements, and personal testimony—each in their unique fashion represents a distinct expression or mediation of the one revelation of God in Christ through the power of the Holy Spirit.

In his influential early commentary on the document, Joseph Ratzinger (the future Pope Benedict XVI) wrote:

> The Council's intention in this matter was a simple one. . . . The fathers were merely concerned with overcoming neo-scholastic intellectualism, for which revelation chiefly meant a store of mysterious supernatural teachings, which automatically reduces faith very much to an acceptance of these supernatural insights. As opposed to this, the Council desired to express again the character of revelation as a totality, in which word and event make up one whole, a true dialogue which touches man in his totality, not only challenging his reason, but, as dialogue, addressing him as a partner, indeed giving him his true nature for the first time.[2]

The trinitarian grammar of divine revelation continues to unfold in *Dei Verbum* as the council teaches that the eternal Word that God shares with us is, in turn, received within our hearts by the power of the Holy Spirit. It is the Holy Spirit "who moves the heart and converts it to God, and opens the eyes of the mind and 'makes it easy for all to accept and believe the truth'" (DV 5). The Spirit leads us into an ever deeper understanding of that revelation. This reflects an important theological insight, namely, that it is in the very nature of revelation to require a human response. Revelation must be received in faith if it is to be effective. Attending to the Spirit-assisted reception of God's revelation in an act of faith highlights the dialogical character of the council's account of revelation.

The council taught that God's Word was addressed to the whole people of God. Firmly rejected is the view that God communicates divine revelation primarily to the magisterium (the authoritative teaching office of the college of bishops in communion with its head, the Bishop of Rome) that then transmits that revelation to the rest of the church. Rather, the Word of God emerges within the whole church through a complex set of ecclesial relationships in which all the baptized, professional theologians, and the college of bishops play vital and neces-

---

[2] Joseph Ratzinger, "Revelation Itself," chap. 1 in *Commentary on the Documents of Vatican II*, 5 vols., ed. Herbert Vorgrimler (New York: Crossroad, 1989, originally published, 1969), 3:172.

sary roles. This was proposed in a number of ways. First, in its treatment of tradition the council affirmed the role not only of the bishops but of all the baptized in the processes by which tradition grows and develops. Second, the council reminded us that the magisterium was not superior to the Word of God but rather its servant:

> This magisterium is not superior to the word of God, but is rather its servant. It teaches only what has been handed on to it. At the divine command and with the help of the holy Spirit, it listens to this devoutly, guards it reverently and expounds it faithfully. All that it proposes for belief as being divinely revealed it draws from this sole deposit of faith. (DV 10)

Much of this conciliar teaching will be developed further in later chapters.

REVELATION IS SYMBOLICALLY MEDIATED

The council's theology of revelation can be further developed by appealing to a philosophy of symbol that proposes we view all revelation as in some way being symbolically mediated.[3] In its primary mode, revelation is not the transmission of information, as with the propositional model, but the sharing of divine life. In revelation, God "addresses us as friends" and invites us into relationship. This revelation is not, however, just a subjective experience; revelation does possess some genuine objective content, as the propositional approach rightly affirms. But here lies the difficulty. God is infinite, incomprehensible mystery, and we are finite creatures. Consequently, God's communication of God's self to us cannot be like my communicating a bus schedule to a friend. Surely as limited creatures we cannot receive God as God is. God cannot be known and mastered the way a beginning chemistry student might strive to master the periodic table. If God really wishes to communicate with us, God must communicate God's self in a manner appropriate to our status as finite, embodied creatures. This is reflected in a medieval dictum, "That which is received is received according to the mode of the receiver" (*quidquid recipitur, recipitur ad modum recipientis*). God comes to us in a manner appropriate to our nature as finite,

---

[3] For a fuller development of this understanding of revelation, see Avery Dulles, *Models of Revelation* (Garden City, NY: Doubleday, 1983), 131–54.

embodied creatures. And as embodied creatures, the primary way in which we come to know our world is through symbols. We learn through language, concepts, images, and metaphors.

It may be helpful to establish a basic distinction between signs and symbols. Signs point to other realities or bits of discrete information (e.g., a red light indicates that we should stop), whereas symbols communicate what the philosopher Paul Ricoeur called a "surplus of meaning."[4] We look at an American flag, a work of art, or a cross—all symbols of one kind or another—and realize that these symbols communicate many different meanings. Indeed, to some extent their meaning changes depending on both the context in which the symbol is encountered and the disposition of the person or community encountering the symbol. An American flag respectfully displayed by a color guard at the beginning of a civic ceremony offers a somewhat different constellation of meanings than an American flag being burned by antiwar protesters. That symbol of a burning flag will also be received differently by an American war veteran than by a diplomat from a foreign country. A cross burning on an African American's front lawn suggests something quite different from a cross leading a liturgical procession at the beginning of a liturgy.

Revelatory symbols also communicate a surplus of meanings. Sometimes these revelatory symbols are linguistic, as with historical narratives, parables, hymns, and doctrinal statements. Sometimes they take the form of distinctive Christian practices, as with the practice of the liturgy. One might also regard art and architecture as potentially revelatory symbols. The Christian community returns time and again to these symbols because it realizes that they draw us into relationship *with* God even as they offer us new insight, new meanings *about* God.

Another way of understanding this approach to revelation is to recall the Catholic understanding of a sacrament. Revelation might be considered sacramental in the sense that, in revelation, as in the sacraments, one encounters God through the medium of some concrete symbol. The Christian enters into sacramental communion with Christ through the eucharistic symbols of bread and wine. The symbols do not just point to Christ; they make Christ present in the sacrament. Yet we acknowledge that this sacramental presence is not the same as a physical

---

[4] See Paul Ricoeur, *Interpretation Theory: Discourse and the Surplus of Meaning* (Fort Worth: Texas Christian University Press, 1976).

presence; we do not encounter Christ in the Eucharist in the same way in which his disciples encountered him along the shores of Galilee before his death and resurrection. In the Eucharist Christ is encountered in a manner that we speak of as "real" and sacramental but not physical. Nor is the encounter with God like an encounter with an object that can be captured and controlled; rather, God meets us in the sacrament as divine Subject who invites us into loving relationship. To take another example, in the sacrament of marriage, I encounter the love of God in my spouse. Yet I recognize that my wife's love for me, while an authentic sacramental mediation of God's love, does not exhaust God's love. God's love is always more and greater than any created mediation of it.

Catholics acknowledge sacramental presence as a unique mode of encountering God. The idea of sacrament affirms that God communicates to us through the mediation of symbols without being reduced to those symbolic expressions as if there were not always "more" of God to be encountered. Now, admittedly, we generally speak of sacraments as mediating God's *grace*, not God's *revelation*. The distinction between grace and revelation is subtle, for both issue from God's desire to share the divine life with us. Perhaps we could say that whereas grace names the offering of God's self to us in the realm of human action, revelation names God's self-communication addressing itself specifically to our consciousness.

Understanding revelation as symbolically mediated also has the advantage of highlighting, more than the propositional approach, the role of human experience in the revelatory process.[5] The term "experience" is an ambiguous one. In contemporary Western culture experience is often used in a purely subjective way, as when we want to emphasize the uniqueness of "my experience." This subjective aspect of human experience is indeed important as it brings to the fore the role of our own personality in shaping how we encounter our world. But experience includes more than this subjective dimension; experience also refers to my engagement with reality. I am always experiencing *something*, and this something names the objective aspect of human experience. Experience does not mean being lost in one's own interiority; it means encountering reality in some determinate way.

---

[5] What follows is indebted to the lucid and concise treatment of human experience in Dermot Lane's *The Experience of God: An Invitation to Do Theology* (New York: Paulist Press, 1981), 4–9.

Another important element in an analysis of human experience is the recognition that human experience is always interpreted. There is really no such thing as a "raw" experience. When we encounter reality, there is a basic dynamism within us that seeks to make sense out of what we have encountered. We try to find *meaning* in our experience. This is never as solitary as we might think. The meanings that we give to our experiences come, at least in part, from the received wisdom of the larger world in which we live—our family, church, and culture. At the same time, we are free to revise these received meanings, to find new insight in what we experience. Finally, we should note that human experience is always partial. As finite creatures, we never encounter reality in its totality. We encounter our world under some aspect or from some particular perspective. Consequently, human experience is never complete; we change and grow in our grasp of reality.

This very cursory consideration of human experience offers much to our understanding of divine revelation. Revelation is God's self-communication, not in some abstract sense, as if revelation were uttered blindly into the cosmos. God communicates *to us*. As humans, we receive that revelation through the prism of historical human experience. Our encounter with the self-revelation of God always has an element of *us* in the encounter. As we receive that revelation we are bound to interpret it, not privately, but from within a number of overlapping interpretive frameworks. Moreover, while from God's side there is nothing lacking in what God communicates to us, from our side, our experience of revelation will always be from a particular perspective and therefore, in some sense, partial or incomplete. This incompleteness must be understood properly. I do not mean that we are missing some vital part of revelation. I am reminded of the Mel Brooks comedy, *The History of the World: Part One*. In it there is this wonderful scene that begins with Brooks playing the role of Moses coming down from Mount Sinai, announcing to the Israelites that he has God's law inscribed on these *three* tablets. Then he stumbles and drops one of them. As it shatters into fragments he pauses, looks up, and says, "Make that *two* tablets!" To say that revelation is incomplete is *not* like that. I do not mean that we are missing a tablet (as if there were an unknown eleventh commandment: "Thou shall not eat asparagus on Tuesdays") but merely that as finite creatures we encounter the revelation of God from our limited human perspective. There is always "more" to be encountered in God's definitive self-revelation in Christ.

SOME BASIC DISTINCTIONS REGARDING
A THEOLOGY OF REVELATION

As theologians have reflected on Vatican II's teaching on revelation, it has been their task to provide a more systematic articulation of that teaching within the larger Catholic theological tradition. This theology of revelation presumes some basic distinctions.[6]

Many theologians will distinguish between *general revelation* and *special revelation*. Revelation, as we have seen, is fundamentally about God revealing God's self with us. This occurs in the most basic or *general* mode of revelation, largely through the beauty and wonder of creation. This is acknowledged in the book of Wisdom. After recalling the beauty of the heavens and the natural wonders that surround us, the biblical author writes: "from the greatness and beauty of created things comes a corresponding perception of their Creator" (Wis 13:5). All peoples should be able to learn of God through an attentive appreciation for the wonder that surrounds us. St. Paul wrote of how even pagans could know of God simply by attending to the world around them: "For what can be known about God is plain to them, because God has shown it to them. Ever since the creation of the world his eternal power and divine nature, invisible though they are, have been understood and seen through the things he has made" (Rom 1:19). Some medieval theologians would speak of God's revelation encountered in two books, the Book of Scripture and the Book of Nature.

This insight has been captured by poets even more profoundly. Elisabeth Barrett Browning invoked the biblical account of God appearing to Moses through a burning bush to suggest that all creation could reveal God if one could but see it:

> Earth's crammed with heaven,
> And every common bush afire with God;
> But only he who sees, takes off his shoes—
> The rest sit round it and pluck blackberries
> And daub their natural faces unaware
> More and more from the first similitude. . . .
>
> If a man could feel,
> Not one day, in the artist's ecstasy,

---

[6] These distinctions are helpfully developed in more depth in Gerald O'Collins, *Rethinking Fundamental Theology* (Oxford: Oxford University Press, 2010).

But every day, feast, fast, or working-day,
The spiritual significance burn through
The hieroglyphic of material shows,
Henceforward he would paint the globe with wings,
And reverence fish and fowl, the bull, the tree,
And even his very body as a man.[7]

Beyond this sense of encountering the revelation of God in nature, there is also another interior sense in which God reveals God's self to us, namely, through the exercise of our conscience. The Second Vatican Council, in its Pastoral Constitution on the Church in the Modern World (*Gaudium et Spes*), eloquently articulates the exercise of conscience as an encounter with the voice of God:

> Deep within their consciences men and women discover a law which they have not laid upon themselves and which they must obey. Its voice, ever calling them to love and to do what is good and to avoid evil, tells them inwardly at the right moment: do this, shun that. For they have in their hearts a law inscribed by God. Their dignity rests in observing this law, and by it they will be judged. Their conscience is people's most secret core, and their sanctuary. There they are alone with God whose voice echoes in their depths. (GS 16)

If God reveals God's self to all humanity in a more general sense, we can also speak of a *special* revelation in which God has revealed God's saving purposes in the history of the people of Israel and preeminently in the incarnation, ministry, suffering, death, resurrection, and ascension of Jesus of Nazareth. Scripture is an inspired testimony or witness to this special revelation.

Regarding this special revelation, it has commonly been held that this revelation ended "with the death of the last apostle." This traditional formulation provided a way of identifying the definitive revelation of God that Christians believe they have received in Jesus Christ and that was testified to by the apostles. This explains why Christians view Scripture as the privileged witness to God's revelation in Christ. Nevertheless, the trinitarian grammar of revelation also illuminates the ways in which the Spirit of Christ continues to "reveal" the love of God to us in the development of tradition. God continues to speak to God's people in

---

[7] Elizabeth Barrett Browning, "Aurora Leigh," in *Mrs. Browning's Complete Poetical Works* (Boston and New York: Houghton, Mifflin and Co., 1900), Book VII, lines 821–26 and 857–64.

worship, in the theological reflection of the great masters, men and women, in the Christian life. God reveals God's self to us in the witness of ordinary believers and in the laments of those who have grappled with all that is not of God—sin, evil, corruption, injustice—even when these occur within the church itself. Gerald O'Collins has proposed that we distinguish between *foundational* revelation that "reached its un-surpassable, once and for all climax with Christ and his apostles" and the *dependent* or ongoing revelation of God encountered through the tradition of the church.[8]

Finally, we can distinguish between *public* revelation and *private* revelations. Public revelation is that revelation that comes to us by way of Scripture and tradition and gives witness to God's saving offer. Private revelations refer to the possibility that individual believers may receive a supernatural revelation in the form of a dream, vision, or apparition, as with the apparition of *La Virgen de Gaudalupe* to St. Juan Diego. Such revelations are given to an individual or group of individuals. The recipients of such revelations may share them with others but believers are not required to accept them as valid. Such revelations should be subject to discernment. It is for those who hear the testimony of an apparition to discern if they believe it to be of God. Occasionally church authorities will enter into a more formal judgment of an apparition's validity. Even when church leaders authenticate the apparition, however, it is still not binding on the church as a whole but is merely being recommended for individual consideration.

In this chapter we have explored the broad outlines of a theology of revelation that we will return to throughout the rest of this book. As we address a number of important topics, our theological context will remain committed to this view of revelation as God's eternal offer of self, rendered definitive in Jesus and made present to the believing community through the power of the Spirit.

---

[8] O'Collins, *Rethinking Fundamental Theology*, 130–35.

DISPUTED QUESTIONS

(1) With regard to Vatican II's theology of revelation, one of the most contentious issues concerns the nature and scope of divine revelation. According to the Second Vatican Council, "Christ is the mediator and sum total of revelation." Some conciliar texts affirm that God can be encountered outside the Judeo-Christian tradition. This raises several important questions. Some theologians have challenged the notion of general revelation for non-Christians. The council certainly affirms the positive value of such religious traditions, they admit. It asserts that they are included in God's "plan of salvation" and that they contain "goodness and truth" (LG 16; see also NA 2). But the council does not directly address itself to the question of whether revelation, properly speaking, is mediated through these traditions. This has been the subject of much debate in the decades since the council.

One school of theologians would read the council texts restrictively, holding that revelation, properly speaking, can be encountered only within the Judeo-Christian tradition. To affirm otherwise, they believe, undercuts the Christian commitment to the uniqueness of Christ. God's offer of salvation to non-Christians manifests itself in ways that can be known only to God. Other theologians contend that the council's recognition of the possibility of salvation for non-Christians presupposes a broader view of revelation. If the non-Christian can be saved, as the council affirmed, doesn't that presuppose that the non-Christian possesses at least some implicit faith? And if they possess an implicit faith, must not that faith be a response to some prior revelation? These theologians wonder, for example, why the Qur'an might not be viewed as a limited mediation of divine revelation. Still other scholars go further and criticize a residual Christian triumphalism in the contention that all revelation finds its term in Christ.

FOR FURTHER READING

Dulles, Avery. *Models of Revelation.* Garden City, NY: Doubleday, 1983.

Dupuis, Jacques. *Toward a Christian Theology of Religious Pluralism.* Maryknoll, NY: Orbis Books, 1997.

Haight, Roger. *Dynamics of Theology*. New York: Paulist Press, 1990.

Knitter, Paul. *Introducing Theologies of Religions*. Maryknoll, NY: Orbis Books, 2002.

Lane, Dermot A. *The Experience of God: An Invitation to Do Theology*. New York: Paulist Press, 1981.

Latourelle, Rene. *Theology of Revelation*. New York: Alba House, 1967.

Levering, Matthew. *Engaging the Doctrine of Revelation*. Grand Rapids: Baker Academic, 2014.

O'Collins, Gerald. *Rethinking Fundamental Theology: Toward a New Fundamental Theology*. Oxford: Oxford University Press, 2011.

Rush, Ormond. *The Eyes of Faith: The Sense of the Faithful and the Church's Reception of Revelation*. Washington, DC: Catholic University of America Press, 2009.

PART TWO

THE AUTHORITY OF
SCRIPTURE AND TRADITION

THREE

WHAT IS THE CANON
OF THE BIBLE?

The word "Bible" conjures a number of images. For some it may call to mind a large family Bible kept in a prominent place in one's home and filled with family genealogical data. Or it may bring to mind one's own personal Bible, with favorite passages marked for easy reference. We might think of a television evangelist, Bible in hand, preaching on the meaning of a particular passage. As I write these words on my laptop in a hotel room, I know there is a copy of the Bible in the drawer of the nightstand, provided by Gideon's International. Whatever the particular recollection, it almost certainly will assume a bound volume, mass-produced for individual purchase and use.

When we consider the appropriate uses of the Bible, many would cite the importance of private Bible reading for spiritual edification. Others might mention its use in faith-based Bible studies constituted by small groups of believers. Many will look to the Bible as a source for particular answers to key decisions or as a warrant for a particular belief. Consequently, it may surprise many to realize that for almost sixteen centuries few Christians owned their own Bible.[1] Indeed, if by Bible we mean a single collection of all the canonical texts, the first true Bible was probably St. Jerome's Vulgate, produced in the late fourth century. For almost a thousand years, copies of biblical texts were compiled in multivolume collections. These collections were relatively rare and kept in monasteries, churches, the private libraries of the nobility, and, later,

---

[1] This brief summary of the history of the Bible is drawn from Christopher De Hamel, *The Book: A History of the Bible* (London: Phaidon Press, 2001).

universities. They were used not for private edification or apologetic disputation but for display, communal worship, and formal study by scholars, monks, and clerics.

The first truly portable Bibles existing as a single bound volume emerged only in the thirteenth century. And only in the thirteenth century did the order of the books within the Bible and the designation of chapter and verse become standardized. Bibles of a size comparable to the modern pocket Bible were developed in Paris in the late thirteenth century. They were made popular by the newly created mendicant religious orders, the Franciscans and Dominicans, who wanted a Bible that could be carried in their habit as they traveled from town to town, exercising their itinerant preaching ministry. These Bibles were produced in the thousands for the friars' use, and the widespread exposure given to these Bibles by the friars undoubtedly led other wealthy and educated persons to obtain copies. Nevertheless, Bibles still would not have been the common possession of individual believers.

The true revolution in the popularity and use of Bibles began with Johannes Gutenberg's invention of a moveable-type printing press. In the mid-fifteenth century, Gutenberg began mass-producing a two-volume Latin Bible that he commercially marketed as a "lectern Bible" to be used in churches and monasteries as well as for private readings in the households of devout, educated laypersons. Between 1520 and 1550, the fortuitous synchronicity of Gutenberg's technology, Luther's vernacular biblical translations, and the Reformation commitment to the priority of the Bible as a religious authority led to what can only be called the "domestication of the Bible in Europe."[2] In consequence, it was only in the sixteenth century that the Bible acquired the authority that many today attach to it, for only in the sixteenth century did the Bible begin to reach thousands of people who had never encountered it outside community worship.

It is one of the truly singular features of the Protestant Reformation that the Bible became an independent source of religious authority to ordinary Christians. Prior to the Reformation the authority of the Bible was, by necessity, conjoined to the authority of the church; it was almost exclusively in the context of church life, in the liturgy, in the university, and in the monastery, that the authority of the Bible was invoked. After

---

[2] Ibid., 216.

the sixteenth century, it would be possible to appeal to the authority of the Bible without having, at the same time, to appeal to the authority of the church. From that time on the question of how to construe the proper relationship between the authority of the church and the authority of the Bible would be a source of division within Christianity.

THE ORIGINS OF THE CANON OF THE BIBLE

Seen from another perspective, the Bible is not just a book that we keep on our nightstand. Christians view the Bible as a defined canon of sacred texts. The term "canon" is derived from the Greek word referring to a reed or instrument of measure. In its early church usage "canon" referred not to the Bible but to the *regula fidei*, the living rule of faith, the preached good news of Jesus the Christ. This was the first measure of the Christian faith. The development of a written canon occurred only very slowly.

The Canon of the Old Testament

The Old Testament itself was composed over a period of almost one thousand years. Much of the literature first appeared in oral form as stories, myths, moral codes, hymns, and aphorisms. What they shared was their testimony to the gracious and faithful activity of the God of Israel in human history. Over time, oral traditions took primitive written form followed by a subsequent process in which these texts were further combined and edited. Particular passages, sometimes placed one after another within a particular book of the Bible, were often written at very different times. Some of the book of Exodus might have been written as early as 1200 BCE only to be combined with other traditions written as late as 500 BCE.

The idea of a collection of sacred writings emerged only gradually among the people of Israel. Many scholars note the significance of the seventh-century Deuteronomic reforms associated with the reign of King Josiah. This period of great reform involved reweaving ancient texts into a new historical framework that offered a master tale of God's dealings with Israel grounded in the giving of the law to Moses. Many of the books of the Old Testament found their final form during this period. The collection of books that resulted went a long way toward shifting the locus of Israelite faith from an oral Torah to a set of sacred writings. An early collection of written texts was likely to have been particularly meaningful for the Israelites as they sought to preserve their identity while in exile. It was during the Babylonian exile and its aftermath that other books would be added to this loose collection.

Judaism preserved from early on, then, a sense of sacred texts that they believed were inspired by God. But they did not engage in any formal process to separate these texts from others. The emergence of a true canon, in the sense of a closed and definitive list of texts that were treated as uniquely authoritative, would come later than was once commonly thought. Disagreement regarding when Judaism moved from a collection of sacred texts to a true canon helps explain the presence of two distinctly different lists of the books contained in the Old Testament.

The Problem of Different Canons

Many Christians are aware that there are differences between the Catholic and Protestant canons of the Old Testament. The traditional explanation for this difference was built on the commonly held assumption that in the first century of Christianity Judaism possessed two different lists of its own sacred texts. One was employed by Palestinian Jews (and referred to as the Palestinian canon) and presupposed the tradition that the Jewish canon was closed at the time of Ezra (ca. fourth to fifth centuries BCE). The second, longer canon was thought to have been adopted by Jews in Northern Africa (often referred to as the Alexandrian canon). This longer canon included books written after the time of Ezra, during the so-called Second Temple period. This canon was enshrined in the Greek Septuagint.

The existence of these two distinct canons was commonly assumed in the fourth century when Christians were compiling their own canon of sacred texts. The majority of early Christian communities followed St. Augustine and the church of North Africa in adopting a list of books thought to be based on the Alexandrian canon. St. Jerome, representing a minority view at the time, proposed acceptance only of the Palestinian canon. Western Christianity ultimately followed St. Augustine and accepted the larger canon of Jewish texts.

This rough consensus would be maintained until the time of the Protestant Reformation. Luther's own views on the canon emerged only gradually. Early in his writing he seems to have accepted those books included in the larger canon. However, in his debates with Johann

Maier of Eck, he was confronted with 2 Maccabees 12:46, which appeared to support the medieval doctrine of purgatory. This raised a question regarding the canonicity of these later Jewish texts and led Luther to adopt the position of Jerome in rejecting the canonicity of all books written after the purported closing of the canon by Ezra. Thus, the distinction between the Protestant and Catholic canons was traced to the assumption of both Augustine and Jerome that there were two canons, one Palestinian, which held for the closing of the canon with Ezra, and a second longer Alexandrian canon. Catholics typically refer to those books included in their canon but not that of the Protestants as deuterocanonical books, while Protestants generally refer to these texts as apocrypha.

Contemporary scholarship, however, has challenged several features of this classical explanation of the different canons. For one thing, it now appears that at the time of Jesus there was, in fact, no fixed Jewish canon of any kind. Judaism certainly believed in a set of inspired writings, but the idea that these writings needed to be definitively set apart from other literature had not yet developed. Bruce Metzger makes a distinction in this regard between "a collection of authoritative books," which Israel had by the Second Temple period, and "an authoritative collection of books," that is, a formal canon, which came much later.[3] Indeed, most scholars now reject the idea, once accepted by both Jerome and Augustine, that there ever were two distinct Jewish canons. It now appears that it was only well after 70 CE, when Judaism shifted "from a temple-based religion to a text-based religion," that Judaism became concerned with identifying a precise biblical canon.[4] And Christianity itself did not focus on the need for a true canon of its own until the late second century. In other words, the early Christian acceptance of later biblical texts like 1–2 Maccabees had nothing to do with assumptions about a prior Jewish canon because there was, as yet, no such canon. Some Jews accepted the later books as authoritative, and others did not. Christian communities seem to have come to their own judgment, largely based on more pragmatic considerations, with the criterion of

---

[3] Bruce Metzger, *The Canon of the New Testament: Its Origin, Development, and Significance* (Oxford: Clarendon, 1987), 283.

[4] Eugene Ulrich, "The Notion and Definition of Canon," in *The Canon Debate,* ed. Lee Martin McDonald and James A. Sanders (Peabody, MA: Hendrickson Publishers, 2002), 21–35, at 24.

liturgical usage playing a significant role. The influential list offered by the North African Council of Hippo in the late fourth century reflects that church's dependence on the contents of the Septuagint manuscripts available to them at the time.

The Development of the New Testament Canon

As with the texts of the Old Testament, many of those of the New Testament, particularly the gospels, likely emerged out of a multistage process beginning with oral materials. Most of the New Testament literature was written between about 50 and 110 CE. St. Paul's letters soon found wide circulation, and later generations would emulate his approach, even to the point of writing under his name, as with at least some of the pastoral letters. Later citations from early church writers suggest that the four gospels and many of Paul's letters were used widely among the churches. As with the Old Testament, for several centuries there were Christian *Scriptures* before there was a Christian *canon*. The eventual need to identify a closed canon developed only gradually. As heretical movements emerged that appeared to threaten the integrity of the Christian faith, two strategies were employed in tandem: (1) the development of a biblical canon that could be used as the measure of authentic Christian faith, and (2) the development of a church office empowered to preserve the one apostolic faith. We will concern ourselves with the second development in part 3 of this volume. The development of a true canon that became not just a collection of texts but a closed list of texts given uniquely authoritative status took place, for the most part, in the third and fourth centuries.

But how did these communities set about determining which texts were or were not canonical? Several criteria came into play. First was the question of *apostolicity*, that is, a text's connection with a known apostle of Christ. In fact, the apostolicity of a text may have been more a matter of legend, but *the claim* to apostolicity remained a significant factor in determining the status of a text. A second criterion concerned the importance of the community from which a text emerged. So, for example, the disruption of early Palestinian Christianity may explain why no strictly Palestinian text ever found its way into the canon, whereas several texts from Syria (Matthew, James, and Jude) were accepted. A third criterion was the text's conformity with the "rule of faith." No text could be accepted into the canon that proposed teachings at odds with the received apostolic faith. This helps explain why certain texts with more idiosyncratic theological perspectives (e.g., Hebrews and Revelation) won acceptance into the canon only at a relatively late date and after considerable debate. Finally, we must acknowledge the importance of liturgical usage. The liturgical use of a text often played a decisive role in its inclusion in the canon.

Within the Orthodox traditions even today, the question of liturgical use has been determinative. The Orthodox see the Bible as the principal "prayer book of the church."[5] For them all questions of canonicity are ultimately questions about which books the church shall proclaim in its liturgy. This position is more distinctive than may first appear. As the Eastern Orthodox biblical scholar Michael Prokurat put it: "In saying Scripture is liturgical, we do not mean to say merely that liturgy is scriptural; but moreover that what was originally liturgy became Scripture. Scripture had its emergence and continued existence in the liturgy, the liturgical life of the Temple and Church, the communal prayers of the people of God."[6]

Although the Christian canon became fixed, for the most part, by the end of the fourth century, we should be careful not to make too much of this. Within that canon a core set of books existed that were broadly accepted and quite influential in sustaining the faith of the early community. Other books were more controversial and, though technically canonical, never received the same weight within the tradition. Still other texts that were not finally included in the canon would remain quite influential for many Christian communities. Even after the canon became "fixed" in the late fourth century, disagreements would continue, in varying degrees, for centuries. Many distinguished figures over the centuries expressed doubts of one kind or another regarding the contents of the canon, including Pope St. Gregory the Great, St. John Damascene, Hugh of St. Victor, and Cardinal Cajetan.

Distinguishing Questions of Canonicity from Questions of Inspiration

The determination of a canon was, at least initially, not about separating inspired books from non-inspired books but a matter of determining

---

[5] Michael Prokurat, "Orthodox Interpretation of Scripture," in *The Bible in the Churches*, ed. Kenneth Hagan, 3rd ed. (Milwaukee, WI: Marquette University Press, 1998), 62.

[6] Ibid.

which books were reliable witnesses to the ancient faith. What distinguishes the canon from other works, in other words, is not inspiration but the church's Spirit-assisted judgment regarding the reliable testimony of these works. As Robert Gnuse puts it: "The ancient church did not bestow authority on the various works incorporated into the canon, it merely recognized the authority which already lay therein."[7]

The idea that only the canonical books of the Bible could lay claim to inspiration now appears to have had its origin in later Jewish literature (after the first century) in which some rabbis taught that inspiration could be found only in the sacred writings from Moses to Ezra. The early Christian community eventually came upon this notion and accepted it. However, the more ancient Christian perspective is described succinctly by Albert Sundberg: "Thus, in forming the canon, the church acknowledged and established the Bible as the measure or standard of inspiration in the church, not as the totality of it. What concurs with canon is of like inspiration; what does not is not of God."[8] To help explore this distinction between canonicity and inspiration, consider the following thought experiment.

Suppose that archaeologists were to discover a lost letter of St. Paul, his *Second* Letter to the Romans, let's say. After careful study, biblical scholars conclude that it is indeed an authentic letter of Paul. What should the Christian churches do? Should they expand the canon of the Bible to include the book? An affirmative answer confuses the question of inspiration and canonicity, for while one might legitimately conclude that the text was inspired, this does not make it necessarily canonical. The canon was established in the early church as a way of designating books whose inspiration was authenticated and therefore *could serve as a norm for the faith of the churches*. A book found only today could not qualify, not because of any questions regarding its "inspired" character, but because it has not served as a norm for the faith of the churches. It has not served as an ecclesial benchmark for the development of our liturgy, theology, spirituality, and church discipline.

---

[7] Robert Gnuse, *The Authority of the Bible: Theories of Inspiration, Revelation and the Canon of Scripture* (New York: Paulist Press, 1985), 110.

[8] Albert Sundberg, "The Bible Canon and the Christian Doctrine of Inspiration," *Interpretation* (1974): 371.

THE SIGNIFICANCE OF A BIBLICAL CANON
FOR AUTHORITY IN THE CHURCH

One of the most important functions of the biblical canon is to remind us that Christianity is a historical religion; it is not grounded in a collection of eternal myths but in a set of historical accounts of God's saving action on behalf of humanity. In other words, Christians do not believe that they can "make it up as they go." Of course, as we shall see in chapter 5, Christianity is also an innovative religion that accepts the possibility of emerging new insight about the faith. The Christian faith is always in some sense tethered to its past, even if that tether can appear quite elastic at times. The canonical books of the Bible anchor that elastic tether. These sacred texts stand as a norm for the Christian faith, a benchmark against which all further expressions of Christian belief and all further Christian activity must be measured. And yet, as we will see in our later chapter on tradition, there is a sense in which, at least for Catholics, Scripture is also *normed* by tradition, at least insofar as it must always be interpreted within the living tradition of the church.

The authority of the Bible is also situated within the life of the community. Our consideration of the formation of the biblical canon can leave no doubt but that the Bible itself emerged out of the prior life of communities of faith (both of Israel and early Christianity). The Scriptures are the end result of a centuries-old process by which human experiences of the saving God were given first oral and then written expression as dynamic traditions, only much later finding their final form in the biblical texts.

It is quite easy for us to forget the extent to which biblical religion was originally non-scriptural. For much of the history of Israel, its faith was rooted not in a set of written texts at all but in the encounter with the living God. Abraham was not confronted with a biblical text. In like manner, it was not a biblical text that was the agent of St. Paul's conversion; both Abraham and Paul were transformed by encounters with God.[9] The origins of the Bible are found in testimony, first oral and then written, to the saving work of God.

Modern Christianity's appeal to the authority of written texts distinguishes it from the biblical communities that produced the Scriptures. Those early communities bequeathed to us the Scriptures, but they were

---

[9] Gnuse, *The Authority of the Bible*, 116–17.

not, by and large, governed by them. That both Augustine and Martin Luther would be converted by reading a text of the Bible demonstrates the fundamental difference between biblical religion and religion founded on the Bible. This insight can perhaps protect us against the temptation to look to the canon of the Bible as a depository of self-contained truths. The authority of the Bible cannot be sustained in this fashion. As we shall see in the next chapter, the authority of the Bible lies in its being a testimony to something prior, something beyond the written text; it is a testimony to the saving and revelatory action of God in history.

Contemporary Catholicism has learned much from the Churches of the Reformation, not the least of which being the importance of the Bible as offering foundational testimony for the Christian faith. Catholicism has generally rejected the classical Protestant view, however, that the authority of the Bible precedes that of the church. For Catholicism, the Bible is the product of the faith of Israel and the early Christian communities. On the other hand, Catholicism has sometimes abused this insight. Certain church attitudes and practices have sometimes given the impression that the chronological priority of church over Bible justifies limiting the authority of the Bible to a kind of remote corroboration for the authoritative teaching of the pope and bishops. This view fails to do justice to the circularity of authority in the church: under the guidance of the Spirit the church authoritatively established the canon but did so with the recognition that this canon would subsequently bind the teaching and practice of the church.

Scripture does not function solely to ground Christian faith in the past; it also orients Christianity toward the future. Our conventional way of understanding the Bible is to see it as giving historical testimony to what God *has* accomplished, and that is true. But the Bible also stands as a testimony to the future, to what God *wishes* to accomplish in the future. We must turn to the Bible to help us interpret our present experience in the light of the future promised us in faith. Those promises appear throughout the Scriptures.[10] By "promise" and "future" I do not mean predictions of future events as one often finds with fundamentalist readings of the book of Revelation. I mean the way in which the biblical texts give testimony to a world yet to be realized, a world of

---

[10] James Barr, *The Scope and Authority of the Bible* (Philadelphia: Westminster Press, 1980), 60–61.

grace and mercy, a world in which "the lion shall lie down with the lamb" and in which "they shall beat their swords into ploughshares."

We must be careful not to oversimplify the significance of a fixed canon in the Christian tradition. As the biblical scholar, James D. G. Dunn has remarked:

> Whatever the theory and theology of canonicity, the reality is that all Christians have operated *with a canon within the canon.* Any who use their New Testament a great deal will at once acknowledge that some pages are more grubby with finger marks than others; how many sermons has the average "person in the pew" heard on Heb 7, say, as against Matt 5–7 or Acts 2 or 1 Cor 13?[11]

For Catholics, however, this undeniable truth simply reinforces the importance of a communal interpretation of Scripture. It is precisely because we are inclined to our favorite passages that we must learn to read Scripture as a community wherein other texts are brought to our attention and we are exposed to the challenging diversity of biblical testimony.

Finally, one of the most important functions of the biblical canon is to remind us that the Bible canonizes Christian diversity. Within the canon, we encounter a dizzying diversity of biblical insight and often a host of not so easily resolved tensions. This too is important, for it reminds us that the necessary unity of the church must not be reduced to a suffocating uniformity. The diversity of testimonies, concerns, and theological insights in the biblical canon affirms the need for a legitimate diversity within the church itself.[12] Yet, even as the canon reminds us of the need for that diversity, it also *"marks out the limits of acceptable diversity."*[13] To assert the authority of the canon is to recognize how early in the history of Christianity there emerged the conviction that not all accounts of the Gospel were equally valid. Some books didn't get in for a reason. This is not to deny that a certain amount of power politics played a role, but most Christians would continue to believe that the determination of the canon was also a Spirit-assisted discernment about the authority or lack of authority of certain ways of understanding the Christian message.

---

[11] James D. G. Dunn, "Has the Canon a Continuing Function?," in *The Canon Debate,* 558–79, at 559.

[12] Ibid., 563.

[13] Ibid., 565; emphasis is mine.

In this chapter, we have explored the formation of the canon of the Bible and have traced the history of the Bible's changing role in the life of the church. Earlier in the chapter we argued that canonicity represented the Christian church's discernment regarding which ancient texts were inspired by the Spirit of God and suitable for norming the faith of the church. In the next chapter, we will consider in more detail what is meant by such terms as "inspiration" and "inerrancy" as they are put to the service of the Christian belief in the Bible's abiding role in the life of the church.

DISPUTED QUESTIONS

(1) The different canons of the Old Testament continue to be a matter of scholarly debate. In the last fifty years, some Protestant scholars have been calling for a reassessment of the Protestant position on this matter. They have challenged their own traditions to consider the consequences of the fact that Luther's justification of a narrower canon seems to have been based on St. Jerome's erroneous assumption regarding the Jewish canon. On the other hand, Catholic scholars have brought to light some complexities involved in the Council of Trent's declaration of canonical books. They note the irony in Trent's having declared St. Jerome's Vulgate normative even though Jerome himself held for a shorter canon. They also point out the alarming lack of scholarly expertise brought to bear on the question by the council.

(2) Feminist biblical scholarship has questioned whether patriarchal assumptions influenced early church decisions regarding the canonicity of certain texts. Did these cultural biases lead the early Christian community to exclude women's perspectives from the canon or to enshrine texts that promote the denigration of women? Some feminists accept the canon as provisionally normative but warn that one should not see the assertion of an authoritative biblical canon as a negative judgment on the spiritual value of other noncanonical texts from the biblical period, some of which cast women in a more positive light.

FOR FURTHER READING

Abraham, William J. *Canon and Criterion in Christian Theology.* Oxford: Clarendon Press, 1998.

Barr, James. *Holy Scripture: Canon, Authority, Criticism.* Philadelphia: Westminster, 1983.

Brown, Raymond E., and Raymond F. Collins. "Canonicity." In *The New Jerome Biblical Commentary*, edited by Raymond E. Brown, Joseph A. Fitzmyer, and Roland E. Murphy, 1034–54. Englewood Cliffs, NJ: Prentice Hall, 1990.

De Hamel, Christopher. *The Book: A History of the Bible.* London: Phaidon Press, 2001.

Gnuse, Robert. *The Authority of the Bible: Theories of Inspiration, Revelation and the Canon of Scripture.* New York: Paulist Press, 1985.

Hagen, Kenneth, ed. *The Bible in the Churches: How Various Christians Interpret the Scriptures.* Milwaukee: Marquette University Press, 1998.

Lienhard, Joseph T. *The Bible, the Church, and Authority: The Canon of the Christian Bible in History and Theology.* Collegeville, MN: Liturgical Press, 1995.

McDonald, Lee Martin, and James A. Sanders, eds. *The Canon Debate.* Peabody, MA: Hendrickson Publishers, 2002.

Metzger, Bruce. *The Canon of the New Testament: Its Origin, Development, and Significance.* Oxford: Clarendon Press, 1987.

Russell, Letty, ed. *Feminist Interpretation of the Bible.* Philadelphia: Westminster, 1985.

Schneiders, Sandra M. *The Revelatory Text: Interpreting the New Testament as Sacred Scripture.* New York: HarperCollins, 1991.

Schüssler Fiorenza, Elisabeth. *In Memory of Her: A Feminist Theological Reconstruction of Christian Origins.* New York: Crossroad, 1983.

Sundberg, Albert. "The Bible Canon and the Christian Doctrine of Inspiration." *Interpretation* (1974): 352–71.

WHAT IS BIBLICAL INSPIRATION AND INERRANCY?

In the Catholic Mass, when the lector has concluded proclaiming one of the first two readings from Scripture, he or she solemnly intones to the assembly: "The Word of the Lord." The belief that Scripture is the Word of God is one of the most basic Christian beliefs. Yet this affirmation needs to be made with some care. Pope Benedict XVI, in his apostolic exhortation *Verbum Domini*, warned that Scripture can only be called the Word of God by way of analogy. For Christians, God's Word comes to us, not initially as a text, but as a Person, the divine *Logos*, who in the fullness of time was incarnate in Jesus of Nazareth. Christianity, moreover, is not properly speaking "a religion of the book," the pope reminded us. Why? Because the Word of God does not reside exclusively in a written text: "the Scripture is to be proclaimed, heard, read, received and experienced as the word of God, in the stream of the apostolic Tradition from which it is inseparable" (VD 7). The contention that Christianity, like Islam (and Judaism), is a "religion of the book" presupposes that what the Qur'an is for Islam, the Bible is for Christianity. But this is not quite right. It would be more accurate to say that what the Qur'an is for Islam, Jesus Christ is for Christianity.

From a different perspective, the feminist biblical scholar and theologian Sandra Schneiders contends that the claim that Scripture is the Word of God is "a metaphor for the *whole process and reality of symbolic divine revelation* culminating for Christians in Jesus."[1] If we literalize the metaphor, she warns, we get a more problematic form of biblical fundamentalism. For fundamentalist Christians, belief that Scripture is the Word of God devolves easily into a belief that Scripture contains the *words* of God. They believe that the particular words of the Bible, in the original languages in which they were written, were given to the biblical authors in a process that can only be described as a kind of spiritual dictation. The closest analog for this in other traditions is Islam, which holds that the words of the Qur'an were dictated to the prophet Mohammed through the angel Gabriel. Consequently, for Islam, only the Arabic text of the Qur'an is considered the inspired text. Few Christians go this far. They readily grant the need for vernacular translations, but many do treat the Bible as the "words" of God. This view cannot be reconciled with the Catholic commitment that while Scripture *mediates* God's Word (recall what we said in chapter 2 about revelation being *symbolically mediated*), that Word is more than a written text; it is a living Word.

The distinctive authority of Scripture is often explained by appeal to the concept of biblical inspiration. The belief in the inspiration of Scripture is as ancient as the church. It was borrowed from ancient Jewish convictions regarding the inspiration of the *Tanak* (the Torah, the Prophets, and the Writings), and some sense of biblical inspiration of the *Tanak* is clearly assumed in several New Testament texts:

> All scripture is inspired by God and is useful for teaching, for reproof, for correction, and for training in righteousness, so that everyone who belongs to God may be proficient, equipped for every good work. (2 Tim 3:16-17)

> So we have the prophetic message more fully confirmed. You will do well to be attentive to this as to a lamp shining in a dark place, until the day dawns and the morning star rises in your hearts. First of all you must understand this, that no prophecy of scripture is a matter of one's own interpretation, because no prophecy ever came by human will, but men and women moved by the Holy Spirit spoke from God. (2 Pet 1:19-21)

Note that these New Testament texts have in mind the Old Testament when they refer to Scripture. The biblical authors were more interested

---

[1] Sandra Schneiders, "Scripture as the Word of God," *Princeton Seminary Bulletin* (1993): 18–35, at 24.

in offering testimony to God's saving work than in offering any particular warrants for the nature of their own authority. We will return to this notion of testimony later in the chapter.

The term "inspiration" refers to Christian convictions that the Bible is "God-breathed," that the texts themselves, or at least their religious content, are the consequence of some special form of the Spirit's influence. The Pontifical Biblical Commission, in its document *The Inspiration and Truth of Sacred Scripture*, made a helpful distinction between revelation and inspiration:

> "Revelation" is presented as the fundamental act of God by which he communicates who he is and the mystery of his will, at the same time rendering human beings capable of receiving revelation. "Inspiration," however, is presented as the action by which God enables certain persons, chosen by him, to transmit his revelation faithfully in writing. Inspiration presupposes revelation and is at the service of the faithful transmission of revelation in the biblical writings.[2]

Insofar as inspiration refers to God's activity, the term is generally only employed with reference to the Spirit's influence on the formation of those sacred texts of Scripture. When theologians speak of other ways in which God influences the mediation of revelation, such as the teaching of the magisterium (the authoritative teaching office of the pope and bishops), they generally refer to such divine influence not as inspiration but as divine "assistance."

THEORIES OF BIBLICAL INSPIRATION

Robert Gnuse contends that most theories of biblical inspiration fall loosely into one of two general categories: verbal inspiration and non-verbal inspiration.[3]

Verbal Inspiration

Theories of verbal inspiration focus on the biblical text itself and the ways in which divine influence can be asserted in the production of the

---

[2] Pontifical Biblical Commission, *The Inspiration and Truth of Sacred Scripture* (Collegeville, MN: Liturgical Press, 2014), 3–4.

[3] Robert Gnuse, *The Authority of the Bible: Theories of Inspiration, Revelation and the Canon of Scripture* (New York: Paulist Press, 1985), 22–65.

biblical text. Following Gnuse, we can divide verbal inspiration into two further subcategories: *strict verbal inspiration* and *limited verbal inspiration.* Strict verbal inspiration assumes there was an identifiable group of biblical authors who could be distinguished from the larger community of Israel and early Christianity and who were subject to a distinct form of divine influence in their authorship. Proponents of this view generally admit that the biblical authors wrote in their own style and in keeping with their own education, but they insist that the authors' intellects were directed by God to communicate divine truth wholly and infallibly. Strict verbal models of inspiration generally presuppose something like the propositional model of revelation discussed in chapter 2. What follows, not surprisingly, is the conviction that Scripture is entirely without error in regard to all of its propositional truth claims. This is often referred to as the belief in the *total or plenary inerrancy* of the Bible. This protection from error extends beyond religious truth to include all biblical truth claims, including those regarding history, geography, science, and culture.

One question this approach immediately raises concerns the problem of the biblical text itself. We do not have any original manuscript of a book of the Bible. Prior to the discovery of the Dead Sea Scrolls, our oldest manuscripts for the Old Testament were dated to the ninth century CE. Even now the oldest manuscripts of the whole New Testament (the *Codex Vaticanus* and *Codex Sinaiticus*) date back only to the fourth century (though we have some small fragments dating all the way to the early second century). Not surprisingly, given the extended period of time between the original authorship of a biblical text and the date of the manuscript copies we possess, these manuscripts do not agree with one another in every detail; individual manuscripts often contain variant readings of a given passage. Proponents of strict verbal inspiration are aware of these difficulties and usually respond that biblical inspiration only concerns the original text and not the copies. They are willing to recognize the fallibility of manuscript copies while insisting that the minor discrepancies that might emerge through scribal errors do not in any way affect the revealed content of the Bible.

Though this view of biblical inspiration and inerrancy is quite popular in Christian circles, there are significant difficulties with this approach. Strict verbal inspiration focuses on the divine origins of biblical texts without attending sufficiently to the humanity of the authors who actually composed them. The popular consequence of this approach to inspiration will often be to use the Bible as a kind of owner's manual intended to provide authoritative answers on matters as diverse as the origins of human life, investment strategies, parenting skills, and the choice of a spouse. Moreover, advocates of strict verbal inspiration, by emphasizing the absolute inerrancy of the Bible, often focus more on defense of the text itself rather than on the message the biblical texts are supposed to communicate.

Many mainstream churches, including contemporary Catholic teaching, uncomfortable with the fundamentalist tendencies of strict verbal inspiration, have pursued a more moderate perspective, what Gnuse refers to as limited verbal inspiration. This approach draws on the early Christian notion of "divine accommodation" in which it was thought that, while God inspired the biblical authors, it was necessary for God to make "accommodations" to the limited knowledge of those authors. Consequently, Origen, the influential third-century Alexandrian theologian, admitted that some biblical narratives that purported to be historical in fact may have never occurred. This did not mean, however, that they were not inspired. Origen insisted that such texts must be interpreted in the light of a nonliteral, interior reading.[4] Later some medieval thinkers would distinguish between God's role as the primary cause in the authorship of biblical texts and the role of human authors as the instrumental causes of the same texts.

Current proponents of this more moderate view of verbal inspiration have incorporated significant contemporary developments in biblical studies, often referred to as *historical-critical methods*. These methods do not preclude biblical inspiration, but they do presuppose that discovering the meaning of a text requires the rigorous application of tools for historical investigation and literary analysis. For example, it is now commonly acknowledged by mainstream biblical scholars, Catholic and Protestant, that the adequate interpretation of a biblical text requires that the interpreter attend to the following: (1) the intention of the author as best as it can be discerned; (2) the historical, social, and cultural context in which a text was written; (3) the particular literary genre or form that was employed in the text; (4) the history of a particular

---

[4] Origen's approach to biblical interpretation is developed in his *On First Principles*. An excellent guide to understanding his thought is Peter W. Martens, *Origen and Scripture: The Contours of the Exegetical Life* (New York: Oxford University Press, 2012).

text that might have developed from an early oral stage and gone through various revisions on the way to the final form encountered in the Bible; (5) the various symbolic and mythological uses of narrative; (6) the interpretation of a particular text within the context of the whole of biblical testimony; (7) the way the text has been read within the tradition of the church.

Adherents of this view may acknowledge a unique divine influence on the biblical authors but contend that this influence would not have precluded the biblical authors writing from within a historically and culturally conditioned framework. Many advocates of limited verbal inspiration remain committed to the inerrancy of the Bible, although usually with the significant qualification that the Bible be considered without error only as regards divine revelation but not as regards historical or scientific matters. We will have more to say about biblical inerrancy later in the chapter.

NONVERBAL INSPIRATION

Advocates of verbal inspiration share a preoccupation with the production of the biblical texts themselves. Problems with manuscript discrepancies and our knowledge of the long, multistage historical process that produced many biblical texts have, however, led some scholars to pursue other approaches, what Gnuse calls nonverbal models of inspiration. One way to do this is to distinguish between the human words that form the biblical text and the underlying ideas or religious content that the text communicates. This theory holds that God does not actually form the words in the mind of the author but rather inspires an idea or insight that the authors then communicate in their own words. Again, going back to the third century, Origen understood inspiration as entailing a kind of "illumination" of the biblical author. This theory accommodated a more expansive role for the human agency of the biblical author. In the nineteenth century, some theologians, like Cardinal John Henry Newman, held that the Bible was inspired only as regarded faith and morals. In the same century, influential Catholic neoscholastic theologians like Giovanne Perrone and Johann Baptist Franzelin affirmed that the biblical authors received ideas by way of divine assistance but that the words chosen by the authors were of completely human origin.

Another variant of nonverbal inspiration has focused, not on the idea communicated in a particular text, but rather on some religious experience that had a broader impact on the author. For example, one might link the inspiration of St. Paul to his own conversion experience on the road to Damascus. To say that the Bible is inspired in this sense is simply to say that the Bible gives testimony to the religious experiences of its authors. The principal danger of this approach is the possible reduction of the Bible to a collection of subjective accounts of religio-mystical encounters with very little objective content. It also makes it very difficult to distinguish between an "idea" and the verbal expression of that "idea." This approach has the obvious advantage, however, of avoiding the problems of inerrancy that accompany a claim that the biblical text itself is inspired.

Up to this point, all of the theories of inspiration that we have considered have focused on the Holy Spirit's influence on a particular biblical author. As such, we may consider these psychological theories of inspiration. But such theories face a fundamental challenge in the face of modern biblical scholarship: if many biblical texts emerged out of a multistage process of development, sometimes being preserved through generations of oral transmission before being transcribed as a written text, then how does one identify the author who is the subject of divine inspiration? One solution is to resituate inspiration within the life of ancient Israel and the early Christian community. Social inspiration theories highlight the activity of the Spirit at work within all the complex human interactions of ancient Israel and the early Christian community, social interactions that ultimately gave rise to the biblical texts.[5]

In our world today, concerns about plagiarism and copyright violations reflect the importance we give to the individual authorship of a literary work. This was not the case in the ancient world. Many biblical texts were written anonymously, with biblical authorship ascribed to them only generations after they were written. Given this reality it only makes sense, proponents of this theory contend, to focus on the Spirit's activity within the whole community. This social theory accords well with a significant but generally overlooked feature of the very origins of Christianity. Jesus of Nazareth did not bequeath to his followers a written text of any kind. He wrote no memoirs, no autobiography, no

---

[5] For different versions of this approach, see Paul J. Achtemeier, *The Inspiration of Scripture: Problems and Proposals* (Philadelphia: Westminster Press, 1980); John L. McKenzie, "The Social Character of Inspiration," *Catholic Biblical Quarterly* (1962): 15–24; Karl Rahner, *Inspiration in the Bible, Quaestiones Disputatae* 1 (New York: Herder, 1961).

written rules of conduct. Rather than leave a written text, Jesus called forth a community of disciples. Jesus' own actions suggest that he put higher stock in community formation and witness than the production of a written text.

VATICAN II'S TREATMENT OF BIBLICAL AUTHORITY

In the nineteenth century, Catholic scholars like Newman and Franzelin grappled with ways to affirm the Bible's inspiration while allowing some room for non-revelatory error. However, Pope Leo XIII's encyclical *Providentissimus Deus* (1893), which offered a modest encouragement for contemporary biblical scholarship, appeared to put an end to such theories with its assertion that the Bible was without error in all matters. The climate for biblical scholarship improved considerably when Pope Pius XII published his encyclical, *Divino Afflante Spiritu*, in 1943. Pope Pius reasserted Pope Leo's conviction regarding the total inerrancy of Scripture, yet he also took the important step of permitting Catholic biblical scholars to make full use of modern historical-critical methods. When the Second Vatican Council opened nineteen years later, the Catholic Church was only just beginning to experience the firstfruits of this development. Consequently, the council members were inclined to proceed quite cautiously on questions related to the authority of the Bible.

Biblical Inspiration in *Dei Verbum*

The explicit treatment of biblical inspiration in *Dei Verbum* was actually relatively cautious and did not break much new ground. The biggest development in the presentation of biblical inspiration actually came from the new context for considering divine revelation that was presented in the first two chapters of the dogmatic constitution. There, revelation was presented in relation to its trinitarian origin, as we saw in chapter 2, and with a greater emphasis on the economy of salvation. As Denis Farkasfalvy notes, this emphasis on God as revealed in salvation history "did not allow the notion of 'revealed truth' to be reduced or restricted to propositional statements."[6] It also allowed for a broader

---

[6] Denis Farkasfalvy, "Inspiration and Interpretation," in *Vatican II: Renewal within Tradition*, ed. Matthew L. Lamb and Matthew Levering (New York: Oxford University Press, 2008), 77–100, at 79.

notion of divine inspiration, one that moved away from strict verbal inspiration and toward something closer to limited verbal inspiration.

Dei Verbum's consideration of biblical inspiration emphasized the role of human agency in the authorship of Scripture. Where an earlier version of article 7 referred to the "dictation of the holy Spirit," the final text refers to a "prompting of the holy Spirit," a much more circumspect description of God's action and one that left more room for human freedom. The council proposed a "two author" theory, referring to God as the "author" of Scripture while also insisting that the biblical writers were "true authors" who made full use of their own powers and abilities. How the collaboration between the divine and human authors was to be conceived was left largely unconsidered. The council members seemed well aware that there was much more constructive theological work to be done on the topic. Consequently, they were content to make several general assertions while leaving the door open for further theological development.

Biblical Inerrancy in *Dei Verbum*

The council did feel it necessary to address the question of biblical inerrancy. For much of the modern period, including in the encyclicals of Popes Leo XIII and Pius XII, assertions of total biblical inerrancy were cast defensively in response to rationalist attempts to undermine the credibility of the Bible by pointing out its various errors. This defensive posture no longer appeared adequate.

An early version of the document on revelation still included previous teaching on total inerrancy, holding that the Scriptures were, in their entirety, completely without error regarding all truths, "religious or profane" (*re religiosa et profana*). Many bishops saw in this view of inspiration and inerrancy echoes of an ancient heresy about Christ, monophysitism, in which Christ was thought to have one divine nature, his humanity effectively being absorbed into the divine—the humanity of the biblical text was in danger of being absorbed into divine authorship. This tendency presented difficulties for those bishops who were well aware of certain historical difficulties found in the Bible.

On October 2, 1964, Cardinal König of Vienna gave a provocative speech in which he warned the bishops not to ignore what many biblical scholars already knew, namely, that certain scientific and historical claims and/or assumptions in the Bible were "deficient." The classic example often cited was Mark 2:26 in which Jesus mentions David's entering the house of God under the high priest Abiathar to eat the "bread of the presence" with his soldiers. This conflicted with the account in 1 Samuel 21:1-6, which said that David did so, not under Abiathar, but under his father Ahimelech. In this instance clearly someone was mistaken, either Mark or Jesus! One could also list inconsistencies in the gospels regarding the timing (at the beginning or the end of Christ's ministry) of the so-called cleansing of the temple, geographic inaccuracies in the Gospel of Mark, or the disagreement among the gospels regarding whether Christ's last supper occurred on Passover or not.

In response to this recognition of certain "deficiencies" in the biblical text, the general sentiment of the bishops was, on the one hand, to avoid any sense that only parts of Scripture were inspired, while, on the other hand, allowing for these deficiencies (bishops were still reluctant to speak of biblical "errors") in the text. Finally, the council simply avoided the religious/profane truths distinction altogether. The official formulation of the council's teaching was arrived at after tortuous negotiation in which even the pope weighed in with his views on the matter. The final text reads:

> Since, therefore, all that the inspired authors, or sacred writers, affirm should be regarded as affirmed by the holy Spirit, we must acknowledge that the books of scripture, firmly, faithfully and without error, teach that truth *which God, for the sake of our salvation, wished to see confided to the sacred scriptures.* (DV 11, emphasis is mine)

The key was the formulation "for the sake of our salvation." This shifted the emphasis from the content of Scripture, that is, the biblical text itself, to the divine intention. Rather than risk dividing Scripture into religious and profane truths, or inspired and non-inspired passages, the council held that inspiration and inerrancy be viewed from the perspective of God's salvific intention. *All* Scripture was inspired, but inspired with a view to communicate God's saving offer, not with a view to historical or scientific accuracy. The scientific and historical framework of biblical texts are to be read as a medium for the communication of God's offer of salvation.

This position represented a subtle but important departure from the commitment to total inerrancy found in the teaching of Popes Leo XIII and Pius XII. The council's perspective was carefully crafted to admit the possibility of human limitations and deficiencies entering into the authorship of the sacred texts but in such a way that God's saving truth was still faithfully communicated through the medium of the entire biblical testimony.

DEVELOPMENTS SINCE THE COUNCIL

Since the council, questions of biblical inspiration and inerrancy have received relatively little attention, at least directly. Broader considerations of the authority of Scripture have often drawn on modern hermeneutical theory, particularly in the work of figures like Paul Ricoeur.[7] Sandra Schneiders, for example, draws considerably on Ricoeur's understanding of *testimony*.[8] For Schneiders and others testimony is a fundamental category for grasping the character of Scripture. We have an explicit statement of the testimonial character of Scripture near the end of the Gospel of John:

> Now Jesus did many other signs in the presence of his disciples, which are not written in this book. But these are written so that you may come to believe that Jesus is the Messiah, the Son of God, and that through believing you may have life in his name. (John 20:30-31)

The gospel author insists that the fundamental orientation of the Gospel of John was *not* toward the factual communication of names, places, and dates. Rather, the gospel gave faithful witness to God's saving offer made real and effective in Jesus. Testimony means more than offering a historical account of an event. When a witness gives testimony "the witness stakes her or his personal integrity on the truth of the testimony, even calling on God by oath to guarantee its veracity."[9] This testimonial character of Scripture is evident as well in the opening of 1 John:

> We declare to you what was from the beginning,
> what we have heard,
> what we have seen with our eyes,
> what we have looked at and touched with our hands,
> concerning the word of life—this life was revealed,
> and we have seen it and testify to it,
> and declare to you the eternal life
> that was with the Father and was revealed to us—

---

[7] Paul Ricoeur, "The Hermeneutics of Testimony," in *Essays on Biblical Interpretation* (Philadelphia: Fortress Press, 1980), 119–54.

[8] Schneiders, "Scripture as the Word of God," 25–29.

[9] Ibid., 25.

we declare to you what we have seen and heard
so that you also may have fellowship with us;
and truly our fellowship is with the Father
and with his Son Jesus Christ. (1 John 1:1-3)

The biblical authors, in giving testimony to the Good News, grounded
their testimony in their own faith convictions. To read something as
testimony is to presume the fundamental truthfulness of what is witnessed to, at least from the witness's perspective. But what of the accuracy of that testimony? Schneiders notes that the very category of
testimony presupposes "limits" since testimony, however much inspired
by God, still draws from the particular witness/witnessing community's
perspective and experience. And all human perspectives, however inspired, are necessarily limited.

> The original witnesses were testifying to their own experience which, of
> necessity, involved their personal and therefore somewhat idiosyncratic
> participation in the events, their selection and arrangement of the ele-
> ments of their experience, and their languaging of that experience in
> literary genres that shaped it decisively.[10]

This appeal to the category of biblical testimony, in turn, has implications for how one might think about biblical inspiration.

> Inspiration . . . could not have saved the biblical text from the limitations
> inherent to human testimony without destroying its character as testi-
> mony, which is precisely what makes it valuable for us as later believers.
> Just as surely as Jesus, because he was a human being, had to age and
> eventually die, so the text, because it is human testimony, has to involve
> incompleteness, perspectival particularity and thus limitation, and even
> errors.[11]

Finally, with regard to the inspiration of Scripture, this emphasis on
testimony draws our attention back to the decisive role of the witness
of the apostolic community.

In the postconciliar period, alongside this appropriation of contemporary philosophical hermeneutics, there has been a certain reaction to
the predominance of historical-critical methods in Catholic biblical studies. Certain critics complain that the dominance of modern historical-
critical methods has led to a disparagement of patristic and medieval

---

[10] Ibid., 26.
[11] Ibid., 27.

exegesis, which, they insist, still has much to offer the church.[12] These scholars would remind us that *Dei Verbum* affirmed *two* sets of principles for biblical interpretation in article 12. The first was "historico-literary" in character and represented the new opening represented by Pope Pius XII's 1943 encyclical. Following *Divino Afflante Spiritu*, the council encouraged biblical scholars to consider a text's historical and cultural context and to take into account its distinctive literary genre. The council also called for a second set of interpretive principles, however, which could be characterized as "theological-ecclesial."[13] These principles attend more to the deeper unity of Scripture and its theological appropriation in the tradition of the church. Some have complained that, in the postconciliar period, the first set of principles has been employed to the neglect of the second. Pope Benedict XVI's apostolic exhortation *Verbum Domini* certainly expressed this concern.[14]

Pope Benedict vigorously reaffirmed the necessity of historical-critical methods for biblical interpretation. In his apostolic exhortation, he considered the inspiration of Scripture according to the analogy of the incarnation. Much as God became human in Jesus of Nazareth, so, in an analogous sense, the *Logos* became human word in Scripture. It is Christianity's commitment to the "realism" of the incarnation that makes use of historical-critical exegesis necessary (VD 32). If the *Logos* has entered human history, not only in Jesus Christ but also in Scripture, then a study of those scriptural texts will require attentiveness to their full humanity, that is, their historical and cultural conditioning. Nevertheless, the analogy of the incarnation also requires that we attend to the revelatory character of Scripture as a whole and as read with the eyes of faith. The pope insisted that we should not be content to simply juxtapose historical-critical exegesis with more theological forms of biblical exegesis; the two sets of interpretive principles/methods must be fully integrated (VD 35). Pope Benedict, while drawing valuable insight from historical-critical scholarship, insists "that the interpretation

---

[12] Examples of such authors would include Denis Farkasfalvy, Matthew Levering, Francis Martin, William Wright IV, and, most significant, Pope Benedict XVI.

[13] The specific terminology here is taken from William M. Wright IV, "*Dei Verbum*" in *The Reception of Vatican II*, ed. Matthew L. Lamb and Matthew Levering (New York: Oxford University Press, 2017), 61–112.

[14] This document can be accessed online at: http://w2.vatican.va/content /benedict-xvi/en/apost_exhortations/documents/hf_ben-xvi_exh_20100930 _verbum-domini.html.

of the bible as Scripture is a theological and ecclesial practice."[15] This led him to insist on a recovery of the church's rich patristic and medieval tradition of exegesis as a necessary complement to historical-critical studies.

CONCLUSION

We should not be surprised to discover some of the difficulties that theologians have had in arriving at an adequate account of biblical inspiration. The dynamics of human discovery and the workings of the creative process have always had a mysterious and ineffable quality that resists schematization. Artists have long struggled to explain how some creative idea came to them. Theology, however, brings to light further difficulties. The daunting task of developing an adequate theory of biblical inspiration is really but one example of a larger theological quandary that has occupied theologians from the beginning of Christianity—how to explain the mysterious collaboration of divine and human agency.

The temptation is to succumb to a kind of zero-sum theory. Here, the human and the divine are placed in a zero-sum relationship such that the emphasis on one term in the equation requires de-emphasizing the other. An excellent historical example of this can be seen in the so-called *De Auxiliis* controversy between Dominicans and Jesuits in the sixteenth and seventeenth centuries. The Dominicans emphasized divine initiative in the life of grace, often at the expense of human freedom, while the Jesuits emphasized human freedom at the expense of divine initiative. Christological controversies betrayed similar tendencies. Overemphasis on Christ's divine nature inevitably compromised Christ's humanity and vice versa. Difficulties raised by the question of biblical inspiration are similar in nature. The British Catholic theologian Nicholas Lash has put the matter well:

> It therefore becomes clear that the real difficulty in saying that Christianity, or theology, is about both God and man, the real difficulty in *verus God et verus homo*, consists not in knowing what we mean by *God* or what we mean by *man* (though these are not small questions), but in the difficulty of knowing what we mean by *and*.[16]

---

[15] Wright, "*Dei Verbum*," 101.
[16] Nicholas Lash, *His Presence in the World: A Study in Eucharistic Worship and Theology* (London: Sheed & Ward, 1968), 4.

Too often forgotten is the Christian conviction that God is not another created agent competing with physical causal events or the work of human agents. God is the ground and source of all forms of human agency. God is the source of life and freedom that makes it possible for a human person to exercise his or her freedom. Applied to our understanding of divine inspiration, this suggests that the influence of the Holy Spirit need not be set off against the biblical authors' created, historically and culturally circumscribed freedom. Rather, inspiration can be understood as God's revealing what God wishes "for the sake of our salvation" precisely through the very real limitations and even biases of the biblical authors and/or their communities. This is the enduring mystery of God-with-Us.

Theories of strict verbal inspiration, and the preoccupation with total inerrancy that accompanies them, are the result of a reliance on a more propositional model of revelation. When we consider revelation as symbolically mediated, the problems of inerrancy are, to a certain extent, sidestepped. If Scripture is the symbolic mediation of divine revelation, then it faithfully communicates divine revelation through the created human medium of biblical testimony. An honest admission of the human authorship of biblical texts does not in any way negate the genuine influence of the Spirit; nor does it undermine the integrity of what is communicated through the Scriptures, namely, God's self-gift to humankind in love. God's revelation may be disclosed in Scriptures, but we appropriate it only through the hard work of critical and communal interpretation. We must set aside any simplistic views of revelation that see it as nothing more than a set of propositions to be proved and defended.

This is what Christians mean when they hold that the Bible must be read in faith. They recognize, of course, that the Bible can be read and comprehended apart from faith. Many colleges and universities offer courses on the Bible as literature, an altogether legitimate undertaking. Christians believe, however, that the same texts read by one person solely as literature can also be read through the lens of faith in such a way that the literary content is not denied but becomes the medium for encountering divine revelation. The fruit of that encounter is an experience of communion between the reader/hearer and the God who addresses him or her. To say that Scripture is "inerrant" is to affirm that the Bible gives faithful testimony to God's saving offer and, when read in faith, brings one into saving communion with God.

DISPUTED QUESTIONS

(1) Questions about the meaning of the council's assertion of two authors—one divine, one human—have continued since the council. Some scholars feel this recourse to two authors was an uneasy compromise, leaving many questions unanswered. For example, in what sense is God to be thought of as "author"? Surely God is not the author of Scripture in a *literary* sense. If God is the originator of the biblical text in such a way as to predetermine what the human authors were to write, then how can we still affirm the genuine freedom of the human authors?

(2) Since Vatican II, new questions have been raised about problems concerning biblical inspiration and inerrancy. Whereas the council was grappling with the possibility of errors in the biblical text of a historical, geographical, and scientific nature, now questions were being raised regarding deeper problems with the text. What does the reader do with texts that appear to be anti-Semitic or misogynist in their treatment of women? How is the reader to come to terms with the Bible's attitude toward slavery?

These problems have given rise to the application of a "hermeneutic of suspicion" in the interpretation of biblical texts. By "hermeneutic of suspicion" is meant a critical criterion that requires the biblical interpreter to adopt a stance of deliberate "suspicion" toward the possibility of bias in a given text. Feminist theologians, in particular, have employed this hermeneutic with respect to the appearance of patriarchal bias (patriarchy refers to a set of cultural, legal, economic, and political relationships that assert male superiority and dominance over women). Such a bias is reflected in biblical assumptions, whether implicit or explicit, that maleness is somehow the norm for understanding human experience and, to that extent, also for understanding God. For many feminist scholars, the pervasive presence of such a patriarchal bias in the Bible raises particular difficulties for any claim to biblical inspiration. At the minimum, it suggests that the acknowledgment of human deficiencies in biblical texts must go beyond the spheres of science and history to include systemic cultural bias. These scholars also wonder whether patriarchal views of authority in the church will not influence how Christians understand the authority of the Bible. They contend that, too often, appeals to the authority of the Bible have been used to assert the dominance of church leadership over members of the community and particularly women.

In response to this critique, other scholars have contended that the appropriate Christian hermeneutic for interpreting biblical texts should be governed, not by systemic suspicion, but by trust. Without denying the historically and culturally conditioned nature of the Bible, these voices insist that the inspired character of such texts precludes systemic bias and requires that one accept the essential trustworthiness of biblical texts as faithful testimonies to the Word of God.

(3) Some contemporary scholars question, in the light of contemporary interreligious dialogue, whether it is necessary to speak of divine inspiration as unique and exclusive to Christian biblical texts. If, with Vatican II, we can affirm the truth and goodness to be found within other religious traditions,[17] and if all truth and goodness find their ultimate source in God, then is it not possible to assert divine influence, in some fashion, in the production of sacred texts within other religious traditions, e.g., the Qur'an for Islam or the Upanishads for Hinduism? Critics would respond that such a position seriously weakens the traditional Christian understanding of biblical inspiration and threatens traditional Christian claims regarding the unique revelation of God in Christ testified to in the Scriptures.

(4) Most of the approaches to biblical inspiration have focused on divine influence with respect to individual authors, communities, or texts. But some scholars today contend that one must also consider the possibility of inspiration or divine assistance with respect to the contemporary *reader* or *hearer* of a biblical text. They ask whether the process of reading or hearing a text and interpreting it within a contemporary context might also be subject to divine influence.

FOR FURTHER READING

Achtemeier, Paul J. *The Inspiration of Scripture: Problems and Proposals.* Philadelphia: Westminster, 1980.
Barr, James. *Holy Scripture: Canon, Authority, Criticism.* Philadelphia: Westminster, 1983.

[17] See the teaching of Vatican II in *Nostra Aetate*, the Declaration on the Relation of the Church to Non-Christian Religions, art. 2.

Benedict XVI, Pope. *Post-Synodal Apostolic Exhortation on the Word of God in the Life and Mission of the Church* (*Verbum Domini*), 2010.

Burtchaell, James Tunstead. *Catholic Theories of Biblical Inspiration since 1810: A Review and Critique.* Cambridge: Cambridge University Press, 1969.

Countryman, William. *Biblical Authority or Biblical Tyranny?* Philadelphia: Fortress Press, 1981.

Farkasfalvy, Denis. *Inspiration and Interpretation: A Theological Interpretation to Sacred Scripture.* Washington, DC: Catholic University of America Press, 2010.

Gnuse, Robert. *The Authority of the Bible: Theories of Inspiration, Revelation and the Canon of Scripture.* New York: Paulist Press, 1985.

Law, David R. *Inspiration.* New York: Continuum, 2001.

Lienhard, Joseph T. *The Bible, the Church, and Authority: The Canon of the Christian Bible in History and Theology.* Collegeville, MN: Liturgical Press, 1995.

Pontifical Biblical Commission. *The Inspiration and Truth of Sacred Scripture.* Collegeville, MN: Liturgical Press, 2014.

———. *The Interpretation of the Bible in the Church.* London: SCM Press, 1995.

Rahner, Karl. *Inspiration in the Bible. Quaestiones Disputatae* 1. New York: Herder, 1961.

Schneiders, Sandra M. *The Revelatory Text: Interpreting the New Testament as Sacred Scripture.* New York: HarperCollins, 1991.

Schüssler Fiorenza, Elizabeth. *Bread not Stone: The Challenge of Feminist Biblical Interpretation.* Boston: Beacon Press, 1984.

Vawter, Bruce. *Biblical Inspiration: Theological Resources.* Philadelphia: Westminster, 1972.

FIVE

WHAT IS THE AUTHORITY OF TRADITION?

In this chapter we explore the distinctive authority we associate with tradition in the Catholic Church. We will begin by considering two basic features of tradition: the role of memory and the reality of change. These reflections on memory and change will help us distinguish between healthy and unhealthy understandings of tradition. From there we will consider the Second Vatican Council's teaching on tradition and its relationship to Scripture. Finally, we will explore four different dimensions or senses of tradition that will help us understand the various ways that memory, change, and development function in the living tradition of the church.

REFLECTIONS ON TRADITION: MEMORY AND CHANGE

The role of tradition in Roman Catholicism can be thought of as a form of communal memory. This memory reminds us of who we are as Christians. The Greek word often used for "memory" in the New Testament is *anamnesis*. If you squint a little you can see embedded within it the root of a word we use today, *amnesia*. Amnesia, of course, refers to the loss of memory. Yet, as television and film remind us, an amnesiac can remember a lot. Recall the series of Jason Bourne spy movies. At the beginning of the first film Jason Bourne is found by fishermen floating in the ocean, shot and close to death. After he is rescued and slowly recovers his health, his strength returns but not his memory. Bourne, in a very real sense, doesn't know who he is. But he does remember a lot. He remembers how to break down a pistol in thirty seconds. He remembers enough martial arts to disarm two police officers. He remembers how to speak French and German. What Bourne has forgotten, and it is this forgetting that so haunts him, is his identity. If amnesia is the loss of identity then *anamnesis*, "memory" in its Christian sense, is about recalling our identity.

When we emphasize in the Catholic Church the importance of tradition we are in effect making claims about why it is important to be a "community of memory." Robert Bellah, a sociologist of religion, has spoken of the importance of belonging to "communities of memory":

> Communities, in the sense in which we are using the term, have a history—in an important sense they are constituted by their past—and for this reason we can speak of a real community as a "community of memory," one that does not forget its past. In order not to forget that past, a community is involved in retelling its story, its constitutive narrative, and in so doing, it offers examples of the men and women who have embodied and exemplified the meaning of the community. These stories of collective history and exemplary individuals are an important part of the tradition that is so central to a community of memory.[1]

Yet this memory involves more than narratives.

> People growing up in communities of memory not only hear the stories that tell how the community came to be, what its hopes and fears are, and how its ideals are exemplified in outstanding men and women; they also participate in the practices—ritual, aesthetic, ethical—that define the community as a way of life.[2]

Indeed, a vital part of memory, and therefore the tradition of the church, is a set of embodied practices, preeminent among which is the worship of the church.

One of most common assumptions regarding the place of religious ritual in the life of the community is that rituals encode belief. We might think that a religious community first possesses a set of beliefs and then encodes those beliefs in its ritual worship. Applied to Christianity this approach to ritual assumes that Christians first held some beliefs regarding, for example, the nature of the triune God and the salvific character

---

[1] Robert Bellah, et al., *Habits of the Heart: Individualism and Commitment in American Life* (New York: Harper and Row, 1985), 153.

[2] Ibid., 154.

of Christ's life, death, and resurrection. These beliefs were subsequently encoded in Christian rituals such as baptism and the Eucharist. In this schema, belief holds primacy over ritual.

Many ritual studies scholars now challenge this view. Theodore Jennings contends that, although it is true that beliefs may be mediated through ritual, this does not occur through a process of ritual encoding and decoding. Rather, ritual involves a unique form of symbolic expression that is rooted in our experience of ourselves as embodied. Jennings writes that "ritual knowledge is gained through a bodily action which alters the world or the place of the ritual participant in the world."[3] What Jennings is saying is that there is a unique form of knowledge that is not primarily cerebral but corporeal. Certain practices, when undertaken, give us a "body knowledge" that disposes us to encounter our world in new ways. This reverses the way in which we tend to view such things. We conventionally believe that we first "think" something and then "perform" it. But, in fact, it is often the reverse. We engage in some bodily activity that affects us in profound ways and then we try to "cerebrally 're-cognize'" the action. Although we often think of our memory as residing in our brain, this is true only in a very limited way. Our most profound memories are often visceral; they are filled with affect and emotion that elude rational analysis.

Within the life of a faith community ritual action produces a corporate body memory often more powerful than any mere transmission of propositional beliefs. As the liturgy of the church is celebrated from generation to generation, the ritual knowledge gained by the corporate performance of the ritual funds the community's memory. Moreover, to the essential role of ritual we must add a wide range of other ecclesial practices that also help sustain the embodied memory of the Christian faith: almsgiving, visiting the sick and prisoners, a wide range of devotional practices. The role of such embodied knowledge has been much neglected in a theology of tradition.

As important and necessary as communal memory is, we must not romanticize it, however. We need to acknowledge the hard truth that memory is capable of distortion. We know too well of communities that keep alive stories of hate and bigotry. We also know well the ways in which certain communal memories can become a social poison prevent-

---

[3] Theodore W. Jennings, "On Ritual Knowledge," in *Readings in Ritual Studies*, ed. Ronald L. Grimes (Upper Saddle River, NJ: Prentice-Hall, 1996), 327.

ing any possibility of communal healing and reconciliation. One need only consider long-standing conflicts in Northern Ireland or the Balkans or the disputes between Israelis and Palestinians. Here the memory of a particular grievance actually has impeded the necessary work of communal reconciliation. This is why the church must always be discerning in its judgment about its communal memory. Not all memories are life-giving.

As the corporate memory of the church, tradition helps us remember who we are. The authority of tradition is, then, decisive for Christianity. We Christians do not simply make things up as we go. The church is not its own Lord. In baptism, we are claimed by a story not of our making, a story of a God who addresses us as friends and invites us into his company. It is a story of scandalous, profligate love embodied in the person of Jesus of Nazareth; it is a story of a God who showers us with mercy and forgiveness and requires us to extend that mercy and forgiveness to others. This church, constituted by baptism and nourished at the Lord's Table, is a school of discipleship wherein we learn how to both live this story and keep it alive for others. Out of our recollection of this story we are sent into the world with hearts aflame with the love of God. We call this story "Good News," the announcement of the Spirit-led in-breaking of God's reign in Jesus of Nazareth. It is a story that must be told and retold, heard and reheard, enacted and adapted to time and place. And yet, even as the story acquires new forms, it must remain grounded in its initial telling. The story we tell today, in all its freshness, must remain faithful to its origins in the Christ Event.

Since the apostles were the first tellers of that story, we use the term "apostolicity" to name this enduring connection between the story once told by tongues of fire and the story we tell today. We believe in a formal ministry of memory, the office of the bishop, heir to the authority of the apostle, and charged with maintaining the integrity and fidelity of the church's communal memory.

Tradition, as the communal memory of the church, is both necessary and dangerous. When people appeal to tradition as a kind of communal memory, whether in matters of politics, family, social custom, or religion, it is often as an argument against change. Regardless of the particular form the argument takes, lurking under the surface is often some version of "this is the way we have always done it." This is no less true for Catholicism. The Catholic faith does lay claim to a two-thousand-year-old tradition, but it is hardly a faith frozen in time. Only those ignorant of history think that Catholicism has been immune to substantial change and development. As the nineteenth-century theologian and cardinal John Henry Newman famously put it, "In a higher world it may be otherwise, but here below to live is to change, and to be perfect is to have changed often."[4] An authentic appeal to tradition is an appeal to a living faith with long historical roots reaching back to the testimony of the apostles. It recognizes the value of a shared community memory, but it is always open to the present moment. The great church historian Jaroslav Pelikan distinguished between healthy and unhealthy attitudes toward tradition by distinguishing between tradition as an icon and as an idol. An *icon* is an object of contemplation that "bids us look at it, but through it and beyond it, to that living reality of which it is an embodiment." An *idol*, however, "purports to be the embodiment of that which it represents, but it directs us to itself rather than beyond itself."[5] For a segment of the church, there is always the danger of tradition becoming an idol. Pelikan warns:

> Tradition becomes an idol, accordingly, when it makes the preservation and the repetition of the past an end in itself; it claims to have the transcendent reality and truth captive and encapsulated in that past, and it requires an idolatrous submission to the authority of tradition, since truth would not dare to appear outside it.[6]

The alternative, of course, is not the rejection of tradition altogether but a recovery of tradition as a living icon:

> Tradition qualifies as an icon . . . when it does not present itself as co-extensive with the truth it teaches, but does present itself as the way that we who are its heirs must follow if we are to go beyond it—to a universal truth that is available only in a particular embodiment, as life itself is available to each of us only in a particular set of parents.[7]

Pelikan famously sums up his reflections on tradition with this observation: "Tradition is the living faith of the dead; traditionalism is the dead

---

[4] John Henry Newman, *An Essay on the Development of Christian Doctrine*, 6th ed. (Notre Dame, IN: University of Notre Dame Press, 1989), I.1.7.

[5] Jaroslav Pelikan, *The Vindication of Tradition* (New Haven, CT: Yale University Press, 1984), 55.

[6] Ibid.

[7] Ibid., 56.

faith of the living. And, I suppose I should add, it is traditionalism that gives tradition such a bad name."[8]

In a living tradition, change is necessary, not because God changes, but because we do. As humans we grow and develop, both as individuals and in our communities, in particular historical and cultural contexts. Our appropriation of God's revelation will be shaped by the time and place in which we live. The community's reception of the gift of God's very self that we call divine revelation will look different for those who received the Gospel in fourth-century Ethiopia, thirteenth-century Paris, nineteenth-century Manila, or twenty-first-century New York.

There is a mystery at work in the development of tradition. On the one hand, we believe that with each retelling of the Christian narrative in new historical and cultural contexts that story takes on new elements, new insights. And yet we believe the original story, at least in its essential features, is somehow carried forward with each retelling. It is important that we hold a balanced appraisal of this process. For even as we assert the broader continuity of tradition as it seeks to be faithful to the original story, we need to appreciate the extent to which the Christian story represents what the Belgian theologian Lieven Boeve calls an "open narrative."[9] The Christian story is one uniquely open to interruption, an interruption, we dare to believe, instigated by the Spirit of God.

Consider the story of St. Peter recounted in Acts 9–10. Humbled by his threefold betrayal of Jesus, yet knowing himself to be both a sinner and forgiven, Peter has committed himself to preaching the good news of Jesus Christ to the children of Israel. He has fully embraced the story of Jesus *as he understood it*. Then, as so often happens in the Bible, Peter has a dream in which a sheet filled with what Jews believed to be unclean foods is lowered from heaven and Peter is commanded to eat the unclean food. Peter refuses, but a voice responds, "What God has made clean, you must not call profane" (Acts 10:15). This is repeated three times.

Now, at the same time, a Gentile centurion named Cornelius also receives a vision. He is told to send some men to call for Simon Peter

---

[8] Ibid., 65.

[9] For more on Boeve's view of interruption as a moment in the traditioning process of the church, see Lieven Boeve, *Interrupting Tradition: An Essay on Christian Faith in a Postmodern Context* (Louvain: Peeters, 2003); idem, *God Interrupts History: Theology in a Time of Upheaval* (New York: Continuum, 2007).

to come to him. Peter arrives and asks what Cornelius desires from him. Cornelius asks Peter to share the Gospel. In response to their remarkable invitation and the insight he has only now gained from his vision, Peter comes to a profound new realization that God's plans are much larger than he had realized. He boldly proclaims, "I truly understand that God shows no partiality, but in every nation anyone who fears him and does what is right is acceptable to him" (Acts 10:34-35). Peter's understanding of the story of Jesus is interrupted and transformed by both his vision and his encounter with Cornelius. For Peter, the story of God's offer of salvation has to be revised in light of this unexpected "interruption."

This is how tradition works. Perhaps the interruption comes by way of an encounter that appears foreign and threatening, presenting us with an invitation to consider some aspect of the narrative of God's saving love in a new way. Imagine a white middle-class Catholic family that moves to a predominantly Latino neighborhood and begins to be active in the local Catholic parish. There they encounter a very different experience of the Eucharist celebrated predominantly in Spanish and with music that is foreign to them. Major Christian feasts are celebrated with long processions through the neighborhood. Images of La Virgen de Guadalupe are everywhere in evidence. This experience of Latino Catholicism "interrupts" their sense of the Christian story they have received in their previous experiences of Catholicism. Now they are faced with a choice: they can reject this new experience of the faith as simply too foreign, or inauthentic, or they can begin the work of re-imagining the Christian story in light of this new experience.

The living Christian tradition is often propelled forward by the Spirit through such "interruptions." This does not mean that every retelling of the Christian story that emerges from such interruptions is of equal value. This living tradition must always be subject to discernment. That discernment takes many forms. It occurs among ordinary Christian believers who have a supernatural gift for recognizing the authentic faith. Theologians refer to this as "the sense of faith" (*sensus fidei*). It must be discerned by the scholarly study of theologians. Finally, Catholics believe that in a distinctive fashion it must be discerned by the bishops who, by virtue of their ordination, have a special responsibility for safeguarding the integrity of the Christian tradition. We will explore each of these in more detail in the third and fourth sections of this book.

CONSIDERING THE RELATIONSHIP BETWEEN SCRIPTURE AND TRADITION

The word "tradition" comes from the Latin verb *tradere* and means "to pass or hand something on." Tradition may be understood both as the content of what is handed on—it is in this sense that we have thought of tradition as a form of communal memory—and as the process by which the faith is handed on. When we think of tradition in this basic sense, as the process of handing on the faith, it becomes clear from our discussion in chapter 3 on the canon of the Bible that the Bible is itself the fruit of tradition. If we recall the formation of the Bible, before there were written texts, there were stories that were handed on from generation to generation and community to community. If we understand tradition in this way, as the handing on of the good news of salvation, then tradition precedes and even gives rise to the Bible. The Bible is both the fruit of this "traditioning" process, and, in the postbiblical period, the vital reference point for any and all subsequent handing on of the faith.

Recalling our earlier discussion about the memory of the church, Scripture and tradition might be seen as distinct but interrelated cells in the corporate memory of the people of God. Through most of the first thousand years of Christianity few conceived of tradition as something completely separate from Scripture. Tradition was the faith of the church testified to in Scripture and now preserved and developed through the example of martyrs, the witness of ordinary believers, the celebration of the liturgy and sacraments, daily practices of Christian discipleship, theological reflection, and Christian art. Only in the Middle Ages does tradition begin to acquire a more independent status as a collection both of church teachings and customs separate from Scripture.

The question of the proper theological relationship between Scripture and tradition did not arise in a formal sense until the Protestant Reformation and the Reformers' espousal of the *sola scriptura* doctrine. The Reformers objected to the haze of accumulated customs, practices, and speculative propositions that had proliferated in late medieval Catholicism, all of which, in their view, clouded over and even distorted the evangelical message of the Bible. The first formal Catholic articulation of its own understanding of the relationship between Scripture and tradition came at the Council of Trent, largely in response to the

Reformers. In one of its decrees the council tried to articulate the proper relationship between Scripture and the various traditions of the church. An early draft proposed that divine truths were contained partly in the "written books" and partly in unwritten traditions (the Council of Trent did not refer to "tradition" in the singular). The final text, however, was changed to read that truth was found "*both* in the written books *and* in unwritten traditions."[10] The first formulation suggested that these were two distinct sources of divine truth, yet the final formulation was at least open to the interpretation that they were not different *sources* of truth at all but only different *modes of expression*. Unfortunately, many theologians and clerics would, after the Reformation, maintain the view more reflective of the first formulation. In other words, with important exceptions (e.g., Bossuet, Möhler, Newman), many Catholic theologians would continue to hold the view that Scripture and tradition were distinct sources of revelation.

This view was indirectly strengthened in the nineteenth century. Popes Gregory XVI, Pius IX, and Leo XIII greatly expanded the teaching office of the papacy. These three popes began to use encyclicals as a vehicle for delivering authoritative doctrinal pronouncements. In 1854 Pope Pius IX "solemnly defined" the dogma of the Immaculate Conception. There is even a story that, during the First Vatican Council, Pius IX learned of the desire of some bishops to have the council affirm that the pope's teaching must be in accord with church tradition. The pope is said to have retorted in exasperation, "Tradition? *I am* tradition!" Whether this story is true or not, it reflects a then-common view of the papacy as the principal "organ of tradition." This growing tendency to identify the teaching of the magisterium in general, and that of the papacy in particular, with tradition strengthened the sense that tradition was a source of divine truth entirely separate from Scripture.

As a consequence of this historical development, Catholics living on the eve of Vatican II often imagined Scripture and tradition as if they comprised a two-drawer filing cabinet holding all the "truths" of divine revelation. One drawer contained the truths found in the Bible; this drawer was shared by all Christians. The second drawer, however, included another set of truths not explicitly found in the Bible. This drawer was tradition and it was commonly thought to be in the exclusive

---

[10] The emphasis is mine.

possession of the Roman Catholic Church. This imaginary construct, though never enshrined in official Catholic teaching, dominated the Catholic consciousness for almost four hundred years. As we will see, the Second Vatican Council went a long way toward dismantling it.

VATICAN II ON SCRIPTURE AND TRADITION

In the decades prior to Vatican II many theologians had already begun to challenge the overly static sense of tradition that predominated. They recognized that the schematization of Scripture and tradition as two different sources was foreign to the Christian heritage of the first thousand years. They knew well that while the late medieval and baroque theologians would speak of traditions in the plural, there was a more ancient insight reflected in the use of tradition in the singular as a way of naming the whole of the Christian faith passed on from generation to generation. Individual customs and traditions served as concrete and particular expressions of the one great tradition. They also contended that it was unfaithful to the witness of the early church to imagine that only the pope and bishops had responsibility for handing on the apostolic faith.

The preparatory draft on divine revelation, given to the bishops at the beginning of the council, ignored all of these developments. That document made the two-source theory (akin to the two-drawer cabinet image) the centerpiece of its theology of revelation. Many bishops roundly criticized the draft, noting that while theologians had often assumed the theory of two sources, it had never been proposed as the authoritative teaching of the church. After a debate filled with accusation and intrigue, Pope John XXIII ordered that the entire preparatory document be removed and that an alternative document be drafted by a newly created mixed commission. That new draft, after undergoing considerable revision, would eventually reflect the fruit of the theological development that had emerged in the preceding decades.

Instead of two sources of divine revelation, the council wrote that Scripture and tradition "make up a single deposit of the word of God, which is entrusted to the church" (DV 10). Here the ancient unity of Scripture and tradition was restored. Perhaps most significant, however, is the broader framework in which Scripture and tradition were considered. As we saw in chapter 2, *Dei Verbum* shifted away from a propositional view of divine revelation. When revelation was understood as a set of individual truths, the two-source theory made sense. But once the council focused instead on revelation as the living Word incarnate as Jesus of Nazareth by the power of the Spirit, it became possible to orient both Scripture and tradition as distinct but interrelated mediations of the same living Word.

Consequently, in article 8 we find a remarkably dynamic definition of tradition: "What was handed on by the apostles comprises everything that serves to make the people of God live their lives in holiness and increase their faith. In this way the church, in its doctrine, life and worship, perpetuates and transmits to every generation all that it itself is, all that it believes." It is worth noting that this definition is formal in character; it simply doesn't address what does or does not, materially, belong to tradition. The council then continues:

> The tradition that comes from the apostles makes progress in the church, with the help of the holy Spirit. There is a growth in insight into the realities and words that are being passed on. This comes about through the contemplation and study of believers who ponder these things in their hearts. It comes from the intimate sense of spiritual realities which they experience. And it comes from the preaching of those who, on succeeding to the office of bishop, have received the sure charism of truth. Thus, as the centuries go by, the church is always advancing towards the plenitude of divine truth, until eventually the words of God are fulfilled in it. (DV 8)

There is a wealth of insight in this brief passage. First, the council affirmed that the pope and bishops were not the exclusive "organs of tradition." The passage does mention the indispensable role of the bishops, but not before it cites the role of believers who, by way of their spiritual experience, allow church tradition to "progress." Elsewhere the council will explicitly affirm the *sensus fidei*, the supernatural sense or instinct of the faith possessed by all believers through baptism:

> Through this sense of faith which is aroused and sustained by the Spirit of truth, the people of God, under the guidance of the sacred magisterium to which it is faithfully obedient, receives no longer the words of human beings but truly the word of God; it adheres indefectibly to "the faith which was once for all delivered to the saints"; it penetrates more deeply into that same faith through right judgment and applies it more fully to life. (LG 12)

This supernatural sense of the faith is the means by which all the baptized contribute to the church's corporate listening to God's Word and participate in the traditioning process of the church.

Second, included within DV 8's reference to the contributions of all the baptized is an allusion to the necessary contributions of theologians and other scholars. In the phrase "contemplation and study" the words "and study" were inserted in the third draft of the document as a way of acknowledging, even if only indirectly, the distinctive contributions of scholars.

Third, the traditioning process active in the life of the whole church is grounded in the triune life of God and, in particular, the work of the Holy Spirit. If it is God who in the fullness of love "addresses us as friends," and it is Christ who is the "mediator and sum total of revelation" (DV 2), it is the Holy Spirit

> who moves the heart and converts it to God, and opens the eyes of the mind and "makes it easy for all to accept and believe the truth." The same holy Spirit constantly perfects faith by his gifts, so that revelation may be more and more deeply understood. (DV 5)

Attention to the Holy Spirit in the life of the church was one of the more important contributions of the Second Vatican Council.

Finally, *Dei Verbum* 8 reminds us that divine truth is not something that the church ever really possesses. As befits a "pilgrim church," the council modestly acknowledged only that the church was "advancing towards the plenitude of divine truth." This passage reflects a kind of eschatological humility that was typical of the council. It is one thing to say that the church abides in the truth as it abides in God. It is altogether something different to say that the church possesses the fullness of truth. According to the council, truth is never fully in the church's possession this side of the second coming of Christ.

For all its many contributions, this key text was not without its shortcomings. Cardinal Albert Meyer of Chicago, in one of his council speeches, criticized the text for a failure to mention the distinction between tradition and traditions that the Dominican theologian Yves Congar, among others, had emphasized.[11] Meyer warned that within the great tradition of the church there were particular traditions that did not have lasting value. Because the council did not distinguish between

---

[11] See Yves Congar, *The Meaning of Tradition* (New York: Hawthorn, 1964).

the larger tradition and the particular traditions contained within it, it also provided no viable criterion for determining the enduring validity of those particular traditions. Nor did it explicitly articulate how the legitimacy of any tradition had to be measured against the clear teaching of Scripture. Interestingly, while the council was in session, the Fourth World Council on Faith and Order was meeting in Montreal to produce its own document on tradition, *Scripture, Tradition and Traditions*, a document that made precisely the distinction Meyer had in mind.[12]

According to the council's teaching. Scripture and tradition are integrally related, proceeding as they do from the one Word of God, but they are not identical. Scripture, as canon, offers a kind of fixed point, a finite set of normative texts that grounds Christian faith in a set of ancient testimonies to foundational events: the exodus and offer of God's covenant; God's saving deeds on behalf of Israel; Christ's life and ministry, death and resurrection; the early origins of the apostolic community. Tradition always embraces this scriptural testimony while going beyond it in bringing the Scriptures into dialogue with the life of the churches from generation to generation. New insights regarding the significance of biblical testimony for the community of faith in a sense do "add to" tradition. The teaching of the Councils of Nicaea and Ephesus on the Trinity go beyond the biblical testimony even as the members of those councils would have insisted on their fidelity to Scripture. Consequently, we must recognize that while tradition stands in "continuity" with the biblical testimony and shares a common source in the living Word of God, it is not strictly identical to it. The very existence of tradition is a statement that, as then-theologian Joseph Ratzinger put it, while Scripture witnesses to revelation it does not exhaust it.[13] Ormond Rush suggests that we might think of Scripture and tradition as standing within a "hermeneutical circle":

> Scripture and Tradition mutually interpret one another. . . . Tradition is normed by Scripture; but the interpretation of Scripture is to be, in turn, normed by the living tradition which formed Scripture. . . . It is therefore helpful to speak of Scripture as the *primary* norm of revelation,

[12] The document is found in *The Fourth World Conference on Faith and Order*, ed. Patrick C. Roger and Lukas Vischer (New York: Associated Press, 1964).

[13] Joseph Ratzinger, "Revelation and Tradition," in *Revelation and Tradition*, ed. Karl Rahner and Joseph Ratzinger (New York: Herder and Herder, 1966), 26–49, at 35–37.

and of tradition as the *subordinate or secondary* norm, with the *supreme or ultimate* norm being the Christ-reality, the Word of God itself, i.e., God's self-giving through the Christ event revealed in the Spirit.[14]

A DIFFERENTIATED UNDERSTANDING OF TRADITION

As we have already noted, one of the most vexing questions in a theology of tradition concerns the interplay of continuity and change or interruption. As helpful as it is to conceive of tradition as a beautiful, organic unfolding of divine revelation across time, tradition also bears witness to certain breaks or discontinuities with the past. Anyone with knowledge of the history of Catholic doctrine and practice knows that there are significant differences between the forms and manifestations of the Christian faith in the early centuries and those common today. John Thiel, in an influential contemporary study of the theology of tradition, offers a helpful framework for considering how an authentic view of tradition can hold together a sense of continuity over time and cumulative development alongside an honest recognition of substantive change. He does this by recalling the medieval practice of considering four different "senses" of a biblical text. Thiel proposes that one can also identify four different "senses" of tradition.[15]

The Literal Sense of Tradition

The first sense of tradition is what Thiel calls the "literal sense." By this he means those beliefs and practices within the Christian tradition that have endured over long periods of history, give the impression of stability, and are viewed as authoritative. The literal sense of tradition does not preclude any change in these beliefs and practices for, as with all beliefs and practices, there are bound to be variances in interpretation. Nevertheless, when we consider the literal sense of tradition, it is the sense of stability over time that stands out. We can identify a number

---

[14] Ormond Rush, *The Eyes of Faith: The Sense of the Faithful and the Church's Reception of Revelation* (Washington, DC: Catholic University of America Press, 2009), 179–80.

[15] In this section I will be summarizing Thiel's treatment of the four senses of tradition. John Thiel, *Senses of Tradition: Continuity and Development in Catholic Faith* (New York: Oxford University Press, 2000), 31–160.

of core Christian teachings that, even allowing for variances in theological explanation, have been relatively stable throughout church history: the Christian hope for eternal life or the belief that Christ is fully human and fully divine. Such examples of the literal sense of tradition demonstrate that, although theological interpretations have varied, one can recognize enduring insight maintained across several Christian epochs.

The Sense of Tradition as Development-in-Continuity

Thiel's second sense of tradition is that of "development-in-continuity." This second sense highlights those aspects of tradition that do give evidence of significant growth and development. This sense was explicitly affirmed for the first time in an ecclesiastical document in *Dei Verbum* 8: "The tradition that comes from the apostles makes progress in the church, with the help of the holy Spirit. There is a growth in insight into the realities and words that are being passed on."

Although Vatican II offers the first official articulation of the dynamic growth and development of tradition, theories of how doctrine developed over time had been proposed in the nineteenth century by important Catholic thinkers like Johann Adam Möhler and John Henry Newman.[16] This was in part due to the nineteenth-century fascination with the metaphor of the organism that can mature while still preserving its fundamental identity. This sense of tradition assumes that while the fullness of divine revelation was given to the apostolic community, the full significance of this definitive revelation could only be "unpacked" over time in the life of the church. "Ideas" given to the early church are seen as unfolding gradually over time.

This second sense represents an important step beyond a kind of Catholic fundamentalism that focuses on pristine truths and practices thought to be immune to change of any kind. It recognizes the reality of change, but insists that such change occurs while preserving the essential identity of that which undergoes change. The conception of tradition as development-in-continuity has played a key role in Catholic thought because it presents tradition from the perspective of divine providence; the change and development that occur do so by the invisible hand of God's Spirit at work in the church from generation to

---

[16] See especially Newman's *An Essay on the Development of Christian Doctrine.*

generation. Many nineteenth-century thinkers assumed this perspective in their explanations of how the dogma of the immaculate conception could achieve its developed expression only in the nineteenth-century dogmatic definition of Pope Pius IX.

One obvious danger with this reading of tradition is the tendency to read history as if all development were moving easily and surely by God's hand to our present moment. We are inclined to read tradition from "God's perspective," as Thiel puts it. But of course, we do not and will never have access to history from "God's perspective." We are forced, whether we like it or not, to interpret history as historical beings ourselves. We have no privileged reading of history from some ethereal plane.

This suggests the need for caution in appealing to this sense of tradition. That God's hand is at work in the movement of tradition is assumed by all Catholic Christians. But our *recognition* of the work of God's hand is another matter entirely. We are tempted to imagine contemporary church teachings as having been invisibly and inexorably directed toward their present formulation. We stand at the present moment and look back on history, trying to recognize the movements of the Spirit. But our present perspective is always partial, and to a considerable extent, it undergoes revision over time. What today strikes us as an obviously providential development of a given insight might conceivably, one hundred years from now, be viewed as a dead-end street. Up to the nineteenth century, many Christians saw slavery as part of God's divine plan under the conditions of human sin. Today, Christians recognize this position for what it is: a tragic misreading of divine providence.

We do believe in faith that it is possible to recognize the hand of God, both in our own personal faith journeys, and in the history of the church, but with rare exceptions (that we will address in a later chapter) this discernment is not infallible and is often open to revision. A personal example might demonstrate the point. If twenty-five years ago I had written a narrative of how the Spirit of God had been guiding me in a variety of decisions that led me to marry my wife and become a theologian, it would doubtless read quite differently from the narrative of those same events I would write today. Our corporate view of tradition can be understood in much the same way. We look back on our common history and read that history out of the questions and concerns of the present moment.

[handwritten margin note: HISTORICAL EXEGESIS]

Thiel suggests that this retrospective approach actually does more justice to the history of doctrine than an attempt to adopt God's view of history. A good example is the dogma of the immaculate conception. The organic model of development tried to present this teaching as if it matured consistently and without interruption from the time of the New Testament to its eventual definition in 1854. Such a perspective has the disadvantage of having to stretch the historical data to fit the theory. In fact, it is quite difficult to see any early maturation in this dogma at all, particularly before Augustine's articulation of the doctrine of original sin. As late as the thirteenth century, significant theologians like Thomas Aquinas were unpersuaded by it. An honest reading of the history of this doctrine cannot produce a narrative of continuous and unswerving development. This need not deny the legitimacy of the teaching, however. It is quite possible to affirm that in 1854, *looking back on the history of Marian reflection*, the understanding of the immaculate conception emerged, not as a single progressive development, but by fits and starts such that only in the nineteenth century could the fragmentary and partial insights that were peppered through the history of Marian reflection be connected in such a way as to enable the dogmatic *recognition* of Mary's role in salvation history.

The Sense of Tradition as Dramatic Development

The first two senses recognize that at the present moment there is some insight, belief, or practice identified within tradition that the believing community wishes to affirm. But this avoids a tricky question: What happens when the tradition of the church develops in a more "dramatic" fashion? What happens when within tradition there is a change that appears as more of a break or even a reversal of an earlier tradition? Tradition is not always the story of enduring or developing beliefs and practices; sometimes it is the story of beliefs and practices that have been abandoned or rejected over time. Some beliefs and practices simply lose their authority. We might consider how for so long the inferiority of women to men "in the order of nature" was considered fully in accord with both natural law and divine revelation. The grudging rejection of this viewpoint in the consciousness of the church can only be viewed as a communal recognition of dramatic *discontinuity* with its past. In a similar way, the church has found it necessary to dramatically re-conceive its earlier denial of religious liberty to nonbelievers.

What distinguishes this sense of tradition from the previous two is that it is acknowledging not a sense of stability or continuity of belief and practice over time but rather a sense of dramatic discontinuity. Some theories have tried to gloss over such discontinuities by claiming that, if one looks deeply enough, there is a consistent affirmation evident underneath the appearance of change and repudiation. Efforts have been made, for example, to see in the Second Vatican Council's teaching on religious liberty and the universal reach of God's saving offer nothing more than new historical applications of past insights. These insights may have been expressed imperfectly or in an underdeveloped manner, it is held, but they can be found in the tradition. There is a real danger, however, of succumbing to historical dishonesty. Perhaps it is more honest simply to recognize the general fallibility of the church as a pilgrim people (beyond the realm of dogmatic teaching) that is moving toward the "fullness of truth" but is not protected from wrong turns along the way. Indeed, one way of thinking about the church's teaching on the charism of infallibility and the irreversibility of certain of the church's teachings is to see the exercise of infallibility as an exceptional instance in which elements of church tradition are excluded from the possibility of dramatic reversal envisioned in this sense of tradition. How the church comes to this infallible judgment will have to be considered in later chapters.

This third sense of tradition as dramatic development should not be thought of as a kind of failure of tradition or a negation of it. Tradition is sustained by the discernment of the whole church regarding the integrity and authenticity of the received apostolic faith. That this discernment will, on occasion, yield a reversal is not a failure of tradition but the proof of its vitality.

The Sense of Tradition as Incipient Development

If we are to really accept the dynamic character of tradition, we must see it as more than simply the preservation or development of the old but also as the openness to what appears as novel, provocative, prophetic. Although tradition represents an evocation of the church's communal memory, it is also oriented toward the future. Tradition must draw us forward to the fulfillment of God's reign, and that can happen only if, along with the affirmation of ancient and enduring beliefs and practices, there is a place in tradition for the new insight, practice, or perspective that can serve to reinvigorate or reorient tradition. This brings us to Thiel's fourth sense of tradition as embracing the novel. Thiel refers to this as "incipient development."

What we are considering here is the situation in which a new belief or practice is initially advocated by a small minority within the church. Many elements of church tradition that we think of as enduring (and therefore as belonging to the literal sense of tradition) were originally presented by a minority and appeared to many as novel. Thiel reminds us that the Council of Nicaea's view that the *Logos* was "one in being with the Father," a belief that we now accept as an enduring feature of Christian tradition, was actually a minority position in the fourth century. At that time, the majority of Christians accepted the views of the Alexandrian presbyter, Arius, who insisted that the *Logos* was subordinate to the Father within the Godhead. Though St. Athanasius and the bishops at the Council of Nicaea insisted that what they were teaching was in conformity with the ancient apostolic faith, many Christians undoubtedly viewed their unprecedented use of the Greek term *homoousios* (of the same being or substance) as a novelty. Indeed, it took over fifty years for the Nicene position to achieve widespread acceptance.

This fourth sense of tradition as incorporating novelty is inherently *unstable.* When something new is introduced into the life of the church, such introductions are always tenuous and provisional. The novelty will either win wide acceptance over time and lose its novelty or it will eventually be dismissed. Canon law recognizes this dynamic when it notes that certain customs may legitimately arise within a community. If those customs endure for a significant amount of time, they gradually lose their status as custom and take on the force of law.

This sense of tradition often functions prophetically. Precisely because the novel perspective is initially voiced by a small number, there is a temptation to dismiss the novel as unfounded, trendy, politically correct, or unbalanced. Yet it may be that this new insight will call the community to consider some hitherto unexamined aspect of the Christian life. Though the call to radical nonviolence has been voiced throughout the Christian tradition, it has always had more of a prophetic character, considered by many to be unrealistic or out of step with the classical tradition's embrace of Christian views of self-defense, just war theory, and the legitimate exercise of capital punishment. And yet the call to radical nonviolence can also be viewed as a call to believers to embrace a vital yet neglected aspect of gospel living.

These four senses of tradition do not compete with one another. An authentic understanding of Catholic tradition must acknowledge the necessity of all four. Without the literal sense of tradition there would be no unity of Christian belief, no common profession of faith to unite believers. Without tradition as continuity-in-development, it would be impossible to recognize insights and practices whose "traditional" character only emerged over time. Finally, without the senses of tradition as reversal and novelty, there would be no real change at all, for both reversal and novelty are dynamisms that serve to expand, renew, and revise the shared consciousness of the Christian faith. To hold these four senses of tradition together is to affirm with Pope John XXIII that "the Church is not an archaeological museum, but is alive, tireless, and life-giving; and it makes its way forward, often in unexpected ways."[17]

As we have noted at several points in this chapter, the authoritative character of tradition is always a matter of discernment. Just as a community must identify and repudiate distorted, toxic memories, so too the church must discern which of our particular traditions should continue to shape our faith, religious imagination, and practice. Some represent enduring apostolic traditions (e.g., the sacraments of the church) while others are so bound to a particular place and time (one thinks of the practice of "churching" mothers after childbirth or the medieval teaching on limbo) that they may no longer be, if they ever were, life-giving and reflective of Gospel teaching. This discernment is a corporate one. It is a discernment to be undertaken by the church's magisterium, by the whole people of God exercising their sense of faith, and by the critical scholarship of theologians. In parts 3 and 4 we will attend more fully to each of these.

---

[17] *Discorsi Messagio Colloqui del S. Padre Giovanni XXIII*, vol. 2 (Città Vaticano, 1960–1967), 652, as quoted in Giuseppe Alberigo, "The Announcement of the Council," in *History of Vatican II*, vol. 1, ed. Giuseppe Alberigo and Joseph A. Komonchak (Maryknoll, NY: Orbis Books, 1995), 53.

DISPUTED QUESTIONS

(1) The sense of tradition as a reversal or repudiation of past beliefs and practices is controversial. In the minds of some, this view challenges the belief that the Spirit, by Christ's promise, would always be with the church protecting it from error—what theologians refer to as the "indefectibility" of the church. They resist any admission of genuine reversals, preferring to view these so-called reversals within a framework of development and growth.

(2) The acceptance of the possibility of novelty within tradition can also be quite controversial. Feminist proposals regarding new images for naming God or new liturgical practices that emerge from grassroots practice (e.g., holding hands during the Lord's Prayer, use of liturgical dance) are often condemned as "untraditional." Theologians and church leaders can disagree on whether such novelty can be justified in a given instance. Some theologians would reject altogether the idea of novelty within the development of tradition, insisting instead that any legitimate "new" developments in tradition must emerge organically out of the old and not as the result of assimilating genuine novelty.

FOR FURTHER READING

Boeve, Lieven. *God Interrupts History: Theology in a Time of Upheaval.* New York: Continuum, 2007.

———. *Interrupting Tradition: An Essay on Christian Faith in a Postmodern Context.* Louvain: Peeters, 2003.

Congar, Yves. *The Meaning of Tradition.* New York: Hawthorn, 1964.

———. *Tradition and Traditions: An Historical and Theological Essay.* New York: Macmillan, 1966.

Lash, Nicholas. *Change in Focus: A Study of Doctrinal Change and Continuity.* London: Sheed & Ward, 1973.

Levering, Matthew. *Engaging the Doctrine of Revelation.* Grand Rapids: Baker Academic, 2014.

Newman, John Henry. *An Essay on the Development of Christian Doctrine.* 6th ed. Notre Dame, IN: University of Notre Dame Press, 1989.

Nichols, Aidan. *From Newman to Congar: The Idea of Doctrinal Development from the Victorians to the Second Vatican Council.* Edinburgh: T & T Clark, 1990.

Noonan, John T., Jr. *A Church That Can and Cannot Change: The Development of Catholic Moral Teaching.* Notre Dame, IN: University of Notre Dame Press, 2005.

O'Malley, John W. *Tradition and Transition: Historical Perspectives on Vatican II.* Wilmington, DE: Glazier, 1988.

Pelikan, Jaroslav. *The Vindication of Tradition.* New Haven, CT: Yale University Press, 1984.

Thiel, John E. *Senses of Tradition: Continuity and Development in Catholic Faith.* New York: Oxford University Press, 2000.

Tilley, Terrence W. *Inventing Catholic Tradition.* Maryknoll, NY: Orbis Books, 2000.

PART THREE

THE AUTHORITY OF
THE MAGISTERIUM

SIX

HOW DID THE MAGISTERIUM
DEVELOP HISTORICALLY?

Few Catholic institutions have been as misunderstood as that of the magisterium, the teaching authority of the college of bishops under the headship of the Bishop of Rome. The four chapters that comprise the third section of this volume all deal with the authority of the magisterium in some sense. In this chapter we will offer a very brief historical overview that calls the reader's attention to key moments in the development of the apostolic office of the church and in particular the exercise of its teaching authority. In chapter 7 we will look to contemporary ecclesiology for fundamental insights that can help illuminate a healthy understanding of the theological foundations, exercise, and limits of the magisterium. Chapter 8 will consider the various ways in which the magisterium can be exercised, and chapter 9 will shift to the object of magisterial teaching, namely, dogma and doctrine.

The term "magisterium" means, literally, the authority of the master (*magister*) or teacher.[1] The term has a long and complicated history. In classical Latin it simply referred to the dignity, authority, or office of the teacher or *magister*. Its usage in the early church was rare, and it did not have the specialized meaning that it carries today. By the late Middle

---

[1] The classic essays on this topic are both by Yves Congar: "A Semantic History of the Term 'Magisterium'" and "A Brief History of the Forms of the Magisterium and Its Relations with Scholars," in *Readings in Moral Theology*, vol. 3: *The Magisterium and Morality*, ed. Charles E. Curran and Richard A. McCormick (New York: Paulist Press, 1982), 297–313 and 314–31. Much of this chapter will draw on Congar's seminal studies of the topic.

Ages, magisterium primarily referred to the function and authority of all teachers in the church, both bishops and scholars. It was in the early nineteenth century that the term "magisterium" began to refer more narrowly to the function and authority of the pope and bishops in teaching doctrine. Today, the term is employed in reference to the pope and bishops themselves as authoritative teachers of the apostolic faith as when we hear the phrase, "The magisterium teaches. . . ." Throughout this volume we will use the term "magisterium" to refer to both the teaching authority of the pope and bishops and to the pope and bishops as a teaching body.

THE ORIGINS OF AN
APOSTOLIC TEACHING OFFICE

As with almost every other aspect of church life, the New Testament gives witness to only the very beginnings of a distinctive teaching authority exercised within the life of the church. St. Paul acknowledges that "God has appointed in the church first apostles, second prophets, third teachers" (1 Cor. 12:28); however, it is difficult to know what distinguished these ministries from each other. One suspects that initially the responsibility for teaching was not very strictly defined and many would have exercised teaching responsibilities in varying capacities. Even the office of apostle is difficult to identify with any precision. There are more than twenty-five different New Testament references to either "the twelve apostles" or simply to "the Twelve." The biblical tradition presents these as special figures called forth specifically by Jesus from among a larger group of disciples. Some, like Peter, James, and John, will play a more prominent role in the gospels. Others are little more than names. What complicates any consideration of the role the Twelve played in the life of the early church is the fact that, by the time the gospels and Acts were being written, four decades after Jesus' death and resurrection, the Twelve had clearly acquired a symbolic significance beyond their actual historical ministry. Jesus' choice of the twelve apostles was likely a symbolic act suggesting the dramatic reconstitution of the twelve tribes of Israel. If so, the choice of the Twelve, for the biblical authors, reinforced the church's relationship to the people of Israel. The Synoptic Gospels seem to present the Twelve as, in some sense, an extension of Jesus' own ministry and mission. We know little about their ministry after the resurrection save what we find in Acts of the Apostles, a somewhat idealistic portrait of the early church. In Luke's account, the Twelve functioned as leaders of the church in Jerusalem whose authority was acknowledged and respected (though not above challenge) among the other churches.

The word *apostolos* is not limited to the Twelve, however. Paul claimed the title for himself, based on his encounter with the risen Christ. He respected the authority of the "pillars in Jerusalem," but he was neither afraid to claim his own authority nor reluctant to challenge the authority of even someone as revered as Peter (Cephas). Also note-worthy is the reference to Andronicus and Junia, whom Paul said were "prominent among the apostles" (Rom 16:7). The tradition generally understood Junia to be a male, but there is growing evidence that Junia was in fact the name of a female leader of the church. St. John Chryso-stom certainly held this view, praising her in these words:

> It is certainly a great thing to be an apostle; but to be outstanding among the apostles—think what praise that is! She was outstanding in her works, in her good deeds; oh, and how great is the philosophy of this woman, that she was regarded as worthy to be counted among the apostles![2]

Although this is the only specific New Testament reference to a woman as an apostle, early church literature granted this title to other figures, most notably Mary Magdalene, referred to in the East as "the apostle to the apostles" because she was commanded by the angel at the tomb of Jesus to go tell his disciples that he was risen from the dead (Matt 28:7). In John's account it is the risen Christ himself who commands her to "go to my brothers and say to them . . ." (John 20:17).

Later New Testament writings, like those found in the Pastoral Letters (1–2 Timothy and Titus), suggest that already, by the end of the first century, certain more formal offices with official responsibility for teaching were being established. Titles like *diakonos*, *presbyteros*, and *episkopos* emerge, but with unclear distinctions; the latter two titles seem to have been used more or less interchangeably. Early postbiblical evidence suggests that the church in Jerusalem and other Jewish-Christian communities were initially governed by a group of elders, perhaps imitating the leadership structure of Jewish synagogues of the time. Other churches may well have been led by itinerant prophets.

---

[2] Quoted in Ute E. Eisen, *Women Officeholders in Early Christianity* (Collegeville, MN: Liturgical Press, 2000), 48.

What we do know is that, at the beginning of the second century, church leadership began to coalesce around a single leader for each eucharistic community, known as an *episkopos* or "overseer," rendered in modern English as "bishop." The early second-century letters of St. Ignatius of Antioch suggest that at least some churches had developed a tripartite structure of church leadership led by a single bishop (*episkopos*) who was surrounded by a group of presbyters (*presbyteroi*) and deacons (*diakonoi*). Ignatius asserted the authority of the bishop and the importance of the people showing obedience, reverence, and respect to the bishop. At the same time, he saw the bishop not as an external authority over the community but as a leader fully immersed sacramentally within the life of the local church.

The move from the unique authority of those who had witnessed the risen Christ (the apostles) to those who took on formal church office as leaders of local churches occurred only gradually. It is doubtful that the early "bishops" were formally installed by apostles, but it was not long before the churches attributed to these bishops a succession to the unique authority of the apostles. By the end of the second century, the monoepiscopate—one bishop leading each local church—was almost universally accepted. The speed with which this occurred is rather remarkable, particularly since, as Hermann Pottmeyer has observed, "there was no central authority demanding or guiding this development."[3] Pottmeyer suggests its rapid acceptance may have been due to (1) the gradual conjoining of pastoral leadership over a local church and the presidency over the celebration of that church's worship and (2) the success of the monoepiscopate in preserving church unity in the face of growing conflicts.

In response to growing heretical and schismatic groups the late second and third centuries saw expanded assertions of the teaching authority of the bishops. Christianity held that the authentic apostolic faith could be found in the testimony of the apostolic churches, those churches thought to be founded by apostles, and in the public teaching of the bishops who led those churches. In the face of conflicting claims of various groups to possess the truth of the faith, the answer to the question "Where is the sure faith of the apostolic community to be found?" increasingly was "In the teaching of the bishops."

---

[3] Hermann J. Pottmeyer, "The Episcopacy," in *The Gift of the Church*, ed. Peter Phan (Collegeville, MN: Liturgical Press, 2000), 337–53 at 343.

KEY DEVELOPMENTS IN
THE FIRST MILLENNIUM

Not surprisingly, bishops freely exercised their authority within their local churches. The local churches believed themselves to be in a spiritual communion with the other churches, even though there were as yet few centralized bureaucratic structures uniting the churches. In the second and third centuries, local bishops began meeting on a regional basis in gatherings that would become known as synods to address questions of common concern. (The term "synod" stems from the Greek prefix *syn*, which means "together," and *hodos*, which means "way"—a synod is then a medium for local churches to "come together" or "walk together.") Often the matters demanding attention were disciplinary, but occasionally these synods would pronounce on matters of doctrine. One example would be regional synods held in North Africa in the third century to deal with questions regarding the appropriate pastoral care of the *lapsi*, those who had "lapsed" or betrayed the faith in the face of persecution. Yet even these pastoral deliberations included discernment on matters of doctrine, such as whether these *lapsi* should be rebaptized or not. This practice of gathering in regional synods suggests that very early in the history of Christianity it was recognized that bishops who were pastors of local churches bore responsibility for the larger church as well.

At this early stage, mostly as a courtesy, synodal decisions and decrees would be communicated to the Bishop of Rome. The leader of the church of Rome was already acknowledged to possess a distinctive authority. When the church of Jerusalem died out near the end of the first century, Rome gradually supplanted Jerusalem as Christianity's "mother church." The Roman church was granted a certain priority among the churches in virtue of the tradition that it had received the apostolic teaching and martyrdom of not one, but two apostles, Sts. Peter and Paul. There is ancient testimony to the unique prestige held by the church of Rome. At the beginning of the second century St. Ignatius would refer to Rome as the church "foremost in love,"[4] and by the end of the same century St. Irenaeus of Lyons would refer to it as the church "of most excellent origins."[5] It is hard for us to appreciate today the

---

[4] St. Ignatius of Antioch, *Epistle to the Romans* 4.
[5] St. Irenaeus of Lyons, *Against the Heresies* 3.3.2.

significance of this ancient claim to the authority of the apostles. Eamon Duffy, in his study of the papacy, puts it well:

> For the earliest Christians apostolic authority was no antiquarian curiosity, a mere fact about the origins of a particular community. The Apostles were living presences, precious guarantors of truth. The apostolic churches possessed more than a pedigree, they spoke with the voices of their founders, and provided living access to their teaching. And in Rome, uniquely, the authority of two Apostles converged. The charismatic voice of Paul, bearer of a radical authority rooted not in institution and organization but in the uncompromising clarity of a gospel received direct from God, joined with the authority of Peter, symbol of the church's jurisdiction in both heaven and earth, the one to whom the commission to bind and to feed had been given by Christ himself.[6]

Yet Duffy also observes that the authority of Rome, by the end of the third century, differed only in degree and not in kind from the authority of other churches with claims to apostolicity. For example, there was no sense, as yet, that the Bishop of Rome could exercise any veto power regarding synodal decisions outside the Roman province.

In the fourth century, an Alexandrian presbyter, Arius, offered a popular interpretation of the divine origins of Christ that soon became the source of considerable controversy. Emperor Constantine, concerned that the dispute was threatening the unity of the empire, called for a special council to address the controversy. It would be the first of many other imperial interventions. This meeting, held in Nicaea, would later be regarded as the first of a series of "ecumenical councils," so named because the teaching of these councils pertained to, and was eventually accepted by, the *oikoumene*, the universal church.

It was only in the fourth century that bishops of the church of Rome explicitly claimed to be the unique successors to the authority of Peter.[7] The authority of the papacy would grow considerably in the fourth and fifth centuries, with Pope Leo the Great (440–461), for example, having a sizable influence on the Council of Chalcedon's Christological teaching. Moreover, in the face of growing feuds among various regional synods, Rome often became a court of final appeal. Nevertheless, when

---

[6] Eamon Duffy, *Saints and Sinners: A History of the Popes* (New Haven, CT: Yale University Press, 1997), 13.

[7] I say "explicitly" because we do have indirect documentary evidence of the third-century Bishop Steven claiming authority as the unique successor of Peter. This is reported in a letter of Firmilian, bishop of Caesurea, to Cyprian.

it came to teaching on doctrinal matters, bishops continued to see themselves as the primary teachers within their own churches while recognizing that the common teaching shared by all the bishops (including the Bishop of Rome) offered a sure foundation for Christian faith.

When it was felt necessary to make more formal pronouncements on doctrinal matters, this was accomplished either regionally or in ecumenical councils. These gatherings were often quite messy affairs, filled with political intrigue. Nevertheless, there was a general agreement that for the decrees of a council to have binding doctrinal force there needed to be a twofold consensus: first, a consensus with the faith of the ancient church, reflected primarily in the teaching of prior councils, and, second, a consensus among the churches that the council's teaching in fact expressed their faith. Finally, adequate participation and approbation by church leadership was considered necessary. In the East the emphasis was on the participation or at least consent of the pentarchy, the five patriarchal sees of Rome, Constantinople, Antioch, Alexandria, and Jerusalem. In the West, where the authority of Constantinople was disputed, the emphasis was primarily on the participation or approbation of the Bishop of Rome. Often the validity of a council's teaching would only be confirmed at a subsequent council.

In the mid-ninth century a set of forged documents were produced that sought to ground a very expansive set of claims to papal authority in the ancient tradition. These became known as the *False Decretals of Isidore* and included the well-known forgery "The Donation of Constantine," which claimed the papal states had been given to the papacy by the fourth-century Emperor Constantine. These documents were not produced to expand papal authority so much as to undermine the abusive exercise of authority on the part of the regional metropolitans who were often appointed by the princes. The papacy was not nearly so dominant at that time as one might think; it was the metropolitan archbishops who often were most feared for their abuses of power. In spite of the papacy's acquisition of the papal states in the eighth century, it would remain dominated by the Carolingian and Ottonian emperors up through the first half of the eleventh century.

As the church approached the end of the first millennium it underwent significant changes. The Eastern and Western churches had grown further apart. The churches of the East remained under the influence of the Byzantine emperor while the churches of the West initially experienced greater political independence before ultimately casting their lot with the Franks in the eighth century. Theological tendencies and liturgical practice began to diverge considerably. This growing division between East and West would be formalized in the mutual excommunications of the pope and the patriarch of Constantinople in 1054.

Through most of the first thousand years of Christianity, while the attention of popes and bishops was often distracted by matters of a more political nature, at least in the West the conviction perdured that the pope and bishops *together* shared responsibility for preserving the apostolic faith of the churches. As the church moved into the beginning of the second millennium, however, the pastoral role of the bishop would diminish, eventually giving rise to the view that a bishop was simply a priest with greater jurisdiction.

KEY DEVELOPMENTS IN THE TEACHING AUTHORITY OF THE POPE AND BISHOPS IN THE SECOND MILLENNIUM

As Christianity in the West began its second thousand years of existence, the dismal state of church affairs in a feudal society eventually led to a series of papal calls for church reform. These culminated in the so-called Gregorian reforms undertaken in the pontificate of Pope Gregory VII (1073–1085). The general thrust of these reforms was to secure the proper autonomy of the church and its bishops against the unwarranted influence of the lay nobility. To do so Pope Gregory articulated a lofty theology of the papacy that asserted the primacy of the pope's spiritual authority over the temporal authority of princes and emperors. Gregory's goal was not the personal consolidation of power but the restoration of the freedom of the church to fulfill its mission. In service of this goal he sought to restore the free elections of the bishops. Nevertheless, an undeniable, if unintended, consequence of these reforms was the solidification of all ecclesiastical authority in the papacy. Gregory's reforms recast the church as if it were one universal diocese with the pope as its bishop and the other bishops as vicars of the pope. Reflecting an early stage of this new ecclesiology, Peter Damien, an eleventh-century cardinal bishop of Ostia, would write: "The pope is the sole universal bishop of all the churches."[8]

Gregory began measures to standardize canon law for the whole church. He required that all archbishops receive the *pallium* (a band

---

[8] Quoted in Jean Rigal, *L'ecclésiologie de communion* (Paris: Cerf, 1997), 24.

of white wool worn around the neck of the pope and archbishops as a sign of authority) from the pope within three months of their election and widened the use of papal legates in other countries, the authority of whom was often held as superior to that of local bishops and metropolitans.

The Gregorian reforms represent a crucial turning point in the history of the church. In spite of the many changes and developments that transpired over the church's first thousand years, for much of that period the church remained very much a communion of local churches, each led by a bishop. Every bishop was considered a "vicar of Christ" whose authority came from Christ. Popes would make ever more expansive claims to papal authority from the time of Pope Leo on, yet even these popes saw themselves as a "bishop among bishops."

With the Gregorian reforms of the eleventh century, bishops would retain considerable practical autonomy and power at the local level, but the dominant theology of the time presented the bishops more and more as dependent on the pope for their spiritual authority. This is reflected in the changing nature of ecumenical councils. Councils in the first millennium were gatherings of bishops convened by emperors in which the Bishop of Rome exercised varying degrees of influence. In contrast, the medieval ecumenical councils were convened by the popes to pursue predominantly papal agendas.

The eleventh to fifteenth centuries would witness a significant reconfiguration of church leadership. In his history of papal primacy, Klaus Schatz observed:

> It [Rome] became no longer simply the center of Church unity, the norm of true belief, and the measure of authentic tradition. Now, for the first time, the papacy became truly the head of the Church; from it went forth all important decisions, and within it all the functions of the life of the whole Church were coordinated. Now Rome raised (and enforced), to a far greater degree than before, the claim to play an active role in shaping the life of the Church and determining the way it should go—thus not merely by responding to questions or petitions, which until that time had constituted by far the greater part of papal activity outside the ecclesiastical province of Rome. . . . The central concept was no longer simply the Roman church or Roman tradition, with the pope primarily the authentic speaker, witness and administrator of that tradition, and thus responsible more for giving witness than for making new judgments.[9]

---

[9] Klaus Schatz, *Papal Primacy: From Its Origins to the Present* (Collegeville, MN: Liturgical Press, 1996), 78.

Even as papal authority expanded during this period, the majority of doctrinal questions were handled not by the pope and bishops but by competent theological faculties. If a particular theological dispute emerged, it might well fall to the theology faculty at the University of Paris or Bologna, for example, to handle the question. Not surprisingly, then, in the late Middle Ages "magisterium" had a much broader meaning; it was applied to the office and authority of teachers, both bishops and scholars. St. Thomas Aquinas wrote of both the magisterium of the pastoral chair (*magisterium cathedrae pastoralis*), by which he meant the authority of the bishop, and the magisterium of the teaching chair (*magisterium cathedrae magistralis*), by which he meant the authority of the theologian.[10] The teaching authority of the theologian was grounded in his scholarly competence whereas the teaching authority of the pastor or bishop was grounded in his jurisdiction. Popes in the late Middle Ages did arbitrate doctrinal disputes but often through the mediation of papal commissions comprised of both bishops and theologians. The pope would receive the report of the faculty or commission and then issue a doctrinal judgment. This continued well into the seventeenth century.

Consider the sixteenth- and seventeenth-century *de auxiliis* ("regarding the divine helps") controversy between the Jesuits and the Dominicans. The Jesuit flag bearer was a man named Luis de Molina while the Dominicans were championed by Domingo Banez. The controversy itself concerned the relationship between divine grace (emphasized by the Dominicans) and human freedom (stressed by the Jesuits). The papacy inserted itself into the controversy only after representatives of the two religious orders had begun accusing each other of heresy. Pope Clement VIII (1592–1605) initiated an investigation, but it came to a definitive conclusion two papacies later, under Pope Paul V (1605–1621). The investigation itself included seventeen public debates between representatives of the principal theological schools. Paul V finally resolved the matter by way of decree, prohibiting either side from condemning the views of the other.

---

[10] St. Thomas Aquinas, *Quodlibet* III, 9, ad 3.

Three Church "Traumas" That Shaped Modern Views of Church Authority

The development of church authority during the second millennium of Christianity was shaped, according to Hermann Pottmeyer, by a reaction to three great "traumas," the first of which was the conciliarist controversy.[11]

The beginnings of conciliarism can be traced back to the second half of the thirteenth century as a succession of weak and/or corrupt popes began to undermine the authority of the papacy. A series of tragic missteps, like the temporary move of the papacy to the French town of Avignon, soon led, by the end of the fourteenth century, to a major crisis in the church. There arose first two and then three different claimants to the Holy See, further eroding the credibility of the papacy. This situation led to the summoning of the Council of Constance in 1413. This council agreed that the only viable solution was the resignation of all three claimants and the election of a new pope. In the eyes of some, this pragmatic move amounted to an assertion of the authority of a council over that of a pope. Proponents of this view came to be known as conciliarists. Others took a more moderate view, seeing Constance as an extreme measure taken in order to ensure the integrity of the church. At the next council, held first at Ferrara and then at Florence (1438–1445), the increasingly extreme views of the conciliarists led to their marginalization and they soon lost most of their support. With the conciliar decree *Laetentur coeli*, the council dramatically reaffirmed the primacy of the pope over any council.

As papal authority was further extended, not a few bishops wondered about the theological bases for their own authority. At the sixteenth-century Council of Trent, the bishops had several important discussions about the authority of the bishops in relation to the authority of the pope. Some held the ancient view that a bishop's juridical power and authority comes from their ordination as bishop; others held that it was delegated to them by the pope. In spite of a lively exchange on this and other related topics, no formal pronouncement was made. An interesting side note is that at the Council of Trent theologians were given a prominent role in which they debated key propositions extensively in

---

[11] Hermann Pottmeyer, *Towards a Papacy in Communion* (New York: Crossroad, 1998), 36–50.

the presence of the bishops gathered at the council.[12] This practice stands in startling contrast to the rules governing the Second Vatican Council in which theologians were not allowed to speak at all during the council sessions.

The fear of resurging conciliarism would haunt the papacy all the way up to Vatican II. The vigorous condemnation of seventeenth- and eighteenth-century movements, such as Gallicanism in France, Febronianism in Germany, and Josephinism in Austria, were in part an expression of papal suspicions regarding the conciliarist tendencies of these movements.

If the first trauma facing the papacy was primarily ecclesial in nature, according to Pottmeyer, the second was predominantly political. From the late fifteenth to the mid-nineteenth centuries, the rise of absolute monarchies in Western Europe created a situation in which the Catholic Church frequently found itself subject to state control and even persecution. States often restricted or interfered in the church's educational ministry and even in the exercise of its sacramental ministry. The papacy protested this situation vigorously, but, weakened first by the Western schism and then by the Protestant Reformation, the papacy was in no position to do anything about it. Ironically, even as the papacy protested against the control of the monarchs over church offers, it was itself being refashioned as a parallel monarchy.

The church's third trauma was both cultural and intellectual and was occasioned by the rise of the Enlightenment. By championing the autonomy of human reason the Enlightenment challenged the legitimacy of any kind of revealed knowledge. The Bible, church tradition, and any notion of a church teaching office were all called into question. The popes of the eighteenth and nineteenth centuries spoke quite vehemently against the excesses of rationalism.

The nineteenth century witnessed a significant increase in papal activism regarding matters of church doctrine. The exercise of papal teaching authority had grown significantly over the course of the nineteenth century, largely through the use of encyclicals (a letter written by the pope to the universal church, addressing doctrinal, moral, or disciplinary matters). The papal encyclical itself was a relatively modern development, first employed in the eighteenth century by Pope Benedict

---

[12] See John W. O'Malley, *Trent: What Happened at the Council* (Cambridge, MA: Belknap Press of Harvard University Press, 2013).

XIV (1740–1758). His encyclicals, however, were all very brief and largely either disciplinary or exhortatory in character. In the nineteenth century, Popes Gregory XVI (1831–1846) and Pius IX made use of the encyclical to address doctrinal matters, but these too were generally short in length. When they condemned erroneous views, there was no intention of stimulating new theological insight.[13] That would begin to change by the end of the century.

The Teaching of Vatican I

The three traumas of the second millennium cumulatively provided the backdrop to the First Vatican Council called by Pope Pius IX (1846–1878) and held from 1869 to 1870. This council was, in many respects, a council of reaction, intended to condemn the errors of modernity and to reaffirm the authority of the pope. The council promulgated the Dogmatic Constitution on the Catholic Faith, *Dei Filius*, which focused on the challenges raised by the enlightenment, offering a fairly sophisticated consideration of the relationship between faith and reason. They intended to also promulgate a similar constitution on the church. A draft was composed but the bishops found it inadequate and returned it to committee for revisions. Unfortunately, the council was suspended due to the Franco-Prussian War, and, as a consequence, the council was never able to produce a comprehensive document on the church as they had originally intended. They were able to deliberate on the material in the draft that pertained to the papacy and eventually produced a separate constitution on papal authority, *Pastor Aeternus.*

In the third chapter of that constitution the council reinforced the teaching of the Council of Florence that the pope possessed "a preeminence of ordinary power over every other church, and that this jurisdictional power of the Roman pontiff is both episcopal and immediate."[14] The use of the term "ordinary" could be misleading. It was a technical, canonical term that did not carry the modern sense of "ordinary," that is, "frequent" or "regular." In canon law the opposite of "ordinary" is not "extraordinary" but "delegated." In this context, asserting that the pope's jurisdiction over the whole church was *ordinary*

---

[13] Schatz, *Papal Primacy*, 167–68.

[14] *Pastor Aeternus*, chapter 3. The translation is from Norman P. Tanner, *Decrees of Ecumenical Councils* (Washington, DC: Georgetown University Press, 1990), 2:813–14.

meant simply that it was proper to the bishop of Rome; it was not a *delegated* jurisdiction.[15] The pope is not the "first bishop" of each local church. He is *bishop* of only one local church, the church of Rome. As such, he has a pastoral concern and responsibility over the universal church that is ordinary, immediate, and universal inasmuch as it properly belongs to him and involves a constant attitude of vigilant concern for the "unity of faith and communion of the whole church." Since this is often misunderstood, it was important that the constitution included a key text on the authority of the local bishop:

> This power of the supreme pontiff by no means detracts from that ordinary and immediate power of episcopal jurisdiction, by which the bishops, who have succeeded to the place of the apostles by appointment of the Holy Spirit, tend and govern individually the particular flocks which have been assigned to them. On the contrary, this power of theirs is asserted, supported and defended by the supreme and universal pastor; for St. Gregory the Great says: "My honour is the honour of the whole church. My honour is the steadfast strength of my brethren. Then do I receive true honor, when it is denied to none of those to whom honour is due."[16]

Unfortunately, the council did not provide any theological rationale to explain how, in fact, positing a universal ordinary jurisdiction to the pope and a distinct ordinary jurisdiction to the local bishop could be reconciled.

When consideration was given to the council's proposed teaching on papal infallibility, the bishops were loosely divided into different camps. One group, dominated by the French, wished to return to a more ancient ecclesiology that stressed fidelity to tradition, saw the whole church as a communion of churches, and emphasized the importance of the pope's ongoing relationship with his brother bishops. The other group were Ultramontanists, so called because they felt that in all matters one should look "beyond the mountains" (the Alps) to submit to the position of Rome. For them a strong doctrinal commitment to unfettered papal authority in matters both spiritual and temporal was the church's best defense against the liberal spirit of the age. Both groups generally accepted some notion of papal infallibility, but while the French minority wanted to connect the exercise of papal infallibility

---

[15] This was reiterated by the Vatican I relator, Bishop Zinelli, in J. D. Mansi, ed., *Sacrorum Conciliorum Nova et Amplissima Collectio* (Graz: Akademische Druck, 1961), 52:1105.

[16] Tanner, *Decrees of Ecumenical Councils*, 2:814.

explicitly to the infallibility of the whole church, the Ultramontanists wanted to preserve papal autonomy. What resulted was a dogmatic pronouncement on papal infallibility that was relatively moderate in scope and which, at least indirectly, related papal authority to the authority of the bishops.

What did Vatican I finally teach regarding papal infallibility? In the beginning of the fourth chapter of *Pastor aeternus* the council moved from a consideration of papal primacy in general to the supreme teaching authority of the pope as part of that primacy. The purpose of this supreme teaching authority is to make "the saving teaching of Christ" available, uncontaminated, to the whole world. The council then contended:

> The Roman pontiffs . . . defined as doctrines to be held those things which, by God's help, they knew to be in keeping with sacred scripture and the apostolic traditions. For the Holy Spirit was promised to the successors of Peter *not so that they might, by his revelation, make known some new doctrine*, but that, by his assistance, they might religiously guard and faithfully expound the revelation or deposit of faith transmitted by the apostles.[17]

This represented a very important qualification. That which is defined must belong to Scripture and tradition (or be necessary for its faithful exposition); it cannot be a doctrinal novelty. Many both before and since the council have mistakenly thought of papal infallibility as teaching new revelation, the communication of new "truths" about God. Yet the council clearly rejected this view and spoke only of divine "assistance" in recognizing and proclaiming what already belongs to the faith of the church.

The formal definition reads as follows:

> Therefore . . . we . . . teach and define as a divinely revealed dogma that when the Roman Pontiff speaks *ex cathedra*, that is, when, *in the exercise of his office as shepherd and teacher of all Christians*, in virtue of his supreme apostolic authority, he defines a doctrine *concerning faith or morals* to be held by the whole church, he possesses, by the divine assistance promised to him in blessed Peter, that infallibility *which the divine Redeemer willed his church to enjoy* in defining doctrine concerning faith or morals. Therefore, such definitions of the Roman pontiff *are of themselves, and not by the consent of the church, irreformable*.[18]

[17] Ibid., 2:816 (emphasis is mine).
[18] Ibid. (emphasis is mine).

The definition follows the medieval tradition, which relates infallibility to the pope only insofar as he is "shepherd and teacher of all Christians." This infallibility can only be considered "personal" inasmuch as it pertains to the pope as officeholder. Bishop Vincent Gasser, the official relator for the theological commission that drafted the text, provided an official explanation of the intent of the drafters known as a *relatio*. In it he clarified that infallibility did not apply to the pope as private doctor.[19] Moreover, the council connected papal infallibility with that infallibility "which the divine Redeemer willed his church to enjoy." In this sense papal infallibility could be distinguished but not separated from the infallibility given to the church itself. Many of the minority bishops pressed for a more explicit connection between the teaching of the pope and the faith of the church. Although their request was rejected, they were somewhat mollified by Bishop Gasser's insistence that the final text did not preclude the pope's general consultation of the bishops. The council document also made it clear that ordinary papal teaching was not taught infallibly. It is only when the pope speaks *ex cathedra*, from the chair of Peter, that he teaches with the charism of infallibility.

What are we to make of the final clause in the definition, which states that these solemnly defined definitions are irreformable "of themselves, and not by the consent of the church"? This passage was a particularly difficult pill for the French minority to swallow since it was added only at the last minute. Some among the minority viewed this late addition as a blatant act of insensitivity to their concerns. Nevertheless, again following Gasser's authoritative interpretation, what the council actually rejected in this clause was only the "strict and absolute necessity of seeking that consent."[20]

There is a growing agreement among commentators that this final condition must be read in the light of a certain obsession at the council with the possible recurrence of Gallicanism, that seventeenth-century French nationalist movement in which the French bishops called for much greater independence from papal authority. This late addition was

---

[19] Mansi, *Sacrorum Conciliorum*, 52:1213. An English translation of Gasser's *relatio* can be found in James T. O'Connor, *The Gift of Infallibility: The Official Relatio on Infallibility of Bishop Vincent Ferrer Gasser at Vatican I*, 2nd ed. (San Francisco: Ignatius Press, 2008).

[20] Mansi, *Sacrorum Conciliorum*, 52:1216.

a repudiation of the Gallican Articles that had called for a *juridical* determination of ecclesial consensus either antecedent or subsequent to a papal definition. It would appear that it was only this extrinsic juridical requirement that was being rejected. Essentially the view of the bishops was that there were sufficient alternative means by which the pope could discern the sense of the church such that an antecedent or subsequent juridical validation would be both unnecessary and unduly restrictive. We might say that the council believed the pope had a moral obligation to consult the bishops and the whole church, but it was not a juridical requirement.

Between Vatican I and II

After the council there was sufficient misunderstanding regarding what the council had actually taught that in 1875 the German bishops issued an important statement clarifying the meaning of the council's teaching on papal primacy. They insisted that the council teaching did not undermine the legitimate authority of the local bishop. Pope Pius IX would publicly thank them for their clarification, which he affirmed. In spite of this attempt to ward off more extreme readings, it must be said that the overall impact of Vatican I's teaching was to encourage a profound papo-centrism in many corners of the church. There were of course many exceptions to this papo-centrist tendency, but as the church moved toward Vatican II, Catholic ecclesiology seemed to suffer, not from any fundamental defect, but from a certain imbalance.

In the wake of the council, exercises of papal authority became more common. With such noteworthy encyclicals as *Aeterni Patris, Providentissimus Deus, Satis Cognitum,* and *Rerum Novarum,* Pope Leo XIII (1878–1903) instigated a further shift in the teaching role of the pope. Popes had claimed doctrinal authority on matters of faith and morals since at least the fifth century. Yet the actual exercise of that authority had been relatively infrequent and, when employed, was usually limited to fairly terse doctrinal pronouncements. The pontificate of Leo XIII marked the beginning of a modern development in the papacy in which popes began to offer, as part of their teaching ministry, extended theological treatments issued in formal magisterial documents on important topics. Pius X (1903–1914) would follow Leo's precedent with *Pascendi Dominici Gregis,* his encyclical condemning modernism, and both Popes Pius XI (1922–1939) and Pius XII (1939–1958) would issue lengthy encyclicals during their successive pontificates.

This pronounced expansion of papal authority was in keeping with a two-tiered theology of the church. Perhaps the clearest expression of this is found in article 8 from *Vehementer Nos*, a 1906 encyclical of Pope Pius X:

> It follows that the Church is essentially an *unequal* society, that is, a society comprising two categories of persons, the Pastors and the flock, those who occupy a rank in the different degrees of the hierarchy and the multitude of the faithful. So distinct are these categories that with the pastoral body only rests the necessary right and authority for promoting the end of the society and directing all its members towards that end; the one duty of the multitude is to allow themselves to be led, and, like a docile flock, to follow the Pastors.[21]

This passage reflects the predominantly clericalist view of the church that dominated late nineteenth- and early twentieth-century Catholic ecclesiology.

In spite of significant undercurrents of church reform, when Pope Pius XII died in 1958, the overwhelming sense of Catholic life was that of being part of a permanent and unchanging institution that stood as a fortress against a hostile world. That church was pyramidal in structure with the pope at the apex and the laity at the base. The papacy had by then achieved unprecedented authority in all spheres of church life. The Roman Curia now exercised many of the tasks and responsibilities that had belonged to the ministry of the bishop during much of the first millennium. The Catholic Church's outlook on the world was dominated by fear and suspicion.

With the election of Angelo Roncalli as Pope John XXIII, few could have predicted the imminent fulfillment of the words of the famous nineteenth-century theologian, Cardinal Newman. Writing to an Anglican cleric dismayed by the one-sided and authoritarian tone of the teachings of Vatican I, Newman wrote: "Let us have a little faith in [the Church] I say. Pius is not the last of the popes. . . . Let us be patient, let us have faith, and a new Pope and a re-assembled Council may trim the boat."[22]

---

[21] English translation from *The Papal Encyclicals*, vol. 3, ed. Claudia Carlen (New York: McGrath, 1981), 47–48.

[22] John Henry Newman, *The Letters and Diaries of John Henry Newman*, vol. 27, ed. Charles Stephen Dessain and Thomas Gornall (Oxford: Clarendon, 1973), 310.

DISPUTED QUESTIONS

(1) It is obvious that the structures of church authority have gone through significant changes over two thousand years. Some controversy has emerged over the hierarchical character of these structures. The term "hierarchy" has probably contributed much to significant misunderstandings regarding the nature of the apostolic office of the bishop. The term was first coined in the late fifth or early sixth century by the neo-Platonic Christian writer known only by his pseudonym, Denys (often referred to by his Latin name, Dionysius) the Areopagite. Etymologically, the term "hierarchy" means simply "sacred source," or "sacred rule." It was Pseudo-Denys who presented the whole cosmos as consisting of descending levels of being in which the higher levels mediate being and God's very presence to the lower levels. Medieval theologians influenced by Pseudo-Denys presented the church on earth as a reflection of the celestial hierarchy of angels. This would eventually be used to justify a monarchical view of papal authority.

Many theologians reject the notion of hierarchy as a "top-down ladder" and call for the reform of church structures and the development of more participatory forms of governance. Others go further and call for a complete dismantling of church structures. They insist that only the development of a more radically egalitarian approach will suffice. Still other scholars and church leaders insist that these calls for reform mistake the church for a secular political institution and therefore evaluate it inappropriately according to the standards of liberal democracy. The hierarchical structure of the church pertains to its sacramental constitution, they insist, and ought not be confused with its secular, bureaucratic analogs. They also note that the Catholic commitment to hierarchy need not exclude participatory decision making in some form.

(2) Although the New Testament hints that women publicly taught in the early churches (hence the condemnation of the practice), growing cultural pressures seem to have quickly muted the voice of women as public teachers. According to some recent scholarship, this historical judgment must be balanced against epigraphical studies suggesting that some women may have held church office in spite of these pressures. Critics of these studies insist that women officeholders were found only among sectarian religious movements. This question has

taken on new currency with Pope Francis's creation of a papal commission to explore the role of women deacons in the early church.

FOR FURTHER READING

Brown, Raymond E. *The Churches the Apostles Left Behind.* New York: Paulist Press, 1984.

Burkhard, John J. *Apostolicity Then and Now: An Ecumenical Church in a Postmodern World.* Collegeville, MN: Liturgical Press, 2004.

Colberg, Kristin. *Vatican I and Vatican II: Councils in the Living Tradition.* Collegeville, MN: Liturgical Press, 2016.

Congar, Yves. "A Semantic History of the Term 'Magisterium'" and "A Brief History of the Forms of the Magisterium and Its Relations with Scholars." In *Readings in Moral Theology.* Vol. 3: *The Magisterium and Morality.* Edited by Charles E. Curran and Richard A. McCormick, 297–313 and 314–31. New York: Paulist Press, 1982.

Miller, Michael. *The Shepherd and the Rock: Origins, Development and Mission of the Papacy.* Huntington, IN: Our Sunday Visitor, 1995.

Nichols, Terence L. *That All May Be One: Hierarchy and Participation in the Church.* Collegeville, MN: Liturgical Press, 1997.

Oakley, Francis. *The Conciliarist Tradition: Constitutionalism in the Catholic Church, 1300–1870.* Oxford: Oxford University Press, 2003.

O'Gara, Margaret. *Triumph in Defeat: Infallibility, Vatican I, and the French Minority Bishops.* Washington, DC: Catholic University of America Press, 1988.

Pottmeyer, Hermann. *Towards a Papacy in Communion.* New York: Crossroad, 1998.

Schatz, Klaus. *Papal Primacy: From Its Origins to the Present.* Collegeville, MN: Liturgical Press, 1996.

Sullivan, Francis A. *From Apostles to Bishops: The Development of the Episcopacy in the Early Church.* New York: Newman Press, 2001.

SEVEN

HOW DO WE UNDERSTAND THE MAGISTERIUM TODAY?

The question of the appropriate exercise of formal doctrinal teaching authority in the Catholic Church is one of the most controversial in contemporary church life. For much of the postconciliar period more progressive Catholics have vilified the magisterium for its purportedly oppressive and penal tactics. Yet during this same period many conservative voices have blamed an overly passive magisterium for permitting rampant dissent. Few adherents to either view have a fully developed and mature grasp of the ecclesiological foundations for appreciating the proper role of a formal doctrinal teaching authority in the church. In this chapter we hope to redress that shortcoming.

Vatican II gave very little consideration to the teaching authority of the pope and bishops, apart from the third chapter of its Dogmatic Constitution on the Church, *Lumen Gentium,* and, to some extent, the Decree on the Pastoral Office of the Bishop, *Christus Dominus.* The council's most explicitly ecclesiological texts attended in a more general way to the nature, structure, and mission of the church in the world today. It has largely fallen on contemporary ecclesiology to provide a more coherent ecclesiological framework for grasping the proper role of the magisterium, the teaching authority of the pope and bishops, in the postconciliar church.

THE TEACHING OF VATICAN II

When Vatican II opened in October 1962 it had been over ninety years since the last ecumenical council. No one in attendance would have had any firsthand experience of an ecumenical council. As we saw in the last chapter, Vatican I had been unable to complete its agenda and produce a comprehensive statement on the church as a whole. The bishops at Vatican II were committed to addressing that lacuna. In the first session of the council the bishops were given a preparatory draft on the church that reflected the general tendencies of Catholic ecclesiology in the decades between the two councils. This document presented the Catholic Church as a visible, hierarchical institution that was, without remainder, the mystical Body of Christ. The bishops ultimately rejected that draft as inadequate and their final document, *Lumen Gentium*, offered a considerably different vision of the church. Put in its simplest terms, the council recovered the properly *theological* foundations of the church. To do so, the council retrieved an ancient appreciation that the church not only celebrated the sacraments but was itself sacramental in character. The church in mission was a sign and instrument of God's saving offer (LG 1, 48). This attribution of sacramentality to the church itself allowed the council to insist on the necessity of the church's visible features—its institutions and laws—without making them an end in themselves. The sacraments, canon law, church office, daily Christian witness—these visible elements of the church manifested the church's own sacramentality.

The bishops also drew attention to the trinitarian foundations of the church, quoting St. Cyprian who wrote that the church was "a people made one by the unity of the Father, the Son and the holy Spirit" (see LG 4). The church was a spiritual communion of life and love that drew believers into communion with God in Christ by the power of the Holy Spirit.

In continuity with the teaching of Pius XII, the council reflected on the spiritual reality of the church as the mystical Body of Christ, giving that ancient belief a more profound, eucharistic foundation. The council complemented that christological image with reflection on the role of the Holy Spirit "which dwells in the church and in the hearts of the faithful as in a temple." This Spirit "guides the church in the way of all truth and, uniting it in fellowship and ministry, bestows upon it different hierarchic and charismatic gifts, and in this way directs it and adorns it with his fruits" (LG 4). The council recovered a theology of the church as the new people of God. This biblical image emphasized God's initiative in calling forth the church. It also stressed the priority of faith and baptism for establishing membership in the church. In a draft of this constitution, the chapter on the people of God had been placed after the chapter on the hierarchy. Representing one of the most significant changes in a draft text, the council decided to place that chapter *before* the chapter on the hierarchy. The message was clear. Before there could be any consideration of the distinctive roles of clergy and laity in the church, one must first acknowledge that all believers share a common identity and equality by virtue of faith, baptism, and the call to discipleship.

When the council turned its attention to ordained ministry in chapter 3 of *Lumen Gentium*, it reasserted the authority of the bishops, both as individual pastors and as belonging to a universal college that shared, with the Bishop of Rome, responsibility for the welfare of all the churches. Vatican I had considered the role of the bishops largely in the context of the papacy. Vatican II, by contrast, began with consideration of the bishops. In its theological reflection on the ministry of the bishop, the council drew inspiration from the practice of the early church.

First, in article 21 of *Lumen Gentium*, the council affirmed that the office of the bishop was not just the "highest degree" of the priesthood, but the fullness of the sacrament of holy orders. Following ancient practice, it is the bishop, rather than the priest, who is the principal minister of the local church. The council also taught that episcopal power was communicated through episcopal ordination itself. The pope did not delegate power and authority to the bishops, though he could regulate episcopal jurisdiction. Nor was the bishop to be viewed as a "vicar" of the pope. Article 27 taught that every bishop could rightly be called a "vicar of Christ." Regarding the nature of the bishop's pastoral responsibilities, the council wrote:

> The pastoral charge, that is, the permanent and daily care of their sheep, is entrusted to them fully; nor are they to be regarded as vicars of the Roman Pontiff; for they exercise a power which they possess in their own right and are most truly said to be at the head of the people whom they govern. (LG 27)

The bishops, the council taught, have a distinctive responsibility to authoritatively interpret Scripture and proclaim the doctrine of the church, but:

> This magisterium is not superior to the word of God, but is rather its servant. It teaches only what has been handed on to it. At the divine command and with the help of the holy Spirit, it listens to this devoutly, guards it reverently and expounds it faithfully. (DV 10)

Because the bishops do not proclaim a secret gospel but rather give an authoritative proclamation of the apostolic faith shared by the whole church, the bishop must be an effective listener if he is to be an effective teacher. The laity have much to offer to the bishops:

> The laity should disclose their needs and desires to the pastors with that liberty and confidence which befits children of God and brothers and sisters in Christ. To the extent of their knowledge, competence or authority the laity are entitled, and indeed sometimes duty-bound, to express their opinion on matters which concern the good of the church. (LG 37)

Of course, just as the bishop is not simply a mouthpiece for the pope, neither is he a mouthpiece for the opinions of his flock reflected in the latest poll. A "special charism of truth" is given to him, and it is his responsibility, and his alone, to exercise that charism faithfully. Although the bishop serves as a *testis fidei*, a witness to that faith that is professed by those in his community, he is also the authoritative teacher and judge of the faith (*iudex fidei*), responsible for safeguarding the faith from the distortion and error that is always possible within any individual community.

The council also addressed a topic almost completely overlooked by Vatican I, namely, the bishops' relationship to one another as a "college." The council taught that through episcopal ordination each bishop was inserted into the college of bishops (LG 22.1). The bishops, "together with their head, the Supreme Pontiff, and never apart from him" also "have supreme and full authority over the universal church" (LG 22). In other words, the whole college of bishops shares with the pope in the pastoral care of the universal church, including a responsibility for teaching church doctrine. By joining papal authority with the authority of the college of bishops, and recognizing that they share supreme and full authority over the church, the council placed the papacy in a new, or, more accurately, a more ancient, ecclesiological context. Vatican II reaffirmed Vatican I's teaching on papal primacy and papal infallibility, but it situated these teachings within an ecclesial vision in which pope and bishops shared responsibility for the welfare of the whole church.

The council granted the authority to the bishops, both individually and collectively, to teach authoritatively on matters of faith and morals (LG 25). But the council also exhibited a certain "doctrinal humility" as it recognized that, while the church can faithfully teach that which

God has divinely revealed, "the church is always advancing towards the plenitude of divine truth, until eventually the words of God are fulfilled in it" (DV 8). The church is faithful to divine revelation, but it has not mastered the mystery of divine revelation as if there were no more to say:

> The church is the guardian of the deposit of God's word and draws religious and moral principles from it, but it does not always have a ready answer to every question. Still, it is eager to associate the light of revelation with the experience of humanity in trying to clarify the course upon which it has recently entered. (GS 33)

Over the past five decades, popes and theologians have been drawing out some of the implications of the teaching of the council. In the next section we will consider some important insights that are drawn from the teaching of the council, as they relate to the magisterium.

KEY INSIGHTS INTO THE NATURE AND EXERCISE OF THE MAGISTERIUM IN THE CHURCH

The nature and exercise of the church's magisterium has changed significantly over its two thousand years of existence. This has often produced some confusion. Certain assumptions that were common in past ages still hold sway in the minds of many Catholics and non-Catholics alike. Although Vatican II made significant contributions, it offered no systematic treatment of the church or church authority. Consequently, the implications of its teaching have been too easily overlooked. It may be helpful to clarify some oft-neglected aspects of Catholic ecclesiology and their implications for our understanding of the magisterium.

The Church Is Not a Democracy . . . Neither Is It a Monarchy!

North American Catholics often approach their church out of a set of distinct cultural assumptions. Particularly here in the United States, our strong commitment to participative democracy leads many to expect the church to function according to liberal democratic principles. Liberal democracies are built on the principle of one person–one vote, wherein each person is expected to vote for individual desires and preferences and the majority opinion assumes the force of law. Liberal democracies also presume that their leaders are nothing more than elected officials expected to represent the needs and desires of their constituents.

The church is certainly not a democracy in this sense. It has a mission that was given to it by Christ. The church is also a recipient of God's revelation. Consequently, its teaching must be determined, not by individual preferences, but by divine revelation and the guidance of the Holy Spirit. The church's decisions are governed, not by changing opinion, but by the determination to remain faithful to the message and mission it has received from Christ, in the Spirit. The church is also not a democracy, in the political sense, because it possesses a sacramentally constituted structure in which some from among the community are ordained for the unique ministry of apostolic oversight (*episkope*). They may be called forth by the community, but they are not delegates of the community in the sense of an elected functionary responsible for nothing more than communicating the will of his constituents. By virtue of their ordination, bishops bear a special responsibility for the preservation of the apostolic faith of the church.

Of course, just because the church is not a liberal democracy, that does not mean that all democratic values and structures are antithetical to the nature and mission of the church. Over its long history, the Catholic Church has often incorporated democratic elements into its life. Bishops were elected in the early church by the clergy and sometimes by the people. Synods and councils have long employed participatory decision-making procedures. Since the eleventh century popes have been elected by the College of Cardinals. Men's and women's religious communities have often employed democratic structures in their choice of leadership and communal discernment. Indeed, there is every reason to hope that further democratic elements might find their way into the life of the church.

If the church is not a liberal democracy, neither is it a monarchy/oligarchy or an aristocracy. Though many of the customs and titles associated with church leadership reflect a time when monarchical and aristocratic views of church leaders predominated (one still hears the cardinals referred to as "princes of the church"), these do not reflect the true nature of the church.

In truth, the church is neither a liberal democratic republic nor a papal monarchy; it is *sui generis*—an ordered spiritual communion sent in mission in the world. As such it *is* (or at least, according to Vatican II, it is supposed to be) a community of equals, a spiritual communion of persons in which all are called, by virtue of their baptism, to submit themselves to hear God's Word and discern God's will in the concrete circumstances of the community. This was affirmed in the teaching of Vatican II:

> Although by Christ's will some are appointed teachers, dispensers of the mysteries and pastors for the others, yet all the faithful enjoy a true equality with regard to the dignity and the activity which they share in the building up of the body of Christ. The distinction which the Lord has made between the sacred ministers and the rest of the people of God implies union, for the pastors and the other faithful are joined together by a close relationship. The pastors of the church, following the example of the Lord, should minister to each other and to the rest of the faithful; the latter should eagerly collaborate with the pastors and teachers. And so, amid their variety all bear witness to the wonderful unity in the body of Christ: this very diversity of graces, of ministries and of works gathers the children of God into one, for "all these things are the work of the one and the same Spirit." (LG 32)

How different this description of the church is from that of Pius X who, five decades earlier, described the church as an "unequal society . . . comprised of two ranks": the clergy, who are called to lead, and the laity, who are called to follow. Since the Word of God is addressed to the whole church, all Christians have a vital role to play in appropriating, interpreting, applying, and handing on the Christian faith. Although bishops cannot be reduced to mere delegates of the community of the baptized, neither are they free to ignore the community of believers. Bishops must recognize that the faith of the church abides in the life witness of all the faithful as much as in official church pronouncements. We will have more to say about this in chapter 10 on the authority of believers.

Pope Francis has done much to develop this insight by reminding us that the church is, or at least should be, fundamentally synodal in character. In the fall of 2015, while the synod on the family was still in progress, Pope Francis gave one of the most important speeches of his pontificate. The occasion was the fiftieth anniversary of the creation of the synod of bishops.[1] In that speech he spoke not so much of the world

---

[1] The text of this speech can be accessed online at: http://w2.vatican.va/content /francesco/en/speeches/2015/october/documents/papa-francesco_20151017 _50-anniversario-sinodo.html.

synod of bishops as an ecclesiastical institution, even though that synod was currently in assembly, but of the broader ecclesial principle of synodality. He noted that the word "synod" comes from the Greek *synodos*, which could be rendered "traveling on a journey together." Francis insisted that "it is precisely on this way of synodality where we find the pathway that God expects from the Church of the third millennium." This principle, he admitted, "is an easy concept to put into words, but not so easy to put into practice." A church committed to "walking together," he said, must resist the neoscholastic separation of God's people into two separate "churches": the *ecclesia docens* or teaching church, and the *ecclesia discens* or learning church. A synodal church must be, whole and entire, a listening church governed by the practice of mutual listening. He then masterfully linked this listening church to the council's teaching that all the faithful were given a supernatural instinct, a *sensus fidei*, for discerning God's Word, penetrating its meaning, and applying that Word more fully in their lives.

The pope contended that if we are to be a "listening church" the commitment to synodality must be enacted at every level of church life. It must be reflected in local parish and diocesan councils, in diocesan synods, and in provincial gatherings. In perhaps the most important document of his pontificate, his apostolic exhortation *Evangelii Gaudium*, Pope Francis had already challenged bishops to broaden their practice of consultation: "The bishop . . . will have to encourage and develop the means of participation proposed in the Code of Canon Law, and other forms of pastoral dialogue, out of a desire to listen to everyone and not simply to those who would tell him what he would like to hear" (EG 31). What is particularly welcome in this text is the recognition that consultation is more than gathering together safe voices that function as little more than an ecclesiastical echo chamber. I suspect that most bishops and pastors—for that matter, most provincials, theology department chairs, deans and university presidents, and corporate CEOs—think that they are consultative just because they seek out the opinions of others. The pope rightly insists that authentic ecclesial consultation within a synodal church, a consultation that aspires to be more than a pragmatic public relations maneuver, a consultation that wishes to be a genuine listening to the Spirit, must attend to a wide range of voices, including those in ecclesial exile.

The Bishop's Identity and Mission Are Integrally Related to the Local Church He Serves

As Vatican II reminded us, the bishop is not a delegate of the pope but a true "vicar of Christ" (LG 27). His authority comes from episcopal ordination and his ministry is bound to the people he serves. His close relationship to his people is reflected in his ancient role as the principal presider over the Eucharist (SC 41). Just as the presiding bishop gathers together and offers up the gifts and prayers of the community, so too the bishop as apostolic leader gathers up the faith insight of the whole community.

The bishop's constitutive relationship to his local church has deep roots in the practice and self-understanding of the early church. A study of early church documents suggests three widely held convictions: (1) that the bishop was the apostolic leader of the local church; (2) that communion with him was a visible sign of communion in the church; and (3) that the bishop was not above the local church but bound to it as its pastoral leader. By the mid-third century, St. Cyprian of Carthage had developed a very strong theology of episcopal authority. To be united with Christ in the church one had to be united with their bishop. At the same time, he believed that, precisely as their spiritual leader, the bishop was also accountable to his community. In a letter to his clergy, Cyprian wrote:

> From the beginning of my episcopate, I decided to do nothing of my own opinion privately without your advice and the consent of the people. When I come to you through the grace of God, then we shall discuss in common either what has been done or what must be done concerning these matters, as our mutual honor demands.[2]

The spiritual bond between a bishop and his people was reflected in the early church's prohibition against ordaining a bishop without a pastoral charge to a local church. To do so would turn episcopal ordination into an honorific rather than a call to serve a church. It was also commonly held that no bishop could be ordained for a local church without the consent of the people. Cyprian made this point well: "Moreover, we can see that divine authority is also the source for the practice whereby bishops are chosen in the presence of the laity and before the eyes of

---

[2] St. Cyprian of Carthage, *Epistle* 14.4.

all, and they are judged as being suitable and worthy after public scrutiny and testimony."[3] The spiritual bond between bishop and people was often expressed in marital imagery. The bishop was, in a sense, married to his local church. Consequently, bishops were prohibited from transferring from one diocese to another.

Any consideration of episcopal teaching authority must hold together both the Catholic conviction regarding the authority the bishop possesses by virtue of his office and his integral relationship to the local church he serves. Pope Francis has emphasized this relationship between the bishop and the people of his church in his own inimitable fashion. In an address to newly ordained bishops, he invoked one of his favorite ministerial images, exhorting these new bishops to exercise their ministry so as to "have the smell of the sheep on them."[4]

There is still much to be done if we are to recover the ancient church's insight regarding the deep bonds that must exist between the bishop and his local church. Many ecclesiologists and canon lawyers have called for changes in our church discipline that might enable, for example, the faithful of a local church to play a much larger role in the appointment of their bishop.[5] Although it is hard to imagine eliminating all transfers of bishops from one diocese to another, significantly resisting the practice would do much to dampen the tendency toward careerism in the episcopate. A bishop not worried about promotion is far more likely to put the welfare of his flock before the ecclesiastical approval of the Vatican and/or his peer bishops.

The Assistance of the Holy Spirit Works through Human Processes

In *Dei Verbum* the council acknowledged the assistance of the Holy Spirit in the teaching ministry of the bishops. There was little theological development, however, of what this meant practically for the exercise of the bishop's teaching ministry. According to Richard McCormick,

---

[3] St. Cyprian of Carthage, *Epistle* 67.4.

[4] Pope Francis, "Address to a Group of Newly Appointed Bishops Taking Part in a Conference, 19 September 2013," in *The Church of Mercy: A Vision for the Church* (Chicago: Loyola Press, 2014), 85–88.

[5] See Joseph F. O'Callaghan, *Electing Our Bishops: How the Catholic Church Should Choose Its Leaders* (Lanham, MD: Sheed & Ward, 2007); Richard R. Gaillardetz and John Huels, "The Selection of Bishops: Recovering the Enduring Values of Our Tradition," *The Jurist* 59 (1999): 348–76.

two extremes must be avoided.[6] The first extreme would be to subscribe to a rationalism that could not recognize any real influence of the Spirit on human action in general and on the exercise of the bishops' teaching ministry in particular. Yet Vatican II taught that there is a distinct "charism for truth" (DV 8) that is given to the bishops and that distinguishes their ministry from that of other believers.

The second extreme would be to imagine the Holy Spirit working in a quasi-magical fashion, beyond the realm of human inquiry and judgment. For those who hold this view, a bishop's possible lack of education or his unwillingness to study or consult with others would be irrelevant to the effectiveness of his teaching ministry because the bishop is given a special assistance of the Holy Spirit. Those who subscribe to this view tend to downplay human factors in the exercise of the church's teaching ministry. Karl Rahner once observed that this approach to the assistance of the Holy Spirit assumes that the Holy Spirit intervenes "only at that point at which human efforts are suspended. In reality, however, God works precisely in and through these human efforts and his activity does not constitute a distinct factor apart from this."[7] To assert God's divine assistance it is not necessary, nor is it theologically sound, to assume that human processes are somehow suspended. We encountered this difficulty earlier when addressing the role of the Holy Spirit in the inspiration of the biblical authors. The assistance of the Holy Spirit is not an external divine force overlaid on top of human effort; rather the Holy Spirit acts within and through genuine human effort. Vatican II acknowledged this when the council wrote of the magisterium's exercise of its teaching ministry: "The Roman Pontiff and the bishops, in virtue of their office and because of the seriousness of the matter, are assiduous in examining this revelation by every suitable means and in expressing it properly" (LG 25).

But what are the "suitable means" by which the pope and bishops engage in this investigation? McCormick divides the relevant human processes into two categories: *evidence gathering* and *evidence assessing.* Evidence gathering refers to the many ways in which the human person inquires after the truth through study, consultation, and investigation.

---

[6] Richard A. McCormick, *Notes on Moral Theology: 1965 through 1980* (Lanham, MD: University Press of America, 1981), 261ff.

[7] Karl Rahner, "The Teaching Office of the Church in the Present-Day Crisis of Authority," in *Theological Investigations*, vol. 12 (New York: Seabury, 1974), 3–30, at 12.

With respect to the exercise of the bishops' teaching responsibilities, this would involve a prayerful study of the church's tradition (giving primacy of place to the testimony of Scripture), a consultation of scholars and theologians (representing diverse schools of thought and theological/historical perspectives), a consideration of the insights of pertinent related fields (e.g., the contributions of the social sciences or genetics), and an attempt to discern the sense of the faithful in and through whom the Spirit also speaks. Insufficient attention to this evidence gathering can hamper the activity of the Spirit in bringing forth wisdom and insight through the bishops' teaching. Evidence assessing involves the proper consideration and assessment of the evidence gathered. Here again recourse to a diversity of theological scholarship will be important, but so will patient reflection and authentic conversation in contexts where the free exchange of views is clearly welcomed.

Catholics rely on the confidence that the assistance of the Holy Spirit brings, but this must not become an excuse for the church's official teachers to shirk their responsibility to use the human resources at their disposal in the exercise of their teaching ministry.

The Church Is an Ordered Communion of Communions

Some Catholics today still hold to monarchical conceptions of the church that suggest one vast, monolithic institution. They imagine a vertical chain of command moving from the laity up through the priests and bishops to the pope, who stands, as it were, at the apex of a great ecclesiastical pyramid. Popular though it may be, this view cannot be sustained theologically. If we are to grasp something of the nature of the church, we must look to its sacramental constitution. There we discover that the church is first constituted by baptismal initiation into a community of disciples. The community of the baptized gathers together at the Sunday liturgy to be nourished in the life of communion and sent forth in mission. The eucharistic liturgy is "the summit toward which the activity of the church is directed; it is also the source from which all its power flows" (SC 10). Established in baptism and nurtured in the Eucharist, the church is a spiritual communion realized on several levels: (1) communion with God in Christ by the power of the Spirit, (2) communion with the fellow believers gathered at the eucharistic assembly, (3) communion with other eucharistic communities throughout the world, (4) communion with Christians who supped at the Lord's table in times past, (5) communion with the saints who celebrate at the eternal banquet, and (6) communion with the world in which it is sent in mission.

Each local church that hears God's Word proclaimed and celebrates the Eucharist under the presidency of an apostolic minister is more than a mere subdivision of the universal church—it is truly the Body of Christ *in that place.* As the great ecumenist Jean-Jacques von Allmen put it, each local church is "wholly the church, but not the whole church."[8] Since each church is truly Christ's Body in that place, each church stands as well in spiritual communion with every other eucharistic community. This relationship among the churches is no mere federation created by mutual contract; it is a profound spiritual communion sustained by the Holy Spirit. At the same time, the eucharistic identity of each church prevents it from being subsumed into some larger whole. Something of this vision of the church as a communion of churches is reflected in the following diagram:

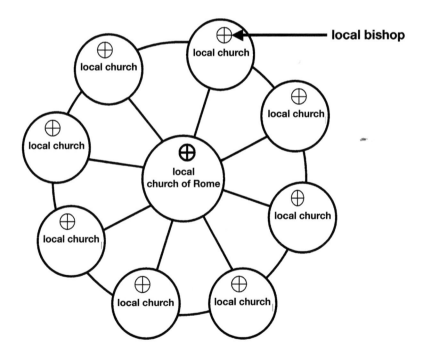

[8] Jean-Jacques von Allmen, "L'Église locale parmi les autres églises locales," *Irénikon* 43 (1970): 512.

Each local church maintains its own integrity even as it stands in spiritual communion with other churches and within the primacy of the church of Rome and its bishop. This insight into the relationship between the local churches and the universal church provides an important foundation for considering the council's teaching on episcopal collegiality.

The Authority of the College of Bishops Is Grounded in the Universal Communion of Churches

When we conceive of the universal church, not as a huge monolith, but as an ordered communion of communions, we find a more helpful theological framework for appreciating the ministry of the college of bishops. Each bishop is both pastor of a local church and member of the college of bishops. As such, each bishop bears a twofold responsibility: (1) he must sustain and nourish the spiritual communion of the local church to which he is charged, preserving it in the apostolic faith, and (2) he is called to extend, celebrate, and nourish the communion that exists between his own church and the other local churches. Consequently, the college of bishops is no external governing board standing above the church. The college of bishops is *the visible expression* of the communion of churches and can never be separated from it. When the bishops gather in an ecumenical council, they are not participating in some extraordinary juridical event outside the life of the church; they are offering a visible expression of what the church in fact always is, a communion of communions.

One helpful way of considering the character of the bishops' episcopal interaction is to conceive it as a kind of ecclesial "gift exchange."[9] Through his participation in the college of bishops, each bishop offers the wisdom of his local church—that unique inculturation of the one Gospel of Jesus Christ in his particular church—to the universal communion of churches. Each shares the insights and challenges that are experienced within his church and receives from the other bishops the gift of their churches' faith testimonies. As such, the ministry of the college of bishops always emerges out of and returns to the communion of the churches.

---

[9] Margaret O'Gara has used the image of the gift exchange to describe ecumenical relations between different Christian communions. See Margaret O'Gara, *The Ecumenical Gift Exchange* (Collegeville, MN: Liturgical Press, 1998).

As Bishop of Rome, the Pope Is Head of the College of Bishops

The pope is neither head of the whole church nor bishop of the whole church. It is Christ and not the Bishop of Rome who is head of the church (see Eph 1:22-23; Col 1:18). Failure to preserve this basic biblical truth is, in part, what paved the way for the monarchical view of the church discussed earlier. Neither is the pope the bishop of the universal church; he is the bishop of the one local church of Rome. There is no such thing as a bishop of the universal church. Every bishop is bishop of a local church.

In this regard, it is worth remembering that papal election is not a sacrament. In other words, no one is ever *ordained* to be pope. The pope is pope only because he is first the bishop of the local church of Rome, a church that from ancient times was granted a distinctive primacy among all the churches. The unique pastoral responsibilities and authority of the pope today are still grounded in his ministry as Bishop of Rome. All papal prerogatives, rightly understood, flow from this Catholic conviction.

If the pope is not head of the church or bishop of the whole church, he *is* the pastor of the universal church by virtue of his role as Bishop of Rome. Moreover, he is head of the college of bishops as a member of that college. Vatican II taught that it is to the whole college of bishops, always under the headship of the Bishop of Rome, that supreme power and authority was given to seek after the welfare of the church. As head and member of this college, the pope can never be separated from and opposed to the bishops. At the same time, neither can the bishops be constituted as a college without being in communion with the Bishop of Rome.

Although the council was somewhat ambiguous on this issue, many theologians now believe that we should consider all significant papal actions exercised for the good of the whole church as, by definition, collegial. This collegiality is made explicit when a pope convenes and presides over an ecumenical council. Yet, they would contend, even when the pope acts alone, as when he promulgates an encyclical, he does so as head of the college of bishops.[10] His role as head of the college presumes that he is maintaining an informed communion with all the bishops. That communion with the bishops should be presupposed

---

[10] For one version of this argument, see Jean-Marie Tillard, *Bishop of Rome* (Wilmington, DE: Glazier, 1983).

in all papal actions. Certainly, Vatican I taught that a pope cannot be legally bound to consult the bishops either before or after a solemn papal definition. As we saw in the last chapter, it is generally accepted (and it was the opinion of many of the bishops at Vatican I) that the pope is still *morally* bound to engage in such consultation.

Vatican II gave relatively little attention to the ministry of the pope, apart from confirming the teaching of Vatican I. Much more important for the development of our understanding of papal ministry was Pope St. John Paul II's encyclical on ecumenism, *Ut Unum Sint*. In that encyclical the pope avoided traditional papal titles like "vicar of Christ" or "sovereign pontiff," preferring instead the title "Bishop of Rome" and, even more profoundly, "the servant of the servants of God." The pope proffered a vision of the papacy that went beyond, without contradicting, the teaching of Vatican I and II. He presented the papacy as a ministry of service within the context of an ecclesiology of communion. Seen from this perspective, the church is neither a federation of autonomous congregations nor a universal corporation with branch offices throughout the world. As a communion of churches, the pope insisted that the primary responsibility for shepherding a local flock lay with the local bishop, the ordinary pastor of the local church. Extraordinary circumstances may require the pope to intervene in the affairs of a local church for the sake of the unity of faith and communion of all the churches. The principal exercise of papal primacy must, however, be to support the bishops in the fulfillment of their pastoral ministry. In this regard, the pope wrote:

> The mission of the bishop of Rome within the college of all the pastors consists precisely in "keeping watch" (*episkopein*), like a sentinel, so that through the efforts of the pastors the true voice of Christ the shepherd may be heard in all the particular churches. . . . All this, however, must always be done in communion. When the Catholic Church affirms that the office of the bishop of Rome corresponds to the will of Christ, she does not separate this office from the mission entrusted to the whole body of bishops, who are also "vicars and ambassadors of Christ." The bishop of Rome is a member of the "college," and the bishops are his brothers in the ministry. (UUS 94–95)

This encyclical represented an important advance, or, perhaps more accurately, an important return, to the ancient ecclesial vision of the papacy in service of the churches.

The Demystification of the Papacy

Since the council, much has been done to reorient the papacy away from its earlier more monarchical trappings and toward a conception of papal ministry more consonant with the ecclesiology of the council. Pope John Paul I reigned as pope for only thirty-three days but he established an important precedent by refusing a papal coronation. Pope John Paul II abandoned the practice of popes speaking with the papal "we." He also abandoned use of the *sedia gestatoria* (a papal throne borne on the shoulders of footmen). Although Pope Paul VI broke with long-standing precedent by making several international trips, it was really John Paul II, with over one hundred international trips (more than all previous popes combined!), who established a new model of papal ministry. The Polish pope saw his many trips as a visible manifestation of the catholicity of the global church.

Although John Paul I ended the practice of papal coronation, it was Benedict XVI who replaced the coronation with a prominent ritual conferring the pallium on the newly elected pope. The pallium, traditionally conferred on new archbishops, is a vestment made of wool that goes around the archbishop's neck and is intended to suggest, among other things, the ministry of the good shepherd carrying the lost sheep on his shoulders. It is a wonderful, symbolic statement of the pastoral character of the papal office.

History may well show that one of Pope Benedict's most significant contributions to a modern understanding of the papacy was his papal resignation. This is not because he was a bad pope but because his papal resignation reminded the church that the papacy is an ecclesiastical office—no more, no less. The last pope to freely resign was Pope Celestine V in the thirteenth century. Many at the time viewed this as a horrific repudiation of his divine call. The action was seen as so detestable by the famous Italian poet Dante that in the *Inferno* he apparently placed him in the antechamber to hell for his "crime." Yet Pope Benedict's resignation in February 2013 can be read in a much more positive light today. One of the likely factors in his resignation was his diminishing stamina due to advanced age. His resignation, in that situation, did much to demystify the papacy. He reminded us that the pope is only pope because he is a bishop and, like other bishops, it would be inappropriate to continue ministering if one's health precluded it.

Pope Francis has undertaken an even more substantive reorientation of the contemporary papacy. This was first signaled when, upon his surprising papal election, he appeared at the loggia of St. Peter's and introduced himself, not as pope, but as Bishop of Rome. In an unprecedented gesture, he then requested the people of Rome first bless him before he offered the traditional papal blessing of the people. This remarkable pattern of behavior, which has had the effect of humanizing the papacy, only continued in the first years of his papacy as he moved out of the papal apartment to stay in a modest room in the Hotel St. Martha (generally used as lodging for Vatican guests). His "cold calling" ordinary believers and frequent participation in extemporaneous interviews with the media are just some of the surprising features of his papacy that have reminded the church that, while the papacy is essential to the life of the church, it is still a ministry exercised by a fellow sinner.

The Need for an Authentically "Pastoral Magisterium"

In Pope St. John XXIII's influential opening address at Vatican II, *Gaudet Mater Ecclesia*, he offered an unambiguous affirmation of the church's fidelity to its doctrinal heritage. He also insisted, however, that this doctrinal fidelity means more than the rote repetition of doctrinal formulas. Pope John then offered a critical assessment of the way in which church teaching authority had been exercised in the past. An emphasis on the vigorous condemnation of error must be replaced, he insisted, by the "medicine of mercy" and by persuasively demonstrating the truth of church teaching. This requires a teaching magisterium, he insisted, that is fundamentally *pastoral* in character.[11]

One of the most important contributions of the pontificate of Pope Francis has been his determination to fulfill Pope John's vision of a truly pastoral magisterium. As we will see in the next chapter, one of the features of a pastoral magisterium is a commitment to decentralization. Pope Francis does not believe "that the papal magisterium should be expected to offer a definitive or complete word on every question which affects the Church and the world" (EG 16). Francis does not deny the

---

[11] Pope St. John XIII, *Gaudet Mater Ecclesia*; his opening address, may be accessed online at: https://jakomonchak.files.wordpress.com/2012/10/john-xxiii-opening-speech.pdf.

need to teach church doctrine authoritatively, but he is committed to what Christoph Theobald once called, in reference to Vatican II's teaching, "the pastorality of doctrine."[12] This means putting church doctrine to the service of the church's pastoral mission of accompaniment with the wounded and marginalized of our world. Pope Francis writes:

> Pastoral ministry in a missionary style is not obsessed with the disjointed transmission of a multitude of doctrines to be insistently imposed. When we adopt a pastoral goal and a missionary style which would actually reach everyone without exception or exclusion, the message has to concentrate on the essentials, on what is most beautiful, most grand, most appealing and at the same time most necessary. The message is simplified, while losing none of its depth and truth, and thus becomes all the more forceful and convincing. (EG 35)

Put simply, Pope Francis does not wish to treat adult Catholics as if they were children. We are adult disciples of Jesus called to exercise our own discernment in living out that discipleship. As disciples, the concrete conflicts we encounter are often "messy," an adjective that Pope Francis uses frequently. Our concrete choices are often circumscribed by factors beyond our control. In such circumstances, we cannot rely on the rigorous application of juridical norms but must engage in the practice of moral discernment.

The pope models here an authority rooted in a ministry of accompaniment. He explores further the demand for individual practice of moral discernment and the formation of conscience in the final chapter of *Amoris Laetitia*. Already in chapter 2 of that document he laments that church leaders, including himself,

> find it hard to make room for the consciences of the faithful, who very often respond as best they can to the Gospel amid their limitations, and are capable of carrying out their own discernment in complex situations. We have been called to form consciences, not to replace them. (AL 37)

Finally, Pope Francis is reluctant to offer premature doctrinal pronouncements on controverted issues. At both the extraordinary and

---

[12] Christoph Theobald, "The Principle of Pastorality at Vatican II: Challenges of a Prospective Interpretation of the Council," in *The Legacy of Vatican II*, ed. Massimo Faggioli and Andrea Vicini (New York: Paulist Press, 2015), 26–37, at 28.

ordinary assemblies of the synod on the family, Pope Francis was insistent that there should be no preemptive effort to remove controversial topics from consideration. He encouraged the synod participants not to be afraid of disagreement. Later, reflecting on the fruit of the synodal assemblies in *Amoris Laetitia*, the pope remarked, "The complexity of the issues that arose revealed the need for continued open discussion of a number of doctrinal, moral, spiritual, and pastoral questions" (AL 2). It followed then that, as the pope put it, "not all discussions of doctrinal, moral or pastoral issues need to be settled by interventions of the magisterium" (AL 3).

Eamon Duffy captures the more circumscribed role of papal teaching in this process: "'Definitive' papal utterances," he writes, "are not oracles providing new information, but adjudications at the end of a wider and longer process of doctrinal reflection, consultation, and debate, often extending over centuries."[13] Magisterial teaching should *conclude* our tradition's lively engagement with a particular question, not preempt its consideration. A pastoral magisterium calls for an exercise of teaching authority that never forgets that, as John Henry Newman put it, "truth is the daughter of time."[14] A pastoral magisterium does not claim to have all the answers; nor does it provide definitive solutions to every controverted issue. A pastoral magisterium acknowledges the here-and-now, normative character of current church teaching while always keeping open the possibility of further insight.

These basic theological insights are crucial for acquiring a more positive and constructive understanding of the role of the magisterium in the church today. As such, they will provide the necessary foundation for our consideration of the concrete exercise of magisterial teaching authority in the next chapter.

---

[13] Eamon Duffy, "Who Is the Pope?," *New York Times Review of Books* (February 19, 2015), accessed online at: www.nybooks.com/articles/2015/02/19/who-is-pope-francis/.

[14] John Henry Newman, *An Essay on the Development of Christian Doctrine*, 6th ed. (Notre Dame, IN: University of Notre Dame Press, 1989), 47. The original source of the dictum may be Francis Bacon.

DISPUTED QUESTIONS

(1) The view of the universal church as a communion of churches and the fundamental identity of the bishop as pastor of a local church has led some theologians to question the practice of ordaining titular bishops who are given "title" to a church that no longer exists while serving either as an auxiliary bishop, a church bureaucrat, or a diplomat. Critics of this practice argue that when someone is ordained bishop without any real pastoral charge to an existing local church, the impression can easily be given that the office of bishop has become an honorific, a rank or title given to enhance an individual's prestige, rather than a ministry in service to a local church. The practice of giving a bishop title to a nonexistent church appears to trivialize the ancient conviction regarding the bishop's vital relationship to a genuine community of faith. These critics suggest that representatives of the church engaging in diplomatic work around the world or functioning as bureaucrats within the Vatican need not be ordained bishop in order to fulfill their assigned tasks.

(2) Born in the twelfth century as a kind of papal court for an imperial papacy, the Roman Curia has functioned for nine centuries as the bureaucratic arm of the papacy. It has provided valuable service, but, in the minds of many, it has also been remarkably resistant to needed reform. According to Vatican II, the Curia was to serve the pope and the bishops in the exercise of their pastoral ministry on behalf of the universal church (CD 9). Many critics of present curial structures and practices believe that for much of the church's modern history, up to the present, curial officials have acted instead as if it were their task to police the local church and their bishops. Admittedly, there have been a number of postconciliar efforts at curial reform (e.g., Pope Paul VI's effort to internationalize the Curia), but many people believe they have not gone far enough. The first years of Pope Francis's pontificate have been marked by a major effort to provide comprehensive reforms of the Curia.

FOR FURTHER READING

Doyle, Dennis M. *Communion Ecclesiology: Vision and Versions.* Maryknoll, NY: Orbis Books, 2000.

Gaillardetz, Richard R. *The Church in the Making:* Lumen Gentium, Christus Dominus, Orientalium Ecclesiarum. Rediscovering Vatican II Series. New York: Paulist Press, 2006.

———. *An Unfinished Council: Vatican II, Pope Francis, and the Renewal of Catholicism.* Collegeville, MN: Liturgical Press, 2015.

Gaillardetz, Richard R., and Catherine E. Clifford. *Keys to the Council: Unlocking the Teaching of Vatican II.* Collegeville, MN: Liturgical Press, 2012.

Granfield, Patrick. *The Limits of the Papacy.* New York: Crossroad, 1987.

Hinze, Bradford. *Prophetic Obedience: Ecclesiology for a Dialogical Church.* Maryknoll, NY: Orbis Books, 2016.

Lakeland, Paul. *A Council That Will Never End:* Lumen Gentium *and the Church Today.* Collegeville, MN: Liturgical Press, 2013.

Mannion, Gerard. *Ecclesiology and Postmodernity: Questions for the Church in Our Time.* Collegeville, MN: Liturgical Press, 2007.

Mannion, Gerard, Richard Gaillardetz, Jan Kerkhofs, and Kenneth Wilson, eds. *Readings in Church Authority: Gifts and Challenges for Contemporary Catholicism.* London: Ashgate, 2003.

Tillard, Jean-Marie. *Bishop of Rome.* Wilmington, DE: Glazier, 1983.

———. *Church of Churches: An Ecclesiology of Communion.* Collegeville, MN: Liturgical Press, 1992.

EIGHT

HOW DO THE POPE AND BISHOPS EXERCISE THEIR TEACHING AUTHORITY?

You awaken on a Saturday morning, get up to check your e-mail, read the daily newspaper online over a cup of coffee, and in the religion section you read that your local bishop has just issued a pastoral letter on immigration policy. A week later, you are watching the evening news and learn that the pope is planning a new encyclical on Catholic just war teaching. Another week goes by and you see an internet post reporting that some Vatican congregation has issued a new document on the recruitment and training of seminarians. A few weeks later your pastor mentions in his homily a recent letter from the US bishops' conference on devotion to Mary and the saints. Each of these represents, in some sense, an official exercise of the church's teaching authority.

One can view this proliferation of church documents as an opportunity for adult education, but it has also become a source of some confusion. How do Catholics assess the significance of these various documents? This is a difficult and, frankly, unprecedented issue. Catholics today are inundated with a number and variety of official church pronouncements unknown to previous generations. This chapter will offer some guidance in sorting through this wide range of magisterial teaching.

One key for assessing the authoritative character of a church document is to look at who promulgated it (e.g., an individual bishop, a bishops' conference, an ecumenical council, the pope) and the manner in which it was proposed. An elaborate set of distinctions regarding the exercise of the magisterium has emerged out of the two-thousand-year history of the Catholic Church. At the most general level, we can distinguish between three modes in which the pope and bishops exercise their distinctive teaching ministry: (1) *the ordinary magisterium* refers to the more common exercises of the pope and bishops' teaching authority when they teach either individually or in groups; (2) *the extraordinary magisterium* refers to the more rare exercise of the pope and bishops' teaching ministry in the form of a solemn definition; (3) *the ordinary universal magisterium* refers to the common judgment of the whole college of bishops (in union with the Bishop of Rome) that a teaching is to be held as definitive. The following chart illustrates these distinctions.

THE EXERCISE OF THE MAGISTERIUM

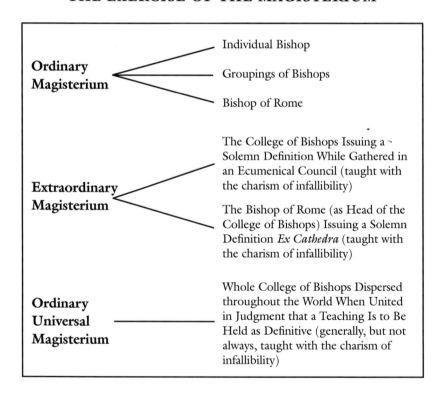

Ordinary Magisterium	Individual Bishop
	Groupings of Bishops
	Bishop of Rome
Extraordinary Magisterium	The College of Bishops Issuing a Solemn Definition While Gathered in an Ecumenical Council (taught with the charism of infallibility)
	The Bishop of Rome (as Head of the College of Bishops) Issuing a Solemn Definition *Ex Cathedra* (taught with the charism of infallibility)
Ordinary Universal Magisterium	Whole College of Bishops Dispersed throughout the World When United in Judgment that a Teaching Is to Be Held as Definitive (generally, but not always, taught with the charism of infallibility)

THE ORDINARY MAGISTERIUM

The ordinary magisterium refers to the many different ways in which the pope and bishops, either individually or in groups, can teach authoritatively. Let us begin with the individual bishop.

The Teaching Ministry of the Individual Bishop

The Second Vatican Council considered the pastoral teaching ministry of the bishop in several texts. *Lumen Gentium* teaches:

> Among the more important duties of bishops, that of preaching the Gospel has pride of place. For the bishops are the heralds of the faith, who draw new disciples to Christ; they are authentic teachers, that is, teachers endowed with the authority of Christ, who preach to the people assigned to them the faith which is to be believed and applied in practice; and under the light of the holy Spirit they cause that faith to radiate, drawing from the storehouse of revelation new things and old; they make it bear fruit and they vigilantly ward off whatever errors threaten their flock. (LG 25)

In the Decree on the Pastoral Office of Bishops, *Christus Dominus* 12, the council teaches that "in the exercise of their teaching office, [the bishops] are to proclaim to humanity the gospel of Christ. This is one of their principal duties."

Individual bishops exercise their teaching ministry in any of a variety of ways. The bishop is the chief evangelist and chief catechist in the local church. He must oversee the preaching and catechetical ministry of the church and ensure that through that ministry all within the local church hear of God's saving offer. The bishop himself will perform his catechetical ministry in his own preaching and catechesis and in the publication of pastoral letters and other ecclesiastical directives. Beyond his direct ministry of preaching and teaching, the bishop is further charged with safeguarding the authentic exposition of church teaching as that ministry is carried out by others within the local church. This means that his responsibility as teacher will include overseeing the catechetical work that takes place within his diocese.

Bishops who are effective teachers always do more than merely reiterate "official church teaching." As Vatican II taught, the bishop is more than a spokesperson for the pope. His teaching should, ideally, illuminate for his people the profundity of the Catholic tradition. The bishop must aspire to advance the cause of the faith through a prayerful and informed presentation of the Catholic tradition that does not simply repeat past formulations but seeks to bring new insight to church teaching. He need not be a professional theologian, but general theological competency and a thorough knowledge of the Christian tradition in its breadth and depth will be important for the effective fulfillment of his teaching ministry.

Frequently, bishops will feel compelled to address complicated and sometimes controversial questions regarding the accepted teaching of the church as it applies to a particular pastoral situation. This is particularly true with respect to the church's moral teaching, where a bishop may need to make concrete moral determinations regarding particular questions and issues arising within a local church. One can easily imagine an individual bishop addressing a wide range of issues concerning immigration or welfare policy, the distribution of contraceptive devices in public schools, etc.

Rarer will be those instances when a bishop will find it necessary to make a formal pronouncement on a doctrinal matter. When a bishop makes a formal doctrinal judgment, he does so specifically with the intent of proclaiming church doctrine in an authoritative and normative manner. In such a situation, according to the teaching of the council (LG 25), a bishop teaches authoritatively but *not* with the charism of infallibility. This means that although he is assisted by the Spirit in his teaching ministry, he is not protected from making an erroneous doctrinal judgment. Nevertheless, in such situations he still teaches with due doctrinal authority and the members of the local church have an obligation to attend carefully and respectfully to his teaching. We will have more to say about this process in chapter 11.

The Teaching Authority of Synods and Episcopal Conferences

As we saw in chapter 6, in the ancient church it was common for bishops to meet in regional synods to deliberate on matters of common concern. Although often preoccupied with pastoral concerns, these synods occasionally considered issues of more wide-ranging doctrinal import. Some of Christianity's most central teachings first emerged out of such regional synods. As a regional assembly of the college of bishops, the synods were considered genuine if partial expressions of episcopal collegiality, even if that specialized language was not yet part of the early church's lexicon. They were also practical examples of what would later be called the principle of subsidiarity, which, put simply, holds that local issues are best dealt with at the local level. A higher authority should intervene only when an issue cannot be resolved at the local level or when the welfare of the larger body is at stake.

Today such regional gatherings of bishops are relatively rare. However, in 1965, in response to several requests from bishops attending the Second Vatican Council, Pope Paul VI established the World Synod of Bishops, a consultative gathering of representative bishops from throughout the world to address a particular topic. Such synods, when meeting on a three-year cycle, are called ordinary synods. Additionally, the pope may call an extraordinary synod to address an issue of particular importance. In 1985 Pope John Paul II convened just such a synod to celebrate the twentieth anniversary of the close of Vatican II and to assess the reception of the council's teaching. More recently, Pope Francis called for an extraordinary synod on marriage and family to prepare the way for the regularly scheduled ordinary synod, which addressed the same topic.

A modern alternative to the ancient practice of regional synods is the episcopal conference, an organization of bishops of a particular region or nation created in order to address regional or national church issues. Episcopal conferences, as we know them today, first emerged in the early nineteenth century. These structures have long been accepted in the church for their practical pastoral value.

Vatican II affirmed their value and, indeed, granted considerable authority to them. In the council's Constitution on the Sacred Liturgy, *Sacrosanctum Concilium*, the bishops granted to episcopal conferences significant authority over a variety of liturgical matters (SC 22, 36, 39). In *Lumen Gentium*, after discussing the ecclesial significance of the ancient patriarchal churches, the council affirmed that "in like fashion, the episcopal conferences at the present time are in a position to contribute in many and fruitful ways to the concrete realization of the collegiate spirit" (LG 23). The decree on bishops also outlined the value of episcopal conferences (CD 37–38).

In the 1980s the US bishops' conference issued several significant pastoral letters, first on war and peace and then on the economy. These documents were viewed as prophetic by some and troubling by others. During this same period, questions were being raised by Vatican officials regarding the nature and limits of the teaching authority of bishops' conferences. Some defenders of the teaching authority of conferences noted that they were structurally equivalent to the regional synods of ancient times, synods that clearly exercised a real if limited doctrinal teaching authority. Others complained that Vatican II's teaching on collegiality affirmed the shared authority of the *whole* college of bishops, but not individual groupings of bishops.[1] The crucial question concerned whether there could be intermediate exercises of episcopal authority between the authority of the individual bishop and the authority of the whole college.

Decades of debate led finally to Pope John Paul II's *motu proprio* (a document issuing at the pope's own initiative) *Apostolos Suos*, issued in 1998. In that document, the pope offered a historical survey of the development of episcopal conferences. He praised their contributions to the life of the church and confirmed the limited doctrinal authority of episcopal conferences. The pope stipulated that episcopal conferences can issue binding doctrinal statements when: (1) they issue the document in a plenary session (not by way of a committee), (2) the document is approved unanimously, or (3) the document is approved by a two-thirds majority and receives a *recognitio* (formal approval) from Rome. Under these conditions the teaching of episcopal conferences becomes a legitimate exercise of the ordinary magisterium. Many critics, however, found these conditions unduly restrictive. Since the issuance of *Apostolos Suos*, episcopal conferences have largely avoided issuing doctrinal statements altogether.

Pope Francis has begun a new chapter in the church's understanding of the teaching role of episcopal synods and episcopal conferences. Soon after his election he announced his intention to convene both an extraordinary and ordinary assembly of the synod of bishops on the topic of marriage and family. He then proceeded to dramatically revitalize the synodal process. He ordered the Vatican secretariat responsible for planning the synod to solicit input from the people of God on the topics under consideration. He boldly insisted that the synod members speak freely in synodal discussions and not be afraid to disagree with one another or to raise difficult questions. It is obvious that Francis sees

---

[1] A good summary of this debate is found in Joseph Komonchak's introduction to *Episcopal Conferences: Historical, Canonical, and Theological Studies*, ed. Thomas Reese (Washington, DC: Georgetown University Press, 1989), 1–22.

such open synodal processes as in keeping with his vision for a truly synodal church.

Francis also believes that elevating the role of episcopal conferences is essential if the church is to achieve a necessary decentralization of church authority. He has taken issue with the outsized role that the modern papacy has taken in the exercise of church teaching. In *Evangelii Gaudium* the pope wrote:

> Nor do I believe that the papal magisterium should be expected to offer a definitive or complete word on every question which affects the Church and the world. It is not advisable for the Pope to take the place of local Bishops in the discernment of every issue which arises in their territory. In this sense, I am conscious of the need to promote a sound "decentralization." (EG 16)

This commitment to the decentralization of church authority has led the pope to give an unprecedented emphasis on the teaching role of regional episcopal conferences. In *Evangelii Gaudium* he writes:

> The Second Vatican Council stated that, like the ancient patriarchal Churches, episcopal conferences are in a position "to contribute in many and fruitful ways to the concrete realization of the collegial spirit." Yet this desire has not been fully realized, since a juridical status of episcopal conferences which would see them as subjects of specific attributions, including genuine doctrinal authority, has not yet been sufficiently elaborated. Excessive centralization, rather than proving helpful, complicates the Church's life and her missionary outreach. (EG 32)

Attached to his reference to the insufficient elaboration of an understanding of the doctrinal authority of episcopal conferences was a footnote to John Paul II's *Apostolos Suos*. This suggests that Francis does not believe that *Apostolos Suos* represents the final word on the doctrinal teaching authority of episcopal conferences.

The high esteem with which Francis holds the teaching ministry of regional episcopal conferences is further reflected in his frequent citation of them in his papal documents. In *Amoris Laetitia* he cites documents from various regional episcopal conferences ten times, and in his encyclical *Laudato Sí*, on care of our common home, he cites regional episcopal conferences twenty times. Clearly our first Jesuit pope believes there is room for episcopal synods and episcopal conferences to play a much greater role in the teaching ministry of the church.

The Ordinary Papal Magisterium

Just as individual bishops and groupings of bishops such as episcopal conferences can share in the church's ordinary magisterium, so too the pope exercises an ordinary teaching authority referred to as the ordinary *papal* magisterium. This teaching, which can take many forms, is a concrete expression of his distinctive ministry as pope to preserve the integrity of the apostolic faith and provide pastoral guidance to his flock. Popes today may exercise their ordinary teaching ministry through the issuance of various kinds of ecclesiastical documents. The chart below mentions a few of these.

Encyclical Letter: Documents offered by the pope as part of his ordinary magisterium and addressed to (a) the whole college of bishops, (b) the whole church, or (c) the whole world. Encyclicals frequently address doctrinal/theological matters but are not normally used to define dogma

Apostolic Letter: Papal letters usually sent to some particular category of persons, e.g., a group of bishops

Apostolic Exhortation: Documents issued by the pope in response to the deliberations of an episcopal synod

Occasional Papal Addresses: Speeches given to various groups who are received by the pope in the Vatican as well as speeches the pope gives on his travels

---

Although these are the main media by which the pope exercises his ordinary teaching office, popes do issue many other kinds of documents that are not normally doctrinal in character (e.g., an apostolic constitution). The publication of any of these documents might constitute an exercise of the ordinary papal magisterium with, however, varying degrees of authority. One would expect, for example, regarding papal attempts to address matters of doctrine, that papal teaching appearing in an encyclical would carry much more weight than that offered in a weekly papal address. Doctrinal pronouncements issued by way of the ordinary papal magisterium represent official church teaching and call for an internal assent by all Catholics (what exactly this means will be discussed in chapter 11). At the same time, it must be noted that the ordinary papal magisterium does not engage the charism of infallibility and thus these teachings are not protected from the remote possibility of error. The development of the modern papacy has created new challenges for appreciating the exercise of the ordinary papal magisterium. Four centuries ago, St. Robert Bellarmine argued that, in dealing with papal authority, one must distinguish between the pope's teaching as guardian of the apostolic faith and universal pastor of the church and his teaching as a "private doctor" or theologian. Pope Benedict XVI provided a relatively straightforward, contemporary example of this distinction. Already a well-respected theologian long before his papal election, Benedict averted to this distinction in the foreword of the first volume of his trilogy, *Jesus of Nazareth*, published while he was pope:

> It goes without saying that this book is in no way an exercise of the magisterium, but is solely an expression of my personal search "for the face of the Lord" (cf. Ps 27:8). Everyone is free, then, to contradict me. I would only ask my readers for that initial goodwill without which there can be no understanding.[2]

This distinction seems to be an important one. Popes are certainly free to enter into extended scholarly conversation, but their contributions need not be seen as normative for Christian faith in the same way as their doctrinal pronouncements would be.

Even when a pope issues formal church documents as expressions of his ordinary papal magisterium, however, the relationship between any binding doctrinal pronouncement contained within the document and the accompanying theological exposition has been considerably complicated in the last fifty years. Popes now frequently offer extended theological treatises in their ecclesiastical documents. This development certainly complicates the task of distinguishing the content in such documents that has binding doctrinal authority from that which represents theological reflection offered for the edification of believers. At present, it is largely left to the theological community to discern, within an ecclesiastical document, where a normative doctrinal pronouncement is being made and where one is encountering supporting theological exposition.

---

[2] Pope Benedict XVI, *Jesus of Nazareth* (New York: Image Books, 2007), 1:xxiv.

A good example of this situation is evident in the popularity of the "theology of the body" often associated with Pope St. John Paul II. Although much of this distinctive theology is found in his magisterial documents, it has its roots in theological and philosophical works written before he was pope. How is a Catholic to receive such teaching? It does not appear that there was really much new *doctrinal* content involved here. Rather, the pope was proposing a new theological framework for appreciating the church's teaching, particularly in the area of sexual ethics and the theology of marriage. On the one hand, while church doctrine on these topics remains formally authoritative for believers, Catholics are not bound to embrace the particular theological framework that the pope presented. On the other hand, it does now appear that in the ongoing development of the papacy, papal theology now aspires to influence the theological conversation in the church on certain topics.

Extended expositions of "papal theology" can be problematic when they acquire a normative character reserved for doctrinal pronouncements, yet they are not without value in the life of the church. Pope Benedict was a master of this form of papal theology, writing three theologically sophisticated encyclicals that offered little new doctrinal content but that offered believers intellectually stimulating and spiritually moving expositions of basic creedal commitments. His learned yet accessible presentation of Christian eschatology in *Spe Salvi* is but one example of papal theology offered for the catechetical formation and spiritual edification of believers.

Even when papal documents provide no new doctrinal content, strictly speaking, their theological and pastoral reflections may still play a role in the gradual development of church doctrine. Consider Pope Francis's *Amoris Laetitia*. In that apostolic exhortation, the pope offered profound yet distinctively pastoral theological reflections on the church's teaching on marriage and family. The text contained no new doctrinal pronouncement, strictly speaking, although it included a chapter that faithfully summarizes current church teaching. As is well known, however, the pope opened the door for a pastoral accommodation regarding the offer of the Eucharist to certain couples in stable, second marriages where the first marriage was not annulled. At no point did the pope reject the church's teaching on marital indissolubility or the inappropriateness of receiving the sacrament outside of a "state of grace." Yet, this pastoral accommodation, proceeding directly from the pope's commitment to a "gospel of mercy," could well contribute to a development of doctrine regarding Christian marriage.

The distinction between pope as private theologian and pope as guardian of the apostolic faith has been blurred in yet another way in our media-saturated culture. John Paul II was the first pope, for example, to take advantage of the popularity of the extended media interview. In the mid-1990s we saw the publication of a series of interviews of the pope by the Italian journalist Vittorio Messori, *Crossing the Threshold of Hope*. In the preface, the interviewer signaled one if the difficulties with this new papal genre:

> It is my duty to guarantee to the reader that the voice that resonates—in its humanity but also in its authority—is entirely that of the successor to Peter. It will now be the job of theologians and analysts of the papal teaching to face the problem of classifying a text that has no precedent and therefore poses new possibilities for the Church.[3]

Messori was right; this did represent a new situation. Bellarmine's distinction doesn't seem to apply in a case in which the pope was being interviewed, not as a private theologian, but precisely *as pope*. What we were dealing with was indeed a new genre of papal teaching.

This new papal genre (the papal interview) has developed in a fascinating way during the Francis pontificate. In the cases of both John Paul II and Benedict XVI, their papal interviews were mostly based on questions submitted in advance, and written responses were, similarly, prepared in advance. Pope Francis, however, is famous for offering both more formal interviews and a wide range of unscripted, informal interviews, often while in transit on a papal trip. Now, it is certainly true that these responses should not be given the same doctrinal authority as a formal magisterial pronouncement. At the same time, I am not convinced that his responses can be dismissed so easily as the comments of a private theologian for, again, the pope is being interviewed *as pope*, that is, as *pastor* of the universal church.

Seen in that light, one could argue that with these interviews we are witnessing simply an exercise of the pope's *pastoral* authority rather than his *doctrinal* teaching authority. Yet this distinction, legitimate in itself, may not entirely do justice to what is happening here. Perhaps

---

[3] Pope St. John Paul II with Vittorio Messori, *Crossing the Threshold of Hope* (New York: Knopf, 1994), viii.

the pope's penchant for informal and unscripted interviews reflects in microcosm a broader attitude regarding the very exercise of church teaching. For a pope committed to the priority of "time over space," and "reality over ideas," doctrine is not to be imposed but rather assimilated through patient dialogue, honest questioning, and prayerful discernment. Perhaps we are seeing here something of what Pope St. John XXIII had in mind when, in his opening address at Vatican II, he called for a magisterium that was authentically "pastoral in character." Pope John did not wish merely to juxtapose pastoral teaching and doctrinal teaching; he wanted them placed in a more fruitful relationship.

With Pope Francis, gone are the days of *Roma locuta, causa finita*— "Rome has spoken, the matter is closed." He recognizes that it may still be necessary, on occasion, to make binding doctrinal pronouncements. Yet Pope Francis appears to concur with Pope John that the church may better meet the needs of the present day "by demonstrating the validity of her teaching, rather than by condemnations." In the synodal listening church of Pope Francis, we are witnessing the gradual emergence of a new exercise of papal teaching, one that is more patient, persuasive, and dialogical. It is an exercise of papal teaching particularly attentive to the complexities and challenges of living the Gospel within the concrete conditions of daily life. It is teaching put directly to the service of discipleship.

THE EXTRAORDINARY MAGISTERIUM

One of the most controversial and, frankly, misunderstood teachings in Roman Catholicism is its teaching on infallibility. In order to grasp this teaching we need to go all the way back to Jesus' parting promise to his followers that "I am with you always until the end of the age" (Matt 28:20). Christians have relied on that promise for over two millennia, believing that Jesus would never abandon the church. We celebrate the feast of Pentecost as a commemoration of Jesus offering his Spirit to the church to guide and direct the community of faith across the centuries. It is the Holy Spirit whom we believe works to keep the church faithful to the Gospel. This fundamental Catholic conviction that through the power of the Spirit Christ will not abandon his church is often referred to as the *indefectibility* of the church.

Long before Christians began using such technical terms as "infallibility" there was an ancient conviction that the Holy Spirit did indeed protect the church from error. Early church writers like St. Irenaeus of Lyons, St. Augustine, St. Vincent of Lérins, and others held that when all the churches were in agreement on a matter of faith, that teaching could be viewed as completely trustworthy by believers. This ancient intuition reflects the broadest and most inclusive understanding of infallibility, namely, the belief that infallibility is given to the whole church in order to keep the church faithful to the Gospel. The Second Vatican Council articulated this belief quite clearly when it wrote: "The whole body of the faithful who have received an anointing which comes from the holy one cannot be mistaken in belief" (LG 12).

The early church also recognized that while the Holy Spirit animated the whole church, the bishops were given a particular gift, "a charism of truth," that would enable them to faithfully proclaim the apostolic faith. By the end of the first millennium, it was commonly held that when all the bishops gathered in an ecumenical council to teach on faith and morals, and their teaching was received by all the churches, that teaching was protected from error and normative for belief. The infallibility given to the whole church was, in a distinctive way, exercised by the college of bishops, especially when they were gathered in an ecumenical council and were intent on definitively pronouncing on a matter revealed by God.

From the beginning of the second century there was also a common conviction that the church of Rome held a special position of privilege among the communion of churches. As centuries went by, the prestige given to the church of Rome was extended more and more to the Bishop of Rome. During that time, history showed that on a number of disputed questions (e.g., when the feast of Easter should be celebrated or whether to rebaptize apostates who returned to the church) Rome was consistently on the side that "won the day." Many looked to Rome as a particularly reliable witness to the good news of Jesus Christ. By the end of the first millennium, the growing recognition that Rome *had not erred* led to the conviction that Rome *could not err*. The belief that the pope could teach with the charism of infallibility would soon be commonly accepted in the church even as there were disagreements regarding the scope and conditions for exercising papal infallibility. Finally, at the First Vatican Council the bishops solemnly defined what is called the dogma of papal infallibility. The Second Vatican Council reaffirmed this teaching on papal infallibility.

According to *Lumen Gentium*, there are three ways in which the magisterium can exercise the gift of infallibility, as indicated in the chart appearing earlier in this chapter. The first two are exercises of what is often called the *extraordinary magisterium*, because it is only exercised relatively rarely and in "extraordinary" circumstances. We will consider the third way in the next section.

First, all the bishops together (including, always, the Bishop of Rome) can solemnly define a dogma when they are gathered at an ecumenical council. In the past, this has generally occurred when the bishops were responding to a serious attack on the faith of the church. So, for example, the Council of Nicaea solemnly defined that the Word, the second person of the Trinity, was "one in being" (*homoousios*) with God the Father. Many of our most basic Christian convictions about Christ and the Trinity were solemnly defined by ecumenical councils in the first millennium. This does not mean, of course, that *every* teaching of an ecumenical council is an exercise of infallibility. The Second Vatican Council, for example, did not invoke the charism of infallibility in its own teaching.

At Vatican I the council explicitly announced its intention to issue a solemn definition with the following formulation, "we teach and define as a divinely revealed dogma . . ."[4] When considering councils before the modern period, however, at a time when these distinctions were not as well established, it is more difficult to know when a council intended to solemnly define a teaching. Scholars must carefully study the wording of conciliar decrees and consider the council *acta* (formal records of council debates) in order to determine the intentions of a council.

Second, the Bishop of Rome, in communion with his fellow bishops, can also solemnly define a dogma of the church. This was first explicitly taught at Vatican I. But, as we saw in chapter 6, the council specified a number of important limits and conditions for the exercise of papal infallibility. The council taught that the pope could teach infallibly only *ex cathedra*, that is, "from the chair of Peter," as universal pastor of the whole church. The council also insisted that popes could not define new doctrine but only that which had been divinely revealed and belonged to the apostolic faith. Consequently, according to Catholic teaching, the pope cannot exercise the gift of infallibility in teaching on any matter he wishes—he cannot solemnly define, for example, that Boston College (my current employer!) is the best Catholic university in the world, true

---

[4] Vatican I, *Pastor Aeternus,* in *Decrees of the Ecumenical Councils,* ed. Norman Tanner (Washington, DC: Georgetown University Press, 1990), 2:816.

though it might be! The pope cannot teach infallibly on matters of politics or science but only on that which directly concerns faith and morals.

Finally, the council taught that the solemn definitions of popes were "irreformable" of themselves and did not require the consent of the church. Here the council was rejecting the need for any *juridical* ratification of a papal definition by the bishops. It is surely significant that before Pope Pius IX solemnly defined the dogma of the Immaculate Conception (1854), and before Pope Pius XII solemnly defined the Assumption of Mary (1950), both popes made a point of first writing to all of the bishops and inquiring after the belief of the church on these matters.

Actual exercises of papal infallibility have been relatively rare in the history of the church. Though lists of papal definitions differ somewhat (before the modern age, popes, like councils, did not explicitly announce when they were teaching infallibly, therefore, determining instances of the exercise of papal infallibility requires careful historical research), one scholar, Francis Sullivan, lists five instances in which popes have solemnly defined a dogma independent of an ecumenical council:[5] (1) Benedict XII's teaching on the beatific vision in *Benedictus Deus* [1336]; (2) Innocent X's condemnation of five Jansenist propositions in *Cum Occasione* [1653]; (3) Pius VI's condemnation of seven Jansenist propositions articulated at the Synod of Pistoia in *Auctorem Fidei* [1794]; (4) Pius IX's definition of the immaculate conception in *Ineffabilis Deus* [1854]; (5) Pius XII's definition of the assumption of Mary in *Munificentissimus Deus* [1950].

THE ORDINARY UNIVERSAL MAGISTERIUM

As we have seen, the two most commonly known ways of exercising infallibility in church teaching are instances of the extraordinary magisterium and are concerned with the solemn definitions of ecumenical councils and of popes. In *Lumen Gentium* 25, however, Vatican II also acknowledged a third engagement of the charism of infallibility in church teaching. In many ways, it is the most ancient.

---

[5] Francis A. Sullivan, *Creative Fidelity: Weighing and Interpreting Documents of the Magisterium* (New York: Paulist Press, 1996), 86.

There are many church teachings that have been commonly accepted as divinely revealed even though they have never been solemnly defined by a pope or council. We should remember that popes and councils generally defined dogmas only if those teachings were being seriously challenged. But what about the many church teachings that Christians have viewed as central to their faith but that were never seriously challenged and therefore were never formally defined by a pope or council? We might think of the church's belief in the communion of saints or in the resurrection of the body. These teachings are central to the Catholic faith even though they have never been solemnly defined.

Vatican II taught that when such teachings have been taught consistently by all of the bishops in their own dioceses as teachings that must be held as definitive and not simply as a probable opinion or as likely to be true, even though the bishops are not formally defining these teachings, they are exercising the charism of infallibility. This third form of exercising the charism of infallibility is referred to as the *ordinary universal magisterium.*

Theoretically, it is also possible for there to be a non-infallible exercise of the ordinary universal magisterium. The best example of this would be the teaching of an ecumenical council when it is not issuing a solemn definition. It would be "ordinary" teaching because there is no solemn definition and "universal" because it engages the whole college of bishops. Other instances of a non-infallible exercise of the ordinary universal magisterium would be the situation in which the bishops, while dispersed throughout the world, held a common judgment regarding a particular teaching but were *not* agreed that the teaching should be held as definitive.

It is not easy for ordinary Catholics today to recognize the distinct modes in which the pope and bishops exercise their teaching office. Sometimes theologians can help identify when these various forms of magisterial teaching are being engaged. For obvious reasons, the most important distinction concerns whether or not the magisterium intends to define a teaching infallibly in a particular teaching act. Canon law provides an important principle in this regard. Canon 749.3 states that "no doctrine is understood to be infallibly defined unless it is clearly established as such." Essentially what this means is that if there is a question as to whether the magisterium has taught something infallibly, the burden of proof is on the magisterium to demonstrate that it is doing so in accord with the accepted conditions established in church tradition. In the face of doubt regarding the possibility of an infallible teaching act, one should presume that the charism of infallibility *has not been engaged* until it is clearly demonstrated otherwise.

This chapter has considered the diverse ways in which the pope and bishops can fulfill their teaching office. For Catholics, this teaching authority is a gift to the church, guiding the community of believers on the path of salvation. Of course, there are those who see the very existence of such a formal and authoritative teaching ministry as out of step with the terms of modernity, in which all forms of authority are subject to challenge. There are others who, fearful of the dizzying atmosphere of change in which we live, cling to easy certitudes and grant to the magisterium an inflated authority that ignores important distinctions in the exercise of authoritative church teaching. It is one aim of this book to help Catholics avoid both tendencies.

DISPUTED QUESTIONS

(1) When the bishops at Vatican II raised the issue of an episcopal synod, many had in mind the kind of structure common to the Eastern churches, that is, a permanent or standing synod of bishops with deliberative authority that would assist the pope in the governance of the church. The offices of the Roman Curia (e.g., the Congregation for the Doctrine of the Faith) would then be responsible to this standing synod. Many critics believe that the synods that emerged out of Pope Paul VI's *Apostolica Sollicitudo* (1965) fell short of this vision.

Pope Benedict XVI began making some changes in the procedures governing synods with a goal of increasing discussion among the synod delegates. Pope Francis has continued along this path, making far more significant changes to the conduct of these synods, including the seeking of formal input from the whole people of God. Nevertheless, these synods still have only a consultative role. They meet for a short period of time every few years and cede to the pope responsibility for issuing a magisterial document based on the synodal deliberations. Many bishops at the council had hoped for the creation of a permanent, standing synod. Pope Francis's creation of the Council of Cardinals has come closer to that model, but with the obvious weakness of relying solely on representation from within the college of cardinals. Moreover, this council is also lacking in deliberative authority. More work needs to be done, it would appear, to realize the vision so many council bishops had for a permanent synod that would assist the pope in church governance.

(2) One of the difficulties with the exercise of the ordinary universal magisterium lies in the problem of verifying when, in fact, the bishops do share a common judgment that a matter is to be held as definitive. Some theologians have suggested that the teachings proposed infallibly by the ordinary universal magisterium have been teachings that have long been accepted in the church without controversy. In the papacies of John Paul II and Benedict XVI, however, appeals to this mode of church teaching were made with regard to more controversial matters. For example, the Congregation for the Doctrine of the Faith, with then-Cardinal Joseph Ratzinger (later Pope Benedict XVI) as its prefect, declared that the pope's apostolic letter on the prohibition of women from ordination to the priesthood, *Ordinatio Sacerdotalis*, was an example of a papal confirmation of the ordinary universal magisterium. But that created the odd situation in which a pope would be exercising his ordinary papal magisterium (which does not engage the charism of infallibility) to confirm that the bishops have taught a particular matter in their ordinary universal magisterium (which does engage the charism of infallibility). The question of how to properly verify the exercise of the ordinary universal magisterium, and what role the papal magisterium can play in that regard, in other words, remains hotly debated.

FOR FURTHER READING

Boyle, John P. *Church Teaching Authority: Historical and Theological Studies*. Notre Dame, IN: University of Notre Dame Press, 1995.
Dulles, Cardinal Avery. *Magisterium: Teacher and Guardian of the Faith*. Naples, FL: Sapientia Press, 2007.
Gaillardetz, Richard R. *Teaching with Authority: A Theology of the Magisterium in the Church*. Collegeville, MN: Liturgical Press, 1997.
———. "The Ordinary Universal Magisterium: Unresolved Questions." *Theological Studies* 63 (September 2002): 447–71.
———, ed. *When the Magisterium Intervenes: The Magisterium and Theologians in Today's Church*. Collegeville, MN: Liturgical Press, 2012.

Huels, John M. "A Theory of Juridical Documents Based on Canons 29–34." *Studia canonica* 32 (1998): 337–70.

Morrisey, Francis G. *Papal and Curial Pronouncements: Their Canonical Significance in Light of the Code of Canon Law.* Second edition revised and updated by Michel Thériault. Ottawa: Faculty of Canon Law, St. Paul University, 1995.

Orsy, Ladislas. *The Church: Learning and Teaching.* Wilmington, DE: Glazier, 1987.

Reese, Thomas, ed. *Episcopal Conferences: Historical, Canonical, and Theological Studies.* Washington, DC: Georgetown University Press, 1989.

Sullivan, Francis A. *Creative Fidelity: Weighing and Interpreting Documents of the Magisterium.* New York: Paulist Press, 1996.

———. *Magisterium: Teaching Office in the Catholic Church.* New York: Paulist Press, 1983.

———. "The Teaching Authority of Episcopal Conferences." *Theological Studies* 63 (September 2002): 472–93.

NINE

WHAT IS THE ROLE OF DOGMA AND DOCTRINE IN THE CHURCH?

At the risk of inviting misunderstanding, particularly in a chapter about doctrine, we begin with an important conviction guiding this entire volume: Christianity is a particular way of life before it is a set of ideas or beliefs. The first Christians were not converted by a set of doctrines. They were grasped by an encounter with the risen Lord that changed everything for them. That experience of the risen Lord led them to reorient their lives—sometimes rather dramatically, often only hesitantly—in accord with what Jesus referred to as the coming reign of God. The good news of Jesus Christ that laid claim on them was not an abstraction or a set of concepts. It was an invitation to submit their lives to the pedagogy of God's love. They were called to "undergo God," as James Alison has put it.[1] The distinctive shape of that divine love was manifest for them in the life, death, and resurrection of Jesus of Nazareth and made possible by the Spirit. This divine pedagogy was a communal enterprise in which the church became for them the school for Christian discipleship. Within that "school," stories, rituals, symbols, practices, emerging ministries, and leadership structures—all worked to re-form believers according to the distinctive pattern of God's love. And although Christianity has become a worldwide religion today with well over a billion adherents, at its core still lies this divine pedagogy.

---

[1] James Alison, *Undergoing God: Dispatches from the Scene of a Break-In* (New York: Continuum, 2006).

As the Reformed theologian James K. A. Smith reminds us, humans are defined more profoundly by what they love than by what they think or believe. Smith contends that we are "liturgical animals" who "cannot not worship."[2] The only question concerns *what* we will worship. Left to our own devices, we are as likely as not to worship material success, pleasure, the esteem of our peers, security, or power. In the church we learn to worship God with our lives (and thereby learn the right enjoyment of all creation). The Christian life is just that then, *a way of life*, one defined by a set of practices (e.g., liturgy, prayer, almsgiving, offering hospitality to the stranger, visiting the sick and imprisoned, working for justice) that train us in the love of God and love of neighbor.

This emphasis on the priority of Christian life over doctrine is a necessary corrective to those for whom the defense of doctrinal orthodoxy trumps all other Christian concerns. In a video message to the Second International Congress of Theology in Buenos Aires, Pope Francis said:

> Doctrine is not a closed system, void of the dynamic capacity to pose questions, doubts, inquiries. On the contrary, Christian doctrine has a face, a body, flesh; it's called Jesus Christ and it is his Life offered to all men and women in all places. To guard doctrine requires fidelity to what has been received and—at the same time—it requires taking into account the one speaking, the one receiving, who is known and loved.[3]

At the conclusion of the Ordinary Synod on the Family the pope pointed out that

> the true defenders of doctrine are not those who uphold its letter, but its spirit; not ideas but people; not formulae but the gratuitousness of God's love and forgiveness. . . . The Church's first duty is not to hand down condemnations or anathemas, but to proclaim God's mercy, to call to conversion, and to lead all men and women to salvation in the Lord.[4]

---

[2] James K. A. Smith, *Imagining the Kingdom: How Worship Works* (Grand Rapids, MI: Baker, 2013), 3.

[3] The text of this address is available on the Vatican website: https://w2.vatican.va/content/francesco/en/messages/pont-messages/2015/documents/papa-francesco_20150903_videomessaggio-teologia-buenos-aires.html.

[4] Pope Francis, "Address at the Conclusion of the Synod of Bishops" (October 24, 2015), accessed at the Vatican website: http://w2.vatican.va/content/francesco/en/speeches/2015/october/documents/papa-francesco_20151024_sinodo-conclusione-lavori.html.

The pope acknowledged the necessity of church formulas but feared those who absolutize them. On yet another occasion, in a papal homily, he derided a Catholic fundamentalism that appears when religious zealots turn church doctrine into ideology and go around saying to everyone who disagrees with them: "Someone who says that is a heretic. You can't say this, or that; this is the doctrine of the Church."[5]

The pope has called us to avoid an ideological abuse of church doctrine. But we must also be aware of an opposing temptation: the repudiation of doctrine altogether. Many today, reacting to instances of a heavy-handed ecclesiastical authoritarianism, have decided to abandon Catholic Christianity altogether. Others take refuge in those elements of Catholicism that appear (wrongly) to be free of doctrinal concerns: spirituality, mysticism, or social justice advocacy.

What is required is a balanced approach to church doctrine that neither turns it into the totality of the Christian faith nor treats it as a necessary evil. The priority of Christianity as a way of life does not negate the role of doctrine, but it does place it in a new context. To grasp this, we might consider some of the ways in which fundamental church doctrines were first employed in the life of the church.

The earliest instances of what we today call doctrine were found in the ancient creeds of the early church. While there were no formal creeds in the New Testament literature, one can find brief confessional formulas like that referred to in 1 Corinthians 12:3, "Jesus is lord!" or that of the Ethiopian eunuch in Acts: "I believe that Jesus Christ is the Son of God" (Acts 8:37). In the postbiblical period, primitive creeds were initially developed for use in sacramental initiation and Christian worship and they were often interrogatory in character, taking the form of a series of questions and answers: "Do you believe in God the Father Almighty, Creator of Heaven and Earth?" "Yes, I do." These early creeds were intended to elicit faith commitment, not affirm factual data; they had a *performative* function. We tend to miss this because of changes in the way we understand the verb "to believe." The Greek verb *pisteuo*, like the Latin *credo*, originally had a performative, promise-making sense (literally "to faith"). To say "I believe in God" was less reporting a matter of fact than it was a personal commitment to a relationship with this God. The profession of faith had the character of a pledge, not

[5] "Pope Francis: Doctrine Unites, Ideology Divides," *Vatican Radio* (May 19, 2017), accessed at: http://en.radiovaticana.va/news/2017/05/19/pope_francis _doctrine_unites,_ideology_divides/1313444.

unlike the pledge that spouses make to one another in their wedding vows. Nicholas Ayo, in his extended meditation on the role of creeds in the life of the church, writes:

> Thus the creed was the confession of faith, the profession of hope, the protestation of a personal love. One bore witness to faith in the mystery of God who is beyond all formulations in this simple and public recitation of the rule or standard of faith that comprises the creed.[6]

Although formal creeds were not included in the celebration of the Eucharist until around the fifth century, their eventual inclusion in the Mass suggests that they were viewed less as a collection of formal truths than as an act of praise and worship. Catherine Mowry LaCugna writes of the *doxological* (from the Greek word *doxa*, which meant glory; doxology is concerned with giving praise to God) function of creeds:

> Although we cannot name God, we can pray the name of God given to us, thereby activating relationship with the God who names Godself. Soteriology culminates in doxology. . . . Praise is never directed to God in an abstract way, as if one could offer praise to God on the basis of speculative attributes such as immutability. Praise is always rendered in response to God's goodness to Israel, or God's majesty in creation, or God's faithfulness to the covenant, or God's peacemaking in the heart of the sinner, or God's face seen in Christ. Praise is offered because in the concrete aspects of God's life with us we experience God's steadfast love, God's gracious and everlasting presence among us.[7]

Creeds give concrete shape to our praise, reminding us of who the object (who is in fact never an "object" but the one great divine "Subject") of our praise really is.

As creeds became more developed, in addition to the performative and doxological functions mentioned above, they also acquired a *catechetical* function and were used as concise summaries of the Christian faith. This catechetical usage is reflected in one of the names given to early Christian creeds, *symbolum*, the "symbol" or summary of the Christian faith. Two of the best examples of this are the Apostles' Creed and the Nicene-Constantinopolitan Creed, both of which remain in use in the church today. Even in their more catechetical employment, these

---

[6] Nicholas Ayo, *Creed as Symbol* (Notre Dame, IN: University of Notre Dame Press, 1989), 2.

[7] Catherine Mowry LaCugna, *God for Us: The Trinity and Christian Life* (San Francisco: HarperCollins, 1991), 335, 337.

creeds were not treated as mere collections of propositional truths to memorize and employ in religious argument. Rather, they were considered shorthand summaries of the basic Christian message.

We can also identify a *regulative function* for creeds in the early church as they were gradually employed as normative expressions of "right belief" in the Christian faith. Many of the key statements in these creeds had emerged at points in the history of the church when fundamental tenets of the faith were being threatened. Their formulation was determined by the controversies to which they were responding. For that reason, properly interpreted within the cultural and historical context in which they first emerged, creedal statements could function as stable reference points for theological discussion and catechetical ministry. Any *alternative* theological formulations would have to be congruent, that is, intellectually reconcilable, with the appropriate doctrinal teaching. Contemporary church doctrine continues to serve this regulative function. It can help the church determine when certain theological, liturgical, spiritual, or pastoral insights or practices may be departing unacceptably from the shared faith of the church.

Finally, we might consider creedal statements' *communicative function*. Divine revelation, as we have seen, is not merely the conveyance of some abstract body of knowledge; it is God's self-communication disclosing to us the deepest reality of God's love and the meaning that love bestows on human life. Formal creedal statements represented the human effort, assisted, we believe, by the Spirit of God, to give a limited but reliable propositional expression to that meaning:

> Even if the personal question (*Who* is revealed?) remains the primary one, the propositional content of revelation (the answer to the question " *What* is revealed?") has its proper place. The personal model emphasizes the *knowledge of* God (a knowledge by acquaintance) which the event of revelation embodies. But this implies that the believer enjoys a *knowledge about* God. The communication of truth about God belongs essentially to revelation, even if always at the service of the personal experience *of* God or encounter *with* God.[8]

For the church today, appropriating the meaning of a given doctrine will always require an attentiveness to the historical and cultural context

---

[8] Gerald O'Collins, *Rethinking Fundamental Theology* (Oxford: Oxford University Press, 2011), 67.

in which that teaching was first articulated. For example, it will not be enough to know that the doctrine of the Trinity denotes belief in three persons in one divine being. The modern meaning of the English word "person" is quite different from the Latin meaning of *persona* and the Greek meaning of *hypostasis*. To properly grasp the meaning of the doctrine of the Trinity will require some historical work to grasp how these terms were understood at the time they were first employed. It will also mean learning how the church's understanding of this teaching has developed over time as it was appropriated in new historical and cultural contexts.

This process continues into the present. In every age, the church will have to reinterpret its formal teaching such that it can speak in language intelligible to the time. This is why, as we saw in our consideration of the dynamic nature of tradition in chapter 5, all church teaching, if it is to effectively communicate the faith in ways appropriate to diverse peoples and cultures, is subject to change and development. Yet, even as we acknowledge the human origins of any church doctrine, these developments also reflect the activity of the Spirit bringing the church to an ever more profound appreciation of the meaning of God's one revelation in Christ.

Clemens Sedmak notes that while there is a danger of relying excessively on propositional truths, nevertheless,

> Doctrines are indispensable guideposts; they have to have the kind of "spiritual clarity" that enables a person to build her life on that doctrine and this clarity cannot be reached by way of narratives alone. There has to be the defining capacity of a proposition. Doctrines are indispensable in upholding the expressions of truth in a propositional form; they are an expression of love of God and loyalty to the gospel.[9]

The danger lies not with a recognition of the necessary role of doctrine but with the kind of reliance on doctrine that sees it as a place of security rather than a call to conversion in service of discipleship. Thus, Sedmak also insists that "doctrines have to be lived so that they can come alive in another person."[10] There is, he suggests, a kind of "existential orthodoxy" that must come before a "doctrinal orthodoxy."[11] Indeed,

---

[9] Clemens Sedmak, *A Church of the Poor: Pope Francis and the Transformation of Orthodoxy* (Maryknoll, NY: Orbis Books, 2016), 146.

[10] Ibid.

[11] Ibid., 161.

for him, this priority is the key to understanding the shift that Pope Francis has effected. Francis wants doctrine to serve a larger reality:

> Pastoral ministry in a missionary style is not obsessed with the disjointed transmission of a multitude of doctrines to be insistently imposed. When we adopt a pastoral goal and a missionary style which would actually reach everyone without exception or exclusion, the message has to concentrate on the essentials, on what is most beautiful, most grand, most appealing and at the same time most necessary. The message is simplified, while losing none of its depth and truth, and thus becomes all the more forceful and convincing. (EG 35)

Although we began this section with a focus on the church's most basic creedal commitments, today the range of formal church teaching has gone beyond that of the church's ancient creeds. The word "doctrine" comes from the Latin noun *doctrina* and its related verb form, *docere*, meaning to teach or instruct. Unless used with a qualifying adjective (e.g., *definitive* doctrine or *authoritative* doctrine), the term "doctrine" is a generic reference to all formal church teaching. A doctrine is any authoritative or normative formulation of a belief of the church, whether revealed or not. A church doctrine is intended to articulate a formal belief of the church that it draws in some fashion from its reflection on divine revelation, even if it may not itself be divinely revealed.

Within this generic category of doctrine, today we can speak more broadly of at least four different categories of normative church pronouncements.

GRADATIONS IN CHURCH TEACHING

Over the course of almost two thousand years, the Christian community has found it necessary to make formal doctrinal pronouncements, sometimes in response to perceived threats to the integrity of the faith. Other pronouncements helped clarify fundamental church tenets. Some dealt with fairly specific issues that later generations would view as peripheral. Not every official church pronouncement is taught with the same degree of authority and therefore not every church pronouncement is equally normative or "binding" for believers. There has gradually emerged within the Roman Catholic communion a set of distinctions regarding church teaching that can help us in assessing the authoritative character of a given church teaching.

GRADATIONS OF CHURCH TEACHING

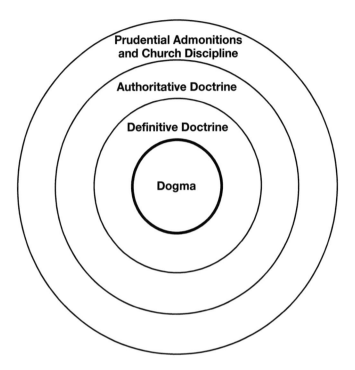

Dogma[12]

Dogma represents the most important category of formal church teaching. These teachings communicate God's saving message as revealed to us in Scripture and tradition. The term "dogma" once carried a wide range of meanings in early Christianity. Beginning in the eighteenth century, however, "dogma" came to refer to those propositional

---

[12] The three basic categories of church doctrine considered here—dogma, definitive doctrine, and authoritative doctrine—are referred to, although not with this nomenclature, in the three additional paragraphs added to the Profession of Faith promulgated by the Congregation for the Doctrine of the Faith in 1989. "Profession of Faith and Oath of Fidelity," *Origins* 18 (March 16, 1989): 661, 663. The fourth category appearing in the accompanying diagram is not technically church doctrine, which is concerned with Christian "belief," but it does pertain to formal church teaching in a more generic sense.

formulations that were taught as "divinely revealed." As such, the church's dogmatic teaching included, but also went beyond, the church's ancient creeds.

> *A dogma is any propositional formulation that is (1) divinely revealed and (2) proposed as such by the magisterium, either through a solemn definition of a pope or council or by the teaching of the college of bishops in their ordinary and universal magisterium.*

There is a curious feature about the place of dogma in the Catholic Church. Ask a Catholic how many sacraments there are and the answer is simple: seven. How many commandments are there? Ten. A little research reveals that in the history of the church there have been twenty-one ecumenical or general councils and 266 popes (with a few of each in dispute). The revised Code of Canon Law contains 1,752 canons. So why is it that there is no standard answer to the question of how many dogmas there are in the Catholic faith? Of course, it is possible to number the articles in the creed, but then the creed does not represent an exhaustive list of dogmatic teachings.

This curious situation brings us back, once again, to the need for an adequate theology of revelation. A strictly propositional view of revelation regards revelation as little more than a collection of individual truths or propositional statements. Those who hold such a view of revelation would expect to be able to identify a set number of church dogmas, if only they look hard enough. But Vatican II taught that revelation cannot be reduced to a collection of statements or discrete truths. Revelation is disclosed, ultimately, not in a statement or a text but in a person, Jesus Christ. Christ is "both the mediator and the sum total of revelation" (DV 2). All church dogma and doctrine are the fruit of the church's communal meditation on the one revelation of God in Christ in the power of the Spirit. For example, the internal unity of the creed is reflected in the diverse ways in which the creeds have been divided. The Apostles' Creed, by tradition, consists of twelve articles. Yet it is also possible to divide it, along with the Nicene-Constantinopolitan Creed, into three articles, each dedicated to a person of the Trinity. Alternatively, one might read the entire creed as the articulation of the one triune mystery of God's saving love made effective through the Word and Spirit.

A simple analogy may help us grasp this peculiarity. Imagine a powerful lamp projecting a single beam of light on a blank wall. What we see is one beam of light. We might think of this light as the unity of the one revelation of God. This one revelation has been communicated into human history from the beginning of time through the divine Word and made effective by the power of the Spirit. In "the fullness of time," Christians believe that this one revelation was expressed in an unsurpassable manner in Jesus of Nazareth. Inasmuch as we reflect on this revelation in terms of its source, the triune God, we will focus on the unity of God's perfect self-communication.

Let us return to the image of the one beam of light. What happens if we place a prism in front of that beam? What we will see projected on the wall is not an undifferentiated beam but a plurality of colors spread across a spectrum. The prism might be thought of as human history. The unity of God's revelation is refracted into a diversity of mediations in human history. As humans, our only access to the unity of the beam of light, the one revelation of God, is through the historical diversity of its manifestations.

Christianity asserts that we have encountered the one revelation of God in the covenants recounted by the ancient ancestors of Israel, in the prophets, and in God's many deeds accomplished on behalf of Israel. For Christianity, the fullness of God's revelation has come to us in Jesus Christ, the testimony to which we find in the written testimony of the early Christians who first walked with Jesus on the shores of the Sea of Galilee and then encountered him as risen. This foundational testimony constitutes our Sacred Scriptures. Yet, we also believe that this revelation continues to be handed on and received in the church's later dogmatic teaching, in the liturgy, in the teachings of councils and popes, in the theological meditations and explorations of great Christian theologians (often called Doctors of the Church), in the dramatic testimony of saints and martyrs, and in the more mundane testimony of simple believers struggling to follow the Gospel in their daily lives. We referred to this earlier as "dependent" revelation. In other words, if we shift our attention from the source of divine revelation to our historical encounter with it, we move from the unity of the one revelation of God in Christ by the Spirit to the plurality of its expression in human history.

This is why we do not number dogmas. Catholics believe that dogmas are but specific historical mediations—specific linguistic, propositional expressions of the one revelation of God. When we forget that, when we treat dogmas as if they were revelation itself instead of limited *mediations* or symbolic articulations of God's revelation, we flirt with a kind of fundamentalism.

Some of these dogmatic teachings are relatively technical, pronounced in general councils or papal decrees to address issues that may not concern us today. Most but not all of the more significant dogmatic teachings are found in the basic creedal statements of the church like the Nicene-Constantinopolitan Creed, which we profess in the Sunday liturgy. They concern such central aspects of our faith as the divinity of Christ, belief in the bodily resurrection and the real presence of Christ in the Eucharist. These teachings, because they are proposed with the charism of infallibility, are held to be irreversible in character. Unfortunately, terms like "infallible," "irreformable," and "irreversible" have often occasioned misunderstanding so it will be worthwhile to consider them in more detail.

The Charism of Infallibility and the Irreversibility of Certain Church Teachings

To say that a dogma is irreversible (some church documents prefer the term "irreformable" or "definitive") means that this teaching is not erroneous—that, adequately interpreted, it will not deceive believers regarding the substance of God's saving offer. At the same time, it is still a human expression that, in its formulation, is subject to all the limits of human communication and therefore can always be improved on. Every dogmatic teaching necessarily makes use of certain cultural, philosophical, theological, and linguistic constructs, all of which are human inventions. Thus, although Catholic Christians believe that an irreversible teaching is a reliable mediation of divine revelation that will never be "wrong," it will always be possible to adopt new and more adequate philosophical, theological, and linguistic constructs aimed at a faithful articulation of revelation. As Karl Rahner writes, "Anyone who takes seriously the 'historicity' of human truth (in which God's truth too has become incarnate in Revelation) must see that *neither the abandonment* of a formula *nor its preservation in a petrified form* does justice to human understanding."[13] The German Jesuit theologian insists that such dogmatic formulas always impel the faith of the church beyond

---

[13] Karl Rahner, "Current Problems in Christology," *Theological Investigations*, vol. 1, trans. Cornelius Ernst (Baltimore: Helicon Press, 1961), 149–200, at 150.

the formula itself to some deeper reality that may eventually require a new dogmatic expression. This new expression, again, doesn't negate the earlier one but carries forward the deep meaning of the former formulation in a new and more adequate expression.

Irreversible dogmas are taught by the magisterium and believed by the whole people of God with the charism of infallibility. Technically speaking, infallibility refers to a charism that assists the church as a whole in a *judgment of belief* and the teaching of the magisterium in a *teaching judgment*. The object of the exercise of the charism of infallibility is a teaching deemed to be irreversible (irreformable or definitive). The gift of infallibility is not some magic wand that popes and bishops get to wield; it is not simply one of the perks that come with the job. According to Catholic teaching, infallibility is God's promise to the church that, *when it comes to the revelation of God's saving offer,* we can be confident that church teaching will be a sure guide.

To understand better how church dogma actually functions, or at least ought to function, in the life of the church, let me suggest a second analogy regarding light. The first analogy demonstrated how revelation is mediated to humankind through the prism of human history. Now we will consider how revealed dogma functions in illuminating, through an act of faith, the mystery of God revealed in Christ by the power of the Holy Spirit. The analogy is different because we are now considering how dogma mediates God's revelation in such a way as to direct our gaze toward God and draw us into the life of communion.

Imagine that a local parish has contracted a world-renowned artist to create a sculpture of Christ, the Good Shepherd. After a long wait the statue is finally to be unveiled in front of the church. Parishioners are invited to come by in the evening to see it beautifully illuminated by a specially designed set of floodlights. I am sure that the pastor (and the artist!) would be quite dismayed if parishioners were to exclaim at the unveiling: "My, what gorgeous floodlights!" The point of the floodlights is not to draw attention to themselves but to illuminate the beautiful statue.

So it is with church dogma. They are like floodlights insofar as their function lies not in drawing our attention to them in their own right but in their ability, by what they communicate, to direct our gaze toward Christ who is himself the indescribable beauty of God and our one true salvation. As with all analogies, there are limits to its applicability. For God is not an object to be observed but a divine Subject encountered in faith as incomprehensible Mystery. Yet dogmas do illuminate for us, however imperfectly, something true and indispensable about the Holy Mystery of God. With that in mind, let us return to the statue and floodlights.

When the floodlights are properly aligned, we don't notice them at all but rather gaze upon the work of art. But what if the floodlights were misaligned and drew our gaze, not to the sculpture, but to the church's rain gutter? For us to encounter the artist's work, we have to trust that the lights will be properly aligned. When it comes to church dogma, we must also trust that they are properly aligned, that they are indeed faithfully and more or less adequately illuminating Christ and the way of salvation. We want to be confident that they will not misdirect our gaze like poorly aligned floodlights. This is the purpose of the charism of infallibility; it gives us the confidence that our gaze is not being misdirected. Church dogma does indeed faithfully and without error mediate divine revelation and illuminate faithfully, if imperfectly, the beauty of God.

There is yet another insight to be drawn from our analogy. If we are standing outside the church at night and the floodlights are properly aligned, they allow us to gaze on the sculpture. It is, however, still possible to improve the floodlights. The artist might ask that more powerful lamps be employed to better illuminate her work. The floodlights, as they are, still function correctly and direct the viewers' gaze to the sculpture, but they can be improved. Perhaps a different style of lamp will remove some of the shadows. So too, while the exercise of infallibility promises us that a dogma will faithfully mediate God's self-gift, it remains possible and often necessary to reformulate our dogmatic definitions. Further study and theological reflection can improve and refine the way we articulate church teaching and deepen our appreciation for the meaning of the dogmatic teaching. To say that a dogma has been taught infallibly means that we can trust that it will not lead us away from the path of salvation; it does not preclude our finding better ways to communicate its abiding truth.

Most of the significant dogmatic teachings of the church are found in the creeds that we recite in the liturgy. Beyond these there are other dogmatic teachings, proposed by popes or councils, generally in response to some controversy. Examples of church dogma include the belief in the divinity of Christ, the law of love, the resurrection of the body, and the affirmation of the real presence of Christ in the Eucharist. All such teachings do, according to Catholic teaching, faithfully mediate some aspect of divine revelation. This does not mean, however, that every dogma is equally foundational to the life of the church.

THE HIERARCHY OF TRUTHS

The Second Vatican Council recognized a certain ordering of church dogma in its teaching on the "hierarchy of truths." In its Decree on Ecumenism, *Unitatis Redintegratio*, the council offered guidelines for how Catholic theologians ought to conduct themselves in formal ecumenical dialogue with other non-Catholic Christians. It then offered this counsel: "When comparing doctrines with one another, they should remember that in catholic doctrine there exists an order or 'hierarchy' of truths, since they vary in their relation to the foundation of the christian faith" (UR 11). The conciliar text insists that church dogmas must be understood and interpreted in the light of their relationship to the foundation of Christian faith. This foundation refers to the entire economy of salvation—what God has done for us in Christ by the power of the Spirit. The council taught that church dogmas have differing relations or links to this foundation. This interpretation is confirmed by the 1973 CDF declaration, "In Defense of Catholic Doctrine," article 4, which affirms that some dogmas or "truths" lean on more principal "truths" and are illumined by them.[14] It is also true that some dogmatic pronouncements addressed questions that were quite important during one period of church history but have diminished in their importance today. This insight can be helpful for catechists who are sometimes tempted to treat every dogmatic teaching as equally weighty.

Let me offer an example from church history. One of the issues with which Christians struggled during the fifth through the seventh centuries was how to hold together both the belief that Jesus was the incarnation of the Second Person of the Trinity and the conviction that Jesus possessed two natures, one human and the other divine. Some theological approaches so emphasized the two distinct natures of Christ that it often seemed that Christ had developed a kind of "split personality." Others so emphasized the unity of Christ as the incarnation of the Word that his distinctive humanity was obscured. Those who chose to emphasize the "oneness of Christ" almost to the point of denying that he

---

[14] This document can be accessed online at: http://www.vatican.va/roman
_curia/congregations/cfaith/documents/rc_con_cfaith_doc_19730705_mysterium
-ecclesiae_en.html.

possessed a distinct human nature were called Monophysites. In the seventh century, as part of an effort to bring the Monophysites back into the church, some theologians offered a compromise theory that affirmed that Christ possessed two distinct natures but had but one "will." This theory came to be known as monothelitism, and it was ultimately condemned at the Third Council of Constantinople, which declared that Christ possessed "two wills." In the context of the debates that raged at the time regarding the integrity of Christ's full humanity, this was an important declaration. In later periods of the church, however, the question of whether Christ possessed one will or two became less significant. Today, if you filled a room with educated Catholics (ordained and lay) and asked them whether Christ possesses one will or two, you would likely find considerable disagreement. This would mean nothing regarding the orthodoxy of one group or another; all it would prove is that this way of formulating ancient Christological teaching no longer has purchase on modern Catholics. It is not that Constantinople III was wrong; it is just that its Christological formulation is no longer central to the faith consciousness of Catholics today.

The council's teaching on the hierarchy of truths holds tremendous potential for the church on a number of fronts. First, it was proposed in the council's document on ecumenism because it seemed important then, and it remains so today, to enter into conversation with members of other Christian traditions with the acknowledgment that not all of our doctrinal differences are equally foundational. Surely, our agreement with other non-Catholic Christians on the doctrine of the Trinity and the resurrection of the body are more significant than our disagreement on purgatory. Second, it holds tremendous promise in catechetical ministry as it can help catechists to realize that they need not go through a laundry list of church dogmas in order to be sure that they have properly catechized their students. Given the potential fruitfulness of this teaching, it is surprising that it actually received relatively little attention in official church teaching in the decades since the council. Pope Francis, however, has given considerable emphasis to the council's teaching on the hierarchy of truths in his pontificate. In *Evangelii Gaudium* he wrote:

> All revealed truths derive from the same divine source and are to be believed with the same faith, yet some of them are more important for giving direct expression to the heart of the Gospel. In this basic core, what shines forth is the beauty of the saving love of God made manifest

in Jesus Christ who died and rose from the dead. In this sense, the Second Vatican Council explained, "in Catholic doctrine there exists an order or a 'hierarchy' of truths, since they vary in their relation to the foundation of the Christian faith." This holds true as much for the dogmas of faith as for the whole corpus of the Church's teaching, including her moral teaching. (EG 36)

For the pope this teaching is about much more than ranking dogmatic teachings; it is about relating these formal teachings to something more basic, the core Gospel message. He is not afraid to affirm church teaching as basic to Christian identity, but he consistently orients that teaching toward the basic Christian kerygma and situates it within the pastoral life of the church.

Definitive Doctrine

There is a tendency among some today to artificially elevate all church teaching to the status of dogma. Yet in fact there are three other categories of church teaching that are not dogmatic, properly speaking. These include a second doctrinal category, which we will refer to as *definitive doctrine*. This category has only recently been explicitly employed by the magisterium. It includes teachings that are not divinely revealed but are *necessary for safeguarding and expounding divine revelation*. Because it is assumed that these teachings are necessary for preserving divine revelation, they are, like dogmas, also taught with the charism of infallibility and, as such, are also irreversible (irreformable). One example of a teaching often placed in this category is the Council of Trent's determination of the books included in the canon of the Bible. The list of books is not itself something that has been divinely revealed, but were the church to be mistaken regarding which books were canonical and which were not, that mistake could put the integrity of divine revelation in jeopardy.

Somewhat more controversially, then-Cardinal Ratzinger and Archbishop Tarcisio Bertone, in a commentary on the new profession of faith that the Congregation for the Doctrine of the Faith had promulgated in 1989, asserted a number of other teachings that they believed had the status of definitive doctrine: the teaching on the illicitness of prostitution and fornication, the canonization of saints, *Evangelium Vitae*'s condemnation of euthanasia, the teaching that priestly ordination is reserved to men, and Pope Leo XIII's declaration that Anglican orders were null and void.[15] Theologians were quick to point out that this commentary was not itself a magisterial document, and some theologians have questioned whether all of these teachings should in fact be considered definitive doctrine.

Authoritative Doctrine

Authoritative doctrine represents a third category of church teaching. This includes teachings that the magisterium proposes authoritatively to guide the faith and practice of believers. Authoritative doctrine is drawn from the wisdom of the church as it reflects on Scripture and tradition. Included among *authoritative doctrine* are many concrete moral teachings, such as the immorality of directly targeting civilians in an act of war or the prohibition of recourse to certain reproductive technologies like *in vitro* fertilization. Yet, even as these teachings are proposed authoritatively, the magisterium is not ready to commit itself irrevocably to them. Practically speaking, this means that, however remote, there is at least a possibility of error with respect to these teachings.

Many people believe that acknowledging the possibility of error in church teaching, even when we are not speaking of church dogma, will undermine the authority of the magisterium. If one admits the possibility of error, they fear, believers would lose confidence in the church's teaching authority. I am inclined to believe that quite the opposite is the case. It is a mistake to think that unless the church's doctrinal teaching authority is infallible, it cannot possess any real authority.

Consider the way in which we view authority in other spheres of our lives. As was pointed out in chapter 1, when I go to a doctor because I am experiencing chest pains, I recognize that there is a remote possibility that the doctor will misdiagnose my condition. I still grant the doctor authority even though I know that her authority is not infallible. I trust that this doctor has been properly trained and certified and has shown herself to be a reliable physician. My recognition of the remote possibility of error is not an impediment to acknowledging her authority. In the same way, the Catholic Church teaches that it is protected from

---

[15] Cardinal Joseph Ratzinger and Archbishop Tarcisio Bertone, "Commentary on Profession of Faith's Concluding Paragraphs," *Origins* 28 (July 16, 1998): 116–19.

error when it pronounces on God's self-gift in revelation. In other instances, it may teach with authority, but that authority does not exclude the possibility of error.

An honest acknowledgment that the magisterium is not always immune from error actually enhances the credibility of the official church teaching. Many Catholics today know enough about past church teachings, like its condemnation of usury, to have already accepted the fact that the magisterium has erred in the past. When church leaders appear reluctant to acknowledge both past errors and the possibility of future ones, they risk undermining the credibility of the magisterium altogether. An honest and forthright acknowledgment of the limits of authority, accompanied by a judicious restraint regarding the frequency with which that authority is exercised, would give subsequent authoritative pronouncements greater weight.

Concrete Applications of Church Teaching, Prudential Judgments, Admonitions, and Church Discipline

Finally, a fourth category of church teaching includes any of a variety of teachings that, technically, would fall short of doctrine, properly speaking. A good example is found in Catholic moral teaching. The American bishops, in their pastoral letter *The Challenge of Peace*, distinguished between binding moral principles and concrete moral applications about which Catholics could disagree in good faith. For example, the bishops' condemnation of any first use of nuclear weapons constituted a quite concrete application of specific moral principles in a particular context. More recently, Pope Francis proposed specific policy assessments and prescriptions in his encyclical on the environment and global climate change, *Laudato Sí*, ranking fossil fuel sources according to the degree of damage they cause and the consequent urgency of replacing them (LS 165) and insisting that market-based approaches such as carbon credits were inadequate solutions to climate change (LS 171). Prudential policy judgments of this kind, regarding the concrete application of church teaching, according to the American bishops, must be given "serious attention and consideration by Catholics as they determine whether their moral judgments are consistent with the Gospel."[16] Nevertheless, they admitted that Catholics might legitimately

---

[16] NCCB, *The Challenge of Peace* 10, available online at: http://www.usccb.org/upload/challenge-peace-gods-promise-our-response-1983.pdf.

differ with the bishops (and even the pope) regarding these moral applications and prudential judgments. This fourth category also includes disciplinary rules varying from the determination of the number of holy days of obligation to the current requirement of celibacy for diocesan priests. Also included in this fourth category would be prudential admonitions by church leaders regarding questionable aspects of certain theological writings. This might include the warning of a bishop or bishops that a particular theologian's treatment of a topic may be doctrinally questionable. Finally, we can place much of church law within this fourth category, such as the determination of the appropriate age to receive confirmation or the prohibition against ordaining married men to the diocesan priesthood in the Latin church *sui iuris*.

As we bring this chapter to a close, we need to address a final matter regarding the authority of church teaching, namely, the authoritative status of the *Catechism of the Catholic Church*. Catechisms have a distinguished tradition in the church going back to the *Catechism of the Council of Trent*, first published in 1566. They can be tremendously helpful in the catechetical ministry of the church and serve as a reliable compendium of church teaching. However, as Pope St. John Paul II made clear in the apostolic constitution, *Fidei Depositum*, by which he officially promulgated the *Catechism*, it "is not intended to replace the local catechisms duly approved by the ecclesiastical authorities. . . . It is meant to encourage and assist in the writing of new local catechisms, which take into account various situations and cultures."[17] As regards the authority of the *Catechism*, the pope writes:

> The *Catechism of the Catholic Church* . . . is a statement of the Church's faith and of catholic doctrine, attested to or illumined by Sacred Scripture, the Apostolic Tradition and the Church's Magisterium. I declare it to be a sure norm for teaching the faith and thus a valid and legitimate instrument for ecclesial communion.

Note that the catechism presents church teaching *already taught* in "Scripture, tradition and the Church's Magisterium"; it is not itself an exercise of the magisterium. In other words, the teachings contained in the *Catechism* carry only the doctrinal authority they already possessed prior to their inclusion in the *Catechism*. Any questions about the authoritative status of a teaching found in the *Catechism* must refer back

---

[17] Pope St. John Paul II, *Fidei Depositum*, accessed online at: http://w2.vatican .va/content/john-paul-ii/en/apost_constitutions/documents/hf_jp-ii_apc _19921011_fidei-depositum.html.

to the original context in which that teaching was first articulated in the life of the church. So, if the *Catechism* presents a teaching of the Second Vatican Council on, for example, religious liberty, for a fuller appreciation of the meaning and authority of that teaching one should turn to its original magisterial source, in this case the council's Declaration on Religious Liberty, *Dignitatis Humanae.*

No taxonomy of church doctrine can do justice to the richness and multitextured character of the Catholic faith. As Catholic teaching has moved away from the propositional emphasis of the dogmatic and moral manuals associated with seminary training before Vatican II and toward a more inductive and dialogical style, it will not always be easy to determine the precise authoritative status of one or another particular teaching. It remains, in no small part, for the theological and catechetical community to assist the whole people of God in the important ecclesial discernment necessary if Catholics are to grasp the proper demands set before them by the teaching of the church.

DISPUTED QUESTIONS

(1) In ecumenical theology the Second Vatican Council's teaching on the hierarchy of truths has tremendous and still largely untapped potential. Many theologians contend that the church has yet to fully exploit this important insight that not every dogmatic teaching in the Catholic Church is equally central to "the foundations of the Christian faith." For example, some scholars have suggested that it need not be necessary to require, as a condition for ecumenical reunion, that non-Catholic Christian communions assent to *every* dogmatic teaching proposed infallibly within the Catholic tradition. These scholars contend that there are certain dogmatic teachings, such as those related to Mary, that, while divinely revealed, simply confirm more basic truths shared by all Christians (e.g., the universality of redemption and the resurrection of the body).

(2) An important disputed question concerns the authoritative status of the church's moral teaching. It is commonly accepted that some moral teachings of the church do have dogmatic status, such as the law of love and the affirmation of the inalienable dignity of the human person. But what about more specific moral teachings like the church's prohibition of artificial birth control, its condemnation

of capital punishment, or its just war teaching? Few theologians believe that teachings of this sort have been taught infallibly, but the more difficult question concerns whether they *could* be taught infallibly. In other words, are pronouncements on more specific moral questions within the scope of the exercise of the charism of infallibility? Those who answer in the affirmative highlight the integrity of divine revelation and the way in which more specific moral teachings, even if they are not technically divinely revealed, are so closely related to divine revelation that they could also be taught infallibly. Other theologians argue that specific moral teachings, like the prohibition of artificial birth control, depend too much on empirical data subject to change (e.g., embryological studies of what transpires in the earliest stages of conception) to be taught infallibly. Of course, they would insist, these teachings would still possess a normative status as authoritative doctrine.

(3) Many questions have been raised regarding definitive doctrine, the second category of church teaching. The assertion that such teachings are protected by the charism of infallibility has been commonly assumed, both at Vatican I and Vatican II. This claim, however, has never itself been taught infallibly.

There are also significant disagreements regarding the scope of definitive doctrine. Pope John Paul II, in the papal document *Ad Tuendam Fidem*, mandated an addition to the Code of Canon Law concerning definitive doctrine. That addition states that definitive doctrines are teachings "*required* for the sacred preservation and faithful explanation of the same deposit of faith" (c. 750.2). Other, less authoritative documents broaden the scope of definitive doctrine considerably to include teachings that are "connected" to divine revelation by "logical or historical necessity." Some theologians have voiced their concern that this broader definition of the scope of definitive doctrine is sufficiently malleable as to allow practically any church teaching to be included in this category.

FOR FURTHER READING

Congregation for the Doctrine of the Faith. "In Defense of Catholic Doctrine" [*Mysterium Ecclesiae*]. *Origins* 3 (July 19, 1973): 97–112.
Crowley, Paul G. *In Ten Thousand Places: Dogma in a Pluralistic Church.* New York: Crossroad, 1997.

Dulles, Avery. *The Craft of Theology: From Symbol to System*. New York: Crossroad, 1992.

———. *Models of Revelation*. Garden City, NY: Doubleday, 1983.

Gaillardetz, Richard R. Chapter 4 in *Teaching with Authority: A Theology of the Magisterium in the Church*, 101–28. Collegeville, MN: Liturgical Press, 1997.

———. "*Ad Tuendam Fidem*: An Emerging Pattern in Current Papal Teaching." *New Theology Review* 12 (February 1999): 43–51.

Helmer, Christine. *Theology and the End of Doctrine*. Louisville: Westminster John Knox Press, 2014.

International Theological Commission. "On the Interpretation of Dogmas." *Origins* 20 (May 17, 1990): 1–14.

John Paul II, Pope. *Ad Tuendam Fidem*. *Origins* 28 (July 16, 1998): 113–16.

Johnson, Luke Timothy. *The Creed: What Christians Believe and Why It Matters*. New York: Doubleday, 2003.

Lindbeck, George A. *The Nature of Doctrine: Religion and Theology in a Postliberal Age*. Philadelphia: Westminster, 1984.

Marthaler, Berard. *The Creed: The Apostolic Faith in Contemporary Theology*. Rev. ed. Mystic, CT: Twenty-Third Publications, 1993.

Ratzinger, Cardinal Joseph, and Archbishop Tarcisio Bertone. "Commentary on Profession of Faith's Concluding Paragraphs." *Origins* 28 (July 16, 1998): 116–19.

Sedmak, Clemens. *A Church of the Poor: Pope Francis and the Transformation of Orthodoxy*. Maryknoll, NY: Orbis Books, 2016.

Segundo, Juan Luis. *The Liberation of Dogma*. Maryknoll, NY: Orbis Books, 1992.

PART FOUR

THE AUTHORITY OF THE BELIEVING COMMUNITY

TEN

WHAT IS THE SENSE
OF THE FAITHFUL?

In some early churches the elect who were being prepared to celebrate the Easter sacraments underwent a ritual known as the *traditio-redditio symboli*, "the handing over and giving back of the creed." A copy of the creed would be handed to the member of the elect and later they would profess that creed before the community. This ritual action aptly symbolized a fundamental dynamic within the life of the church. The *General Directory for Catechesis* (GDC) explains its significance:

> The profession of faith received by the Church (*traditio*), which germinates and grows during the catechetical process, is given back (*redditio*), enriched by the values of different cultures. The catechumenate is thus transformed into a center of deepening catholicity and a ferment of ecclesial renewal.[1]

The GDC recognized that the handing on of the faith was a complex process. On receiving the faith of the church, we make it our own as it takes root in the distinctive cultural soil of our own lives. When we profess that faith, now enriched by our appropriation of it, we offer something of our own lives back to the faith of the church. The Second Vatican Council acknowledges this dynamic and active appropriation of the faith in its teaching on the "sense of faith" (*sensus fidei*).

The term *sensus fidei* appeared in official church teaching for the first time in the documents of Vatican II, but the reality underlying it goes

---

[1] Congregation for the Clergy, *General Directory for Catechesis* (Washington, DC: USCC, 1997), art. 78.

back to the very origins of Christianity. There the biblical tradition presented Christian faith as the fundamental response of the believer to the proclamation of the Gospel. Recall the teaching of St. Paul:

> Now I would remind you, brothers and sisters, of the good news that I proclaimed to you, which you in turn received, in which also you stand, through which also you are being saved, if you hold firmly to the message that I proclaimed to you—unless you have come to believe in vain. (1 Cor 15:1-2)

Christian faith was never understood as a passive acceptance of some body of information but as an active and ongoing appropriation of the good news of Jesus Christ. This faith in Christ was enabled by the power of the Holy Spirit, for, as Paul put it, "No one can say 'Jesus is Lord' except by the Holy Spirit" (1 Cor 12:3). It is this biblical tradition that informed much of the Second Vatican Council's teaching on the *sensus fidei.*

THE TEACHING OF VATICAN II

As we saw above, for St. Paul, Christian faith was enabled by the action of the Holy Spirit in the life of the believer and the believing community. One of the most significant new developments in the council's theological reflection on the church lay in the renewed attention it gave to pneumatology, the theology of the Holy Spirit. For much of the history of Western ecclesiology, the role of the Holy Spirit had been eclipsed by a tendency to think of the church almost exclusively in its relation to Christ: the church instituted by Christ, the church as the Body of Christ, the church as the Bride of Christ. The Holy Spirit received very little attention. This began to change in the decades prior to the council, particularly as Catholic theologians benefited from interaction with Eastern Orthodox theologians whose tradition gave much greater prominence to the work of the Spirit. At Vatican II we find a renewed sense that if Christ laid the foundations for the church, it is the Spirit who continues to animate the church, guiding it along its pilgrim journey.

The council recalled Scripture's testimony to the dynamic activity of the Holy Spirit in the life of the church. At Pentecost, the Holy Spirit both enabled the proclamation of the Gospel by the apostles and facilitated the surprising reception of that Gospel by those in Jerusalem.

Moreover, those who received the apostolic message heard it "in our own languages." The Spirit did not erase the cultural distinctiveness of the hearers of the Gospel, who came from places as diverse as "Mesopotamia, Judea and Cappadocia, Pontus and Asia, Phrygia and Pamphylia, Egypt and the parts of Libya belonging to Cyrene, and visitors from Rome" (Acts 2:8-10). Rather, it enabled each to hear the Gospel within their own cultural frame of reference, drawing these diverse cultural receptions of the Gospel into the spiritual communion of the church. Later in Acts we encounter the deliberations of the church of Jerusalem regarding how best to respond to Paul and Barnabas's mission to the Gentiles. Luke presents the Holy Spirit as the divine agency animating the community's deliberation, as he reports the final judgment of the Jerusalem church's leadership: "For it has seemed good to the Holy Spirit and to us to impose on you no further burden than these essentials" (Acts 15:28).

Although it was far from consistent, the council presented the Holy Spirit, along with Christ, as the "co-instituting principle" of the church, enabling the church's faithful reception of the Gospel and guiding it in its corporate discernment.[2] We see this renewed appreciation for the work of the Spirit in the life of the church in *Lumen Gentium*:

> The Spirit dwells in the church and in the hearts of the faithful, as in a temple, prays and bears witness in them that they are his adopted children. He guides the church in the way of all truth and, uniting it in fellowship and ministry, bestows upon it different hierarchic and charismatic gifts, and in this way directs it and adorns it with his fruits. By the power of the Gospel he rejuvenates the church, constantly renewing it and leading it to perfect union with its spouse. (LG 4)

By appealing to the Holy Spirit as the source of all gifts the council was able to reconcile what had often been opposed.

For almost four centuries Catholicism had rallied around the authority of church office (e.g., pope and bishops) while classical Protestantism stressed the indispensability of charisms given to each of the faithful. In LG 4 the council contended, however, that both church office and individual charism find a common source in the work of the Holy Spirit. And among the many charisms offered to believers, the council highlighted

---

[2] See Yves Congar, "The Church Made by the Spirit," in *I Believe in the Holy Spirit* (New York: Crossroad, 1997), 2:5–14.

the gift of a "supernatural instinct for the faith," a *sensus fidei*, offered by the Spirit at baptism.

The council first considered the role of the *sensus fidei* in the second chapter of *Lumen Gentium* on the church as the new people of God. In that chapter the council employed, as a framework for its reflections, the traditional attribution to Christ of the threefold office: "priest, prophet and king." It did not, however, limit its application to the clergy, as had been common prior to the council, but applied it to the whole people of God. Thus, the council taught that *all* the faithful participated in a common priesthood by virtue of their baptism, and all shared in the kingly office of Christ through their work to bring about God's kingdom. The council taught that the whole Christian faithful shared as well in the prophetic office.

> The holy people of God shares also in Christ's prophetic office: it spreads abroad a living witness to him, especially by a life of faith and love and by offering to God a sacrifice of praise, the fruit of lips confessing his name. The whole body of the faithful who have received an anointing which comes from the holy one cannot be mistaken in belief. It shows this characteristic through the entire people's supernatural sense of the faith [*sensus fidei*], when, "from the bishops to the last of the faithful" it manifests a universal consensus in matters of faith and morals. By this sense of the faith [*sensus fidei*], aroused and sustained by the Spirit of truth, the people of God, guided by the sacred magisterium which it faithfully obeys, receives not the word of human beings, but truly the word of God, "the faith once for all delivered to the saints." The people unfailingly adheres to this faith, penetrates it more deeply through right judgment, and applies it more fully in daily life. (LG 12)

According to the council, each believer, by virtue of baptism, has a supernatural instinct or sense of the faith (*sensus fidei*) that allows each to recognize God's Word and to respond to it. Yet the personal exercise of the *sensus fidei* is not a solitary one. The council also acknowledges a corporate exercise of this gift in its reference to the "whole body of the faithful who have received an anointing which comes from the holy one."

Unfortunately, the council did not develop this theme in any detail. Consequently, some clarifications regarding terminology might be helpful. According to Ormond Rush, we can think of this "sense of faith" first of all as a gift exercised by an individual believer, which we can identify as the *sensus fidei fidelis* (the sense of faith of the individual believer). But, recalling the testimony of the early church, faith is never the private action of a believer; it is always realized in the life of a community. There must also be a communal dimension to one's response to the Gospel in the life of faith. When we have in mind this communal response of the whole Christian faithful, we speak instead of the *sensus fidei fidelium* (the sense of faith of all the faithful).[3] In both instances we are talking about the gift itself as a capacity to receive God's Word. We can also think, however, of the *result* of that communal discernment and speak of *what it is* that, in fact, the faithful believe. In this context, we can speak simply of the "sense of the faithful" (*sensus fidelium*). This term denotes, then, *what* the whole people of God in fact believe. This is not always easy to determine, and there will be many instances when there is, at a given point in time, disagreement among the people. This is more likely to be the case when the church is considering new and emerging issues or older questions being considered in new contexts. Finally, when the faithful are united in their belief, manifesting a true consensus, we can then speak of a *consensus fidelium*. In those instances where there is a *consensus fidelium* ("when, 'from the bishops to the last of the faithful' it manifests a universal consensus in matters of faith and morals") the council taught that the belief of God's people was infallible (LG 12).

REFLECTIONS ON THE "SENSE OF FAITH" GIVEN TO ALL BELIEVERS

This sense or instinct for the faith, in both its individual and communal senses, can be understood in two ways.[4] First, it can refer to a *capacity* to grasp God's revelation. In this regard, we can think of the sense of faith as a kind of spiritual sense or sixth sense. It is this capacity that allows a believer and believing community, almost intuitively, to sense what is of God and what is not. Second, this sense of faith can also be thought of, not only as a capacity, but as an actual perception or imaginative grasp of divine revelation.

---

[3] Ormond Rush, *The Eyes of Faith: The Sense of the Faithful and the Church's Reception of Revelation* (Washington, DC: Catholic University of America Press, 2009), 5. See also International Theological Commission, "*Sensus Fidei* in the Life of the Church" (2014). This document can be accessed at: http://www.vatican.va/roman_curia/congregations/cfaith/cti_documents/rc_cti_20140610_sensus-fidei_en.html.

[4] Rush, *The Eyes of Faith*, 215–40.

Let us return to the analogy of a work of art employed in the last chapter. When we encounter a piece of art like a beautiful sculpture, it has an effect on us; we "receive" the art, encounter it, from our own particular perspective. Our own life story, our storehouse of life experiences, inclines us to understand the work of art in certain ways. The work of the artist is in a sense completed only in our viewing (or, regarding other artistic media, our hearing, touching, or reading) the work as we bring something of ourselves to the encounter with the work of art. So, returning to the sculpture of Christ the Good Shepherd discussed in the last chapter, viewers who might gather around to discuss their impressions of the sculpture will have a shared dimension to their experiences—they are viewing the same sculpture—but their interpretations of it will inevitably differ. For one viewer, the artist may have wonderfully captured childhood images nurtured through repeated stories of the shepherd who leaves the ninety-nine to seek out the one lost sheep. Yet other viewers will experience a shock in the viewing as they recognize something in the sculpture quite at odds with their childhood image. Perhaps the Good Shepherd looks younger or more playful than they had imagined. Perhaps his features seem more Middle Eastern than so many European portrayals of Christ. That experience of shock may work on the viewers at some deep level as their religious imaginations subtly reconfigure themselves around this startlingly new artistic work. Is it too bold to wonder whether the encounter with this sculpture could reshape their faith in Christ, a faith that exists at a level far deeper than that of doctrine, a faith that is enriched in one's imaginative construal of Jesus as Good Shepherd?

Christians encounter God's divine revelation in the context of particular communities of faith. It is within these distinctive communities that we hear the Scriptures preached to us, celebrate the liturgy, meditate before the crucifix. Again, it is the particularity of our lives that allows us to return to the church our culturally informed reception of the Gospel as something that can enrich the community. The council acknowledged this reality in *Dei Verbum*, when it insisted that believers contribute something to the faith consciousness of the church, not only through their passive acceptance of church doctrine but by offering to the church the fruit of their own spiritual experience (DV 8).

The insight and wisdom of ordinary believers often eludes propositional form, embedded as it generally is in the concrete life of Christian discipleship. Here the Christian faith is exhibited in its most basic form, not as academic theology or formal church doctrine, but as a faith sustained in a rich web of narratives, rituals, devotions, artistic productions, exemplary moral witness, and daily human interactions. There is an undeniably aesthetic dimension to the ordinary life of faith, immersed as it is in the sights, sounds, and smells of our daily existence. This is not a primitive or inchoate, predoctrinal stage of the Christian faith. This is the faith as it is customarily lived in the rich humus of daily life. It is constituted by simple prayers, devotional art, virtuous practices in the home, generous expressions of care and hospitality to our neighbor and the stranger, simple stories of faith we share with our children, religious customs of the community, the celebration of the sacraments, etc. Together these practices shape the way we imagine our God and construe the shape of Christian discipleship, but much of this eludes rational explication or recourse to formal church doctrine. And, frequently, this is where faith remains for many, perhaps most, believers who never feel the need to appeal in any formal way to the propositional articulation of the Christian faith.

One of the most important if oft-neglected implications of the council's teaching on the *sensus fidei* is that the lived faith must always have an existential priority in the Christian life since that lived faith is always richer and more compelling than its doctrinal articulation. None of this denies or diminishes the role of formal magisterial teaching authority. But throughout the church's history, formal doctrinal pronouncements have generally been issued in response to serious and enduring controversy regarding the substance of the Christian faith. It does not follow from the occasional need for such normative pronouncements, however, that doctrine represents the most profound expression of the faith. After all, few Christians are moved to heroic exercises of discipleship by simply reading the catechism. Yet, if "the sense of the faithful" (*sensus fidelium*) refers to this ordinary incarnation of the Gospel in the lives of believers, it is still the case that this ordinary faith witness has much to offer the pope and bishops in the exercise of their doctrinal teaching responsibilities.

THE RELATIONSHIP BETWEEN THE SENSE OF THE FAITHFUL AND THE MAGISTERIUM

We have already seen how, in the Dogmatic Constitution on Divine Revelation, the council credited the development of tradition itself to the contributions of the spiritual insights of the faithful.

> This [the growth of tradition] comes about through the contemplation and study of believers who ponder these things in their hearts. It comes from the intimate sense of spiritual realities which they experience. And it comes from the preaching of those who, on succeeding to the office of bishop, have received the sure charism of truth. (DV 8)

This passage proposes that the testimony of the faithful and the ministry of the bishops share in the traditioning process of the church. The council returns to this conviction in *Lumen Gentium* 35 where the bishops write:

> [Christ] fulfils this prophetic office, not only through the hierarchy who teach in his name and by his power but also through the laity. He accordingly both establishes them as witnesses and provides them with an appreciation of the faith (*sensus fidei*) and the grace of the word so that the power of the Gospel may shine out in daily family and social life.

Catholic doctrine teaches that the bishops alone possess doctrinal authority in the church and, by virtue of their apostolic office, are the authoritative guardians of the faith. But Catholic teaching also holds that the bishops, including the Bishop of Rome, do not teach "new revelation" but only what has been passed on. How, then, are we to understand the relationship between the whole people of God who encounter God's Word in their daily lives and the bishops who must *safeguard* that Word? We might consider an image first developed by Cardinal John Henry Newman in the nineteenth century: the *conspiratio fidelium et pastorum*, literally, the "breathing together of the faithful and the pastors."

Newman developed the theological significance of this image in his famous work *On Consulting the Faithful in Matters of Doctrine*.[5] In that essay he pointed out how there were key moments in the history of the church when it was the ordinary faithful who had preserved the integrity of the apostolic faith in their daily witness when many bishops were seduced by error. He was not negating the role of the bishops, but he was warning of the danger of teaching doctrine without drawing on the faith witness of ordinary believers. In our age, it is all too common to see the magisterium pitted against the faithful in a relationship of opposition and subordination. Newman's fine image, *conspiratio*, "breathing together," avoids this in two ways.

---

[5] John Henry Newman, *On Consulting the Faithful in Matters of Doctrine* (1859; reprint, Kansas City, MO: Sheed & Ward, 1961).

First, we must remember that the pastors are also part of the faithful. A common mistake in popular ecclesiology identifies "the faithful" with the laity. But as Vatican II taught, the faithful, the *fideles*, are the *whole* people of God, lay and clergy, so there can be no opposition. The bishop's role of leadership is situated *within* his common Christian identity as a *Christifidelis*, a "Christian faithful." In a sermon in which he reflected on his own office as bishop, St. Augustine said, "When I am frightened by what I am for you, then I am consoled by what I am with you. For you I am the bishop, with you I am a Christian. The first is an office, the second a grace; the first a danger, the second salvation."[6]

Second, Newman's use of the image of "breathing together" reminds us of the Holy Spirit who is the "holy breath" of God. "Breathing together" requires a shared rhythm, if you will, a rhythm established by the Spirit. Newman believed that the one apostolic faith given to the whole church was manifested in different forms in the life of the church. To discover this faith one must look to "the mind of the church."[7] Consequently, in some sense the whole church could be seen as teachers and learners. Newman broke with the tendency in Catholic thought, at least since the sixteenth century, to divide the church into two different groups, the teaching church (*ecclesia docens*) and the learning church (*ecclesia discens*). For Newman, the whole church participated in the handing on of the faith.

This sharing of the roles of teacher and learner was a manifestation of this *conspiratio*. It did not mean for Newman that the bishops abandoned their unique role as authoritative teachers. Rather, it meant that before they taught, along with their careful and prayerful study of Scripture and tradition, they might profitably inquire after the insights of the faithful as part of their preparation for teaching. The early church saw no contradiction in asserting that the bishop was both a teacher and a learner. Jean-Marie Tillard, noted ecclesiologist and ecumenist, wrote that the bishop is "entrusted with the task of *watching over* the way the gift of God is *received* and passed on from one group to the other, one generation to the other."[8] Thus the bishop becomes the minister responsible for serving the corporate "memory" of the church.

---

[6] St. Augustine, *Sermon* 340.1.

[7] Newman, *On Consulting the Faithful*, 163.

[8] J.-M.-R. Tillard, "Tradition, Reception," in *The Quadrilog: Tradition and the Future of Ecumenism*, Festschrift for George Tavard (Collegeville, MN: Liturgical Press, 1994), 328–43, at 336.

POPE FRANCIS AND THE
INTERNATIONAL THEOLOGICAL COMMISSION
ON CONSULTING THE FAITHFUL

More than any of his predecessors, Pope Francis has highlighted the significance of the council's teaching on the "sense of the faith." In his address celebrating the fiftieth anniversary of the Synod of Bishops he echoed the insights of Newman, reminding us that the council's teaching on the *sensus fidei* "prevents a separation between an *Ecclesia docens* and an *Ecclesia discens*, since the flock likewise has an instinctive ability to discern the new ways that the Lord is revealing to the Church."[9] This represents a major theme of his pontificate.

In *Evangelii Gaudium* he stressed its importance in a consideration of the shared responsibility of all the baptized for the work of evangelization:

> In all the baptized, from first to last, the sanctifying power of the Spirit is at work, impelling us to evangelization. The people of God is holy thanks to this anointing, which makes it infallible *in credendo*. This means that it does not err in faith, even though it may not find words to explain that faith. The Spirit guides it in truth and leads it to salvation. As part of his mysterious love for humanity, God furnishes the totality of the faithful with an instinct of faith—*sensus fidei*—which helps them to discern what is truly of God. The presence of the Spirit gives Christians a certain connaturality with divine realities, and a wisdom which enables them to grasp those realities intuitively, even when they lack the wherewithal to give them precise expression. (EG 119)

Francis's affirmation of this long-neglected conciliar teaching is certainly welcome, but even more so is the attention he has given to the concrete implementation of this teaching in structures and practices that allow the insight of God's people to contribute to the formulation of church teaching. In his speech on synodality he called for formal mechanisms for listening at every level of church life. Early in his pontificate, in his much-read interview with Antonio Spadaro, he had called for the recovery and reform of consultative, collegial structures:

---

[9] Pope Francis, "Address at Commemorative Ceremony for the 50th Anniversary of the Synod of Bishops" (October 17, 2015), accessed online at: http://w2.vatican .va/content/francesco/en/speeches/2015/october/documents/papa-francesco _20151017_50-anniversario-sinodo.html.

The consistories [of cardinals], the synods [of bishops] are, for example, important places to make real and active this consultation. We must, however, give them a less rigid form. I do not want token consultations, but real consultations. The consultation group of eight cardinals, this "outsider" advisory group, is not only my decision, but it is the result of the will of the cardinals, as it was expressed in the general congregations before the conclave. And I want to see that this is a real, not ceremonial consultation.[10]

This commitment was also evident in his instruction to Cardinal Baldiserri, then the secretary general of the synod of bishops, that formal efforts should be made to consult the faithful in preparation for the two synods on the family. He has called for this, yet again, regarding preparations for the synodal assembly on youth. Francis has directly challenged bishops to broaden their practice of consultation:

In his [the bishop's] mission of fostering a dynamic, open and missionary communion, he will have to encourage and develop the means of participation proposed in the Code of Canon Law and other forms of pastoral dialogue, out of a desire to listen to everyone and not simply to those who would tell him what he would like to hear. Yet the principal aim of these participatory processes should not be ecclesiastical organization but rather the missionary aspiration of reaching everyone. (EG 31)

What is particularly welcome in this passage is the recognition that consultation involves more than simply gathering together safe voices functioning as little more than an ecclesiastical echo chamber. Most bishops and pastors—for that matter, most university presidents, religious superiors, and department chairs—think that they are consultative just because they seek out the opinions of others. The pope rightly insists that authentic ecclesial consultation that aspires to be more than a pragmatic public relations maneuver, that aspires, that is, to be a genuine listening to the Spirit, must attend to a wide range of voices, including those who labor in something close to ecclesial exile.

Yet another promising development during the Francis pontificate has been the publication of an important study of the *sensus fidei*

---

[10] Antonio Spadaro, Interview with Pope Francis, "A Big Heart Open To God," *America* (September 30, 2013), accessed online at: https://www.americamagazine.org/faith/2013/09/30/big-heart-open-god-interview-pope-francis.

undertaken by the International Theological Commission.[11] Although the ITC is not technically an organ of the magisterium, it is presided over by the prefect of the Congregation for the Doctrine of the Faith and its scholarship was envisioned by Pope Paul VI, who first established it, as a resource for the work of the magisterium. That same commission had addressed the *sensus fidei* a few years earlier, when Benedict XVI was still pope.[12] While the earlier document made some worthwhile contributions, its treatment of the *sensus fidei* was more cautious and emphasized the overriding role of the magisterium.[13] The second document, published in the early years of Francis's papacy, although not without flaws, makes a more helpful contribution to our topic. The ITC listed three principal manifestations of the *sensus fidei fidelis*:

> 1) To discern whether or not a particular teaching or practice that they actually encounter in the Church is coherent with the true faith by which they live in the communion of the Church; 2) to distinguish in what is preached between the essential and the secondary; and 3) to determine and put into practice the witness to Jesus Christ that they should give in the particular historical and cultural context in which they live. (SF 60)

It also mentions the organic relationship between the sense of faith of the individual believer (*sensus fidei fidelis*) and the sense of faith of the entire people of God (*sensus fidei fidelium*). Both individual believers and the discernment of the whole Christian community actively contribute to the development of doctrine (SF 67). Gerard Mannion has highlighted as one of "the more refreshing parts of the document" its consideration of the ecumenical implications of church teaching on the

---

[11] International Theological Commission, "*Sensus Fidei* in the Life of the Church" (2014). References to the document will be made parenthetically as "SF" followed by the article number. This document can be accessed online at: http://www.vatican .va/roman_curia/congregations/cfaith/cti_documents/rc_cti_20140610_sensus -fidei_en.html.

[12] International Theological Commission, "Theology Today: Perspectives, Principles, and Criteria" (2012). This document may be accessed online at: http:// www.vatican.va/roman_curia/congregations/cfaith/cti_documents/rc_cti_doc _20111129_teologia-oggi_en.html.

[13] For a helpful comparison of the two documents, see Gerard Mannion, "*Sensus Fidelium* and the International Theological Commission: Has Anything Changed between 2012 and 2014?," in *Learning from all the Faithful: A Contemporary Theology of the* Sensus Fidei, ed. Bradford E. Hinze and Peter C. Phan (Eugene, OR: Pickwick Publications, 2016), 69–88.

sensus fidei.[14] Any listening to the people's sense of faith must extend to a sympathetic engagement with the wisdom, insights, and concerns of those of other Christian traditions (SF 86).

The ITC asserts the magisterium's distinctive responsibility for judging the sense of the faithful. Yet this text also emphasizes the fundamental obligation of the magisterium to listen to the *sensus fidelium.* Since it is not only the magisterium but the whole people of God who are responsible for the apostolic faith, the commission insisted that the magisterium have appropriate structures for consulting the faithful. The ITC's treatment of potential disagreement between the magisterium and the sense of the faithful brings with it a refreshing new admission that in such instances the problem is not always on the side of the faithful:

> There are occasions, however, when the reception of magisterial teaching by the faithful meets with difficulty and resistance, and appropriate action on both sides is required in such situations. The faithful must reflect on the teaching that has been given, making every effort to understand and accept it. Resistance, as a matter of principle, to the teaching of the magisterium is incompatible with the authentic *sensus fidei. The magisterium must likewise reflect on the teaching that has been given and consider whether it needs clarification or reformulation in order to communicate more effectively the essential message.* These mutual efforts in times of difficulty themselves express the communion that is essential to the life of the Church, and likewise a yearning for the grace of the Spirit who guides the Church "into all the truth" (John 16:13). (SF 80, emphasis is mine)

And what of the situation when the people fail to receive magisterial teaching? The commission held that such a failure to receive the teaching of the magisterium could be due to indifference, a lack of faith, or "an insufficiently critical embrace of contemporary culture." It also admitted, however, that "in some cases it [a failure to receive church teaching] may indicate that certain decisions have been taken by those in authority without due consideration of the experience and the *sensus fidei* of the faithful, or without sufficient consultation of the faithful by the magisterium" (SF 123).

The ITC touched on the proper relationship that must exist as well between the *sensus fidelium* and theologians, for they too must carefully

---

[14] Mannion, "*Sensus Fidelium,*" 78–79.

take into account the witness of the Christian faithful (SF 82). Finally, it highlighted the distinctive way in which the *sensus fidelium* emerged out of the contributions of popular religious practice. The practical wisdom of the people, the commission asserted, is often embedded in their popular devotions, pilgrimages, and processions (SF 107–12).

This emphasis on popular religiosity is also central to Pope Francis's own understanding of the sense of the faithful. As a priest and bishop in Argentina, he was himself greatly influenced by the *teología del pueblo,* "theology of the people," a distinctive form of liberation theology that focused on *religiosidad popular*, the popular religiosity of the people that often preserved the distinctive wisdom and insight of a profoundly inculturated form of the faith. As bishop, Francis once wrote: "*La religiosidad popular* is simply the way of being religious of believers who must express publicly, with sincere and simple spontaneity, their Christian faith, received from generation to generation, and which has formed the life and customs of the whole people."[15]

In the last few decades a number of theologians have challenged the way academic theology has in the past been inclined to dismiss popular religiosity as little more than superstition for the uneducated. Latino theologian Orlando Espín has explicitly connected the notion of the *sensus fidei* with popular religiosity.[16] Too often, Espín contends, we have thought of tradition as sustained exclusively by way of the decrees of ecumenical councils and papal statements. While this contribution

---

[15] Jorge Bergoglio, "Religiosidad popular como inculturación de la fe en el espíritu de Aparecida" ("Popular Religiosity as Inculturation of the Faith in the Spirit of Aparecida"), a pastoral statement promulgated in Argentina, January 19, 2008, following the close of the Fifth General Conference of the Episcopate of Latin America and the Caribbean in Aparecida, Brazil (May 13–31, 2007). Here I use the English translation of Cecilia González-Andrieu found in "Evangelization, Inculturation and Popular Religion," in *Go into the Streets: The Welcoming Church of Pope Francis*, ed. Thomas P. Rausch and Richard R. Gaillardetz (Mahwah, NJ: Paulist Press, 2016), 41–56, at 47.

[16] Orlando O. Espín, *The Faith of the People: Theological Reflections on Popular Catholicism* (Maryknoll, NY: Orbis Books, 1997); *Idol and Grace: On Traditioning and Subversive Hope* (Maryknoll, NY: Orbis Books, 2014). See also Roberto Goizueta, *Caminemos con Jesús: Toward a Hispanic/Latino Theology of Accompaniment* (Maryknoll, NY: Orbis Books, 1995). For a fine distillation and analysis of the contributions of Espín and other Latino/a theologians, see Edward Hahnenberg, "Learning to Discern the *Sensus Fidelium Latinamente*: A Dialogue with Orlando Espín," in *Learning from all the Faithful*, 255–71.

cannot be ignored, it must be augmented by an appreciation for the way in which the church's ecclesial memory is sustained and nurtured in "the living witness and faith of the Christian people."[17] For Espín, popular religious practice is as much a vital bearer of the living tradition of the church as a conciliar decree. Pope Francis would surely agree.

We should be grateful to the contributions, in particular, of Latino/a theologians who have emphasized the deeply inculturated lived faith of ordinary Christians as an expression of the sense of the faithful.[18] They have resisted the idea that only the clarity of logical propositional statements can do justice to the lived faith of the church. Their intention is not to deny the rational element of the life of faith that can benefit from clear doctrinal statements. They simply invite the church to an expanded sense of what counts as "the rational." For them, a properly Christian sense of the rational must be expanded to embrace ordinary human experience, an embodied knowledge that includes a more aesthetic consciousness shaped as much by music and artistic imagery as by logical discourse.

CONCLUSION: THE SENSE OF THE FAITHFUL IN A SYNODAL CHURCH

This chapter has followed four chapters in the previous section that were concerned with the role of the magisterium in the church. In this chapter we pivoted to consider the sense of the faithful. And yet, the legitimate and necessary role of the magisterium still looms large. It is all too easy to define the sense of the faithful primarily by way of its relationship to the magisterium. Of course, the relationship between these two ecclesial realities remains important, and it has justified our careful attention. But that relationship needs to be placed within a more comprehensive framework, that of a church that sees dialogue and discernment as foundational to its existence.

---

[17] Espín, *Faith of the People*, 65.

[18] See also the contribution of Natalia Imperatori-Lee, "Latina Lives, Latina Literature: A Narrative Camino in Search of the *Sensus Fidelium*," in *Learning from all the Faithful*, 272–80; "Unsettled Accounts: Latino/a Theology and the Church in the Third Millennium," in *A Church with Open Doors: Catholic Ecclesiology for the Third Millennium*, ed. Richard R. Gaillardetz and Edward P. Hahnenberg (Collegeville, MN: Liturgical Press, 2015), 45–63.

In his first encyclical, *Ecclesiam Suam*, Pope Paul VI shared a vision of a church constituted by dialogical practices.[19] For Pope Paul, the call to dialogue was grounded in the dialogue of salvation that God extends to humanity (ES 74), and "it must be conducted with all men of good will both inside and outside the Church" (ES 93). The pope presented this dialogue as transpiring within a series of concentric circles, starting from the outermost circle and moving in: dialogue with all humanity; dialogue with those belonging to other world religions; dialogue with other Christians; dialogue within the church.

The pope's encyclical, published while Vatican II was still in session, only reinforced the council's own commitment to the primacy of dialogue. Focusing on the necessary dialogue that must take place in the church, the council wrote:

> The church shows itself as a sign of that amity which renders possible sincere dialogue and strengthens it. Such a mission requires us first of all to create in the church itself mutual esteem, reverence and harmony, and to acknowledge all legitimate diversity; in this way all who constitute the one people of God will be able to engage in ever more fruitful dialogue, whether they are pastors or other members of the faithful. For the ties which unite the faithful together are stronger than those which separate them: let there be unity in what is necessary, freedom in what is doubtful, and charity in everything. (GS 92)

The council bishops were not naïve in their appeal to the practice of dialogue in the church. In a passage exhorting the lay faithful to take the initiative in bringing the Gospel to bear on the concerns of our world in the spheres of family, work, and politics, the bishops encouraged them to turn to the clergy for guidance, "but let them realize that their pastors will not always be so expert as to have a ready answer to every problem, even every grave problem, that arises; this is not the role of the clergy" (GS 43). This represented a remarkable shift away from the predominantly clerical church of the decades before the council.

The council recognized that the exercise of the *sensus fidei* concerning how best to apply the Gospel to the concrete circumstances of their daily lives would be messy and conflictual, with significant disagreements doubtless emerging:

---

[19] This encyclical can be accessed at the Vatican website: http://w2.vatican.va/content/paul-vi/en/encyclicals/documents/hf_p-vi_enc_06081964_ecclesiam.html.

Very often their christian vision will suggest a certain solution in some given situation. Yet it happens rather frequently, and legitimately so, that some of the faithful, with no less sincerity, will see the problem quite differently. Now if one or other of the proposed solutions is readily perceived by many to be closely connected with the message of the Gospel, they ought to remember that in those cases no one is permitted to identify the authority of the church exclusively with his or her own opinion. *Let them, then, try to guide each other by sincere dialogue in a spirit of mutual charity and with a genuine concern for the common good above all.* (GS 43, emphasis is mine)

Bradford Hinze contends that it is this conflictual dimension of Christian life that has been too little explored in a theology of the sense of the faithful. He argues that the exercise of the *sensus fidei* must expand beyond an active reception of the apostolic faith to embrace as well the laments, conflicts, and disappointments of the people of God.[20]

Pope Francis has given new impetus to the challenge of becoming a community of dialogue and discernment. Our first Latin American pope has called for the realization of a synodal church. In his speech commemorating the fiftieth anniversary of the Synod of Bishops that we quoted above, he quickly moved from explicit consideration of the institution of the Synod of Bishops to consider synodality as a more fundamental feature of the church itself:

A synodal Church is a Church which listens, which realizes that listening "is more than simply hearing." It is a mutual listening in which everyone has something to learn. The faithful people, the college of bishops, the Bishop of Rome: all listening to each other, and all listening to the Holy Spirit, the "Spirit of truth" (*Jn* 14:17), in order to know what he "says to the Churches" (*Rev* 2:7).[21]

Lest there be any doubt as to the significance he places on synodality, he goes on to claim that synodality must be "a constitutive element of the Church." This requires a thorough reimagination of the church itself:

In this Church, as in an inverted pyramid, the top is located beneath the base. Consequently, those who exercise authority are called "ministers,"

---

[20] Bradford Hinze, *Prophetic Obedience: Ecclesiology for a Dialogical Church* (Maryknoll, NY: Orbis Books, 2016).

[21] "Address at Commemorative Ceremony for the 50th Anniversary of the Synod of Bishops."

because, in the original meaning of the word, they are the least of all. It is in serving the people of God that each bishop becomes, for that portion of the flock entrusted to him, *vicarius Christi*, the vicar of that Jesus who at the Last Supper bent down to wash the feet of the Apostles (cf. Jn 13:1-15). And in a similar perspective, the Successor of Peter is nothing else if not the *servus servorum Dei*.[22]

According to Clemens Sedmak, Francis has made listening a fundamental "epistemic practice" in the church, by which he means a fundamental way of accessing the truth God wishes to share with us.[23]

Within a synodal church, much greater attention needs to be given to the witness of ordinary believers and the diverse cacophony of voices inhabiting our church. There is always a temptation to dampen that cacophony prematurely, in order to restore a safe and secure sense of ecclesial order. But this diversity of voices in the church must be embraced rather than feared. We must hold in a productive tension both the global and local perspectives on the church. Again, demonstrating his gift for evocative images, Pope Francis proposes:

> Here our model is not the sphere, which is no greater than its parts, where every point is equidistant from the centre, and there are no differences between them. Instead, it is the polyhedron, which reflects the convergence of all its parts, each of which preserves its distinctiveness. . . . Pastoral and political activity alike seek to gather in this polyhedron the best of each. There is a place for the poor and their culture, their aspirations and their potential. Even people who can be considered dubious on account of their errors have something to offer which must not be overlooked. It is the convergence of peoples who, within the universal order, maintain their own individuality; it is the sum total of persons within a society which pursues the common good, which truly has a place for everyone. (EG 235–36)

Pope Francis believes that this diversity of voices, including even those we might view as erroneous, is not something to be feared but welcomed.

As we submit to the demands of ever more patient ecclesial listening, we can discover, with those at Pentecost who had come from the four corners of the world, that amid this diversity, a unity of faith percolates

---

[22] Pope Francis, "Address at Commemorative Ceremony for the 50th Anniversary of the Synod of Bishops."

[23] Clemens Sedmak, *A Church of the Poor: Pope Francis and the Transformation of Orthodoxy* (Maryknoll, NY: Orbis Books, 2016).

just below the surface. Pope Francis's commitment to patient listening, his confidence in the evangelical power of the inculturated faith expressions of the poor, his refusal to use doctrine as a weapon with which to bludgeon one's opponents into submission, his call for humility in building a "culture of encounter"—in all these ways Francis's vision of a synodal church will demand nothing less than a conversion, both personal and ecclesial, from all Catholics.

In an authentically synodal church we must reject the temptation to play the hierarchy off against the laity or to appeal to "the sense of the faithful" as a mere counterposition to official church teaching. Within a truly synodal church, the distinctive authority of the pope and bishops will remain, and at times it will require that they act so as to preserve the integrity of the apostolic faith. But perhaps, following Pope Francis's lead, their ministry might also embrace a more facilitative role, inviting the people of God into a patient, communal listening. Perhaps they might, as Tillard put it, take up "the task of *watching over* the way the gift of God is *received* and passed on from one group to the other, one generation to the other."[24] This synodal church will be faithful to its truest identity when all the baptized—pope, bishops, priests, professed religious, and laity—acknowledge the wisdom of listening before speaking, learning before teaching, praying before pronouncing. In the humility of such a community, the good news of Jesus Christ will reverberate with an unimagined clarity and power before a world hungry for a word of hope and an offer of salvation.

DISPUTED QUESTIONS

(1) Some church commentators have pointed out that the spiritual sense of the faith given to each believer in baptism must be cultivated within the life of the church. One would assume, they suggest, that Catholic Christians who have cultivated their spiritual instincts through the faithful practice of their Catholic faith will exercise a more developed insight than "lapsed" Catholics. Consequently, some have criticized appeals to polling data on the grounds that such polls seldom distinguish between active, practicing Catholics and inactive Catholics. Recourse to polls may be helpful but they are not sufficient

[24] Tillard, "Tradition, Reception," 336.

for assessing the true sense of the faithful. Yet there are also dangers in offering a too strict definition of who constitutes "the faithful." In doing so one risks excluding the voices of persons who may currently feel marginalized within the church (the uneducated, persons of color, LGBT persons, etc.) and/or find themselves, for various reasons, living in "ecclesial exile."

(2) One of the most vexing issues with respect to the sense of the faithful is the problem of verification. There are many controversial matters in church doctrine and practice about which it would be impossible to say that there is a widespread agreement among the faithful. How does one distinguish between mere opinion shaped by the values of the broader culture and a genuine Spirit-led insight? How does one verify whether the *sensus fidelium* actually represents a *consensus fidelium*?

FOR FURTHER READING

Baggett, Jerome. *Sense of the Faithful: How American Catholics Live Their Faith*. New York: Oxford University Press, 2009.

Burkhard, John. "*Sensus Fidei*: Meaning, Role and Future of a Teaching of Vatican II." *Louvain Studies* 17 (1992): 18–34.

———. "*Sensus Fidei:* Theological Reflection Since Vatican II." *Heythrop Journal* 34 (1993): 41–59, 137–59.

Congar, Yves. "Reception as an Ecclesiological Reality." In *Election and Consensus in the Church* [*Concilium* 77], edited by Giuseppe Alberigo and Anton Weiler, 43–68. New York: Herder, 1972.

Curran, Charles, and Lisa Fullam, eds. *The* Sensus Fidelium *and Moral Theology*. New York: Paulist Press, 2017.

Espín, Orlando. *The Faith of the People: Theological Reflections on Popular Catholicism*. Maryknoll, NY: Orbis Books, 1997.

———. *Idol and Grace: On Traditioning and Subversive Hope*. Maryknoll, NY: Orbis Books, 2014.

Gaillardetz, Richard R. "The Reception of Doctrine: New Perspectives." In *Authority in the Roman Catholic Church*, edited by Bernard Hoose, 95–114. London: Ashgate, 2002.

Hinze, Bradford. *Prophetic Obedience: Ecclesiology for a Dialogical Church*. Maryknoll, NY: Orbis Books, 2016.

Hinze, Bradford E., and Peter C. Phan, eds. *Learning from all the Faithful: A Contemporary Theology of the Sensus Fidei.* Eugene, OR: Pickwick Publications, 2016.

Lakeland, Paul. *The Liberation of the Laity: In Search of an Accountable Church.* New York: Continuum, 2003.

Metz, Johann Baptist, and Edward Schillebeeckx, eds. *The Teaching Authority of the Believers* [*Concilium* 180]. Edinburgh: T & T Clark, 1985.

Rush, Ormond. *The Eyes of Faith: The Sense of the Faithful and the Church's Reception of Revelation.* Washington, DC: Catholic University of America Press, 2009.

Sedmak, Clemens. *A Church of the Poor: Pope Francis and the Transformation of Orthodoxy.* Maryknoll, NY: Orbis Books, 2016.

ELEVEN

IS THERE A PLACE
FOR DISAGREEMENT
IN THE CHURCH?

"Am I allowed to disagree with Catholic teaching and still be a Catholic in good standing?" Some version of that question has been posed to countless clergy and pastoral ministers time and time again. The answers, I fear, have been all over the proverbial map. The question deserves a careful response, one informed by the best wisdom of our tradition and a keen awareness of the distinctive character of religious belonging in our contemporary age.

Some will dismiss the question altogether, seeing it as reflective of a toxic "cafeteria Catholicism" born out of an individualistic and consumerist culture. Although this view rather oversimplifies matters, there can be no doubt that Catholic identity has become, in many ways, more tenuous in our world today. In the first half of the twentieth century, particularly for those Catholics raised in Catholic immigrant enclaves, the Catholic faith was mostly inherited from one generation to the next whole-cloth and then perhaps renegotiated in early adulthood. Today, it is far less likely that our youth will be raised in a home with the same caregivers present throughout their childhood, let alone caregivers who consistently practice the same faith and hand it on to their children. The principal consequence of this cultural shift, at least in the United States, is that religious identity is more likely to be acquired in a piecemeal fashion, often by way of the habits of consumption in which the consumer compares religious "products" and chooses to appropriate this religious practice, that religious belief, from among a veritable supermarket of religious options.[1] Consequently, our religious identities will appear more constructed than inherited, and our religious convictions are likely to be more malleable, more subject to change. This is reflected in recent studies that have mapped the much greater fluidity of religious identity in the United States today.[2] People are much more willing to shift from one religious affiliation to another. Beyond this we must also recognize the consequences of living in a much more global, pluralistic world in which we are more likely to come into regular contact with people of dramatically different faiths and belief systems, or with no religious beliefs at all. As Charles Taylor has reminded us, living in a "secular age" does not mean living in a world without belief; it means living in a world where religious belief is simply one option among many.[3] Add to this the fact that, in the eyes of many, the institution of the Catholic Church has a greatly diminished credibility, particularly for young adults.

Three watershed moments mark this growing crisis of institutional credibility: 1968, 1994, and 2002. The first year was marked by the promulgation of Pope Paul VI's encyclical *Humanae Vitae*, in which the pope reaffirmed the church's teaching that every marital sexual act must be open to bringing forth new life. This teaching precluded any use of artificial contraception. The teaching was not new; it had been, more or less, the official teaching of the church for some time. In the wake of the reformist impulse of Vatican II, however, and the fact that a commission established by the pope to study this question had issued a report calling for a certain relaxation of this teaching, many Catholics had expected at least some change in the teaching. Numerous episcopal conferences offered lukewarm receptions of the encyclical, often emphasizing the primacy of one's conscience. The pope's encyclical was simply rejected by many Catholics, giving an unprecedented visibility to those who considered themselves Catholic while disagreeing with a doctrine of the church.

---

[1] See Vincent J. Miller's now classic analysis of the impact of consumerism on religion, *Consuming Religion: Christian Faith and Practice in a Consumer Culture* (New York: Continuum, 2004).

[2] The literature on this demographic shift is voluminous. One could profitably begin with the studies produced by the Pew Research Center on Religion & Public Life. Their website can be accessed at: http://www.pewforum.org/.

[3] Charles Taylor, *A Secular Age* (Cambridge, MA: Belknap Press of Harvard University Press, 2007).

In the decades since the Second Vatican Council multiple expressions of Christian feminism began to emerge as women (and not a few men) chafed against the many strictures in church law and doctrine that limited the full participation of women in the life of the church. Feminist theologies flourished and further influenced many Catholics. Calls for the ordination of women, doubtless spurred by the acceptance of women for ordination in several other Christian traditions (Eastern Orthodoxy being the major exception), became more frequent. In 1976, the Congregation for the Doctrine of the Faith issued a declaration that reasserted the Catholic prohibition of the ordination of women. Yet this appeared only to fuel more theological and historical scholarship bent on refuting the principal arguments proposed by the CDF. Finally, in 1994 Pope St. John Paul II issued an apostolic letter, *Ordinatio Sacerdotalis*, that appeared to be much more definitive in its reassertion of church teaching. With larger numbers of Catholics in North America supporting the ordination of women, the teaching magisterium of the church experienced yet another challenge to its credibility.

The third moment was not concerned with church teaching but it nevertheless marked a devastating blow to the Catholic hierarchy's credibility, namely, the *Boston Globe*'s January 2002 series reporting widespread clerical sexual abuse of children and an even more disturbing pattern of ecclesiastical cover up. This issue had been simmering in the church with various regional reports and dire warnings going back to the 1980s. The *Globe* report, however, gave the crisis an unprecedented visibility. Tawdry tales of abuse and ecclesiastical coverup filled newspaper headlines. New reports of clerical abuse and instances of episcopal malfeasance proliferated through the country and globally, shocking Catholics and further undermining the credibility of church leadership.

This brief summary of our contemporary situation should not be read as an indictment of the Catholic Church's doctrinal teaching authority. Rather, my intention is to situate the seemingly straightforward question—"Can I disagree with Catholic teaching and still be Catholic?"—in its contemporary cultural and ecclesial context. This question has been posed with unprecedented frequency in the last five decades.

How one responds to the question depends a great deal on the stance of the one posing it. On the one hand, it is quite possible for such a question to be posed as little more than a means of identifying the minimum agreement with church teaching required for a Catholic to be "in good standing." This reflects a problematic bottom-line approach to Catholic identity. Catholic identity should never be reduced to a set of affirmations or beliefs that one must minimally "sign off on" in order to be a member. On the other hand, the question can reflect the honest struggles of a faithful Catholic wrestling with a teaching they find deeply troubling.

Consider the fictional case of two young adults who were recently received into the Catholic Church; we'll call them Michael and Marie. Eager to learn more about their newly acquired Catholic faith, they begin attending an adult education program taught by their pastor. In one of those sessions they both hear, for the first time, the Catholic Church's teaching that the use of *in vitro* fertilization to assist a married couple in conceiving a child was, according to Catholic teaching, always morally wrong. On learning this, Michael becomes furious and dismisses the teaching as "ridiculous." He tells the pastor that although he came to the Catholic faith out of a love, in particular, for its liturgy, its rich spiritual tradition, and its prophetic social teaching, this kind of silliness is exactly the kind of thing that almost prevented him from being received into the Catholic faith in the first place. For him this represents simply another example of the Catholic obsession with sex and reproduction. He dismisses the position out of hand and never gives it another thought. Marie was also dismayed to discover, so soon after her reception into the church, that she could not, at least initially, embrace this church teaching. She goes up to the pastor after the session and asks to meet with him to discuss the matter further. At their later meeting, he suggests that they both study a recent Vatican statement explaining the official church teaching. She goes home and does, in fact, read the Vatican statement. Much to her surprise, she finds herself in sympathy with some (but not all) of the arguments. She is particularly influenced by the concern that some reproductive technologies may unintentionally contribute to turning children into a commodity, a product ordered through a catalog of potential sperm and ovum donors. For her this is a valuable insight, but it doesn't fully persuade her that there could not be instances when such technologies might help a Catholic married couple fulfill the church's teaching about the importance of married couples generously welcoming children into their lives. She spends considerable time in prayer and reflection on the matter and finds that she still cannot fully accept the prohibition, at least in every case. She meets again with her pastor to share her concerns with him, and both agree to pray and discuss the matter further.

From the perspective that identifies "being a Catholic in good standing" with being able to give an unambiguous assent to every teaching of the church, one might be inclined to say that Marie ends up at the same place as Michael, who clearly rejected this teaching. Yet Michael did not appear in any way to have been troubled by his disagreement with official church teaching. Discovering that the teaching did not confirm his prior views, he simply dismissed the teaching. One has to wonder whether his facile dismissal reflects a deeper unwillingness to engage any church teaching that might challenge his preconceived views. One must also wonder whether that unwillingness will in the end prevent him from the kind of wrestling with troubling teachings that might be the occasion for real spiritual growth, regardless of the outcome. This unwillingness to wrestle with church teaching suggests a real risk that his Catholic identity will remain relatively superficial. Marie, by contrast, may not have found that she could fully embrace the church's teaching, but her determination to wrestle with the teaching anyway allowed her to arrive at a different spiritual place with both new perspectives and enduring concerns. She has been shaped by church teaching even where she has not fully embraced it.

If, as I have suggested throughout this volume, our response to God's revelation is a response of the whole person to be lived out in gratitude and a determination to engage in a way of living shaped by Gospel values, then the question of Catholic identity cannot be reduced to a simple binary of assent/dissent. Just as authentic church teaching is only discovered within the context of a rich Christian tradition that hands on and receives God's Word in many different forms and contexts, so too the true character of one's response to church teaching will be disclosed only in the daily life of Christian discipleship. It is there, in the ongoing struggle to remain faithful as followers of Jesus, that we give our most profound answer to God's invitation to saving communion.

Church doctrine will doubtless play a role in the formation of Catholic identity, but for the mature Catholic, it will be but one of many factors. For the Catholic life of faith will be formed as much or more by the distinctive practices that constitute our Christian way of life: the faithful celebration of the Eucharist; daily contemplation; fasting and feasting; almsgiving; visiting the sick; keeping the Sabbath; offering hospitality to immigrants, refugees, the homeless, and other strangers; speaking out against injustice. Our identity will also be shaped by the central narratives of the Christian faith: the biblical stories of those who first gave witness to the God of Love and the inspiring testimony of great saints who have not just taught but demonstrated with their lives what identifying oneself as a disciple of Christ might mean. It will be shaped as well by the stories of ordinary Christian heroism lived out in homes, workplaces, and political arenas. Only once we have considered a much thicker account of the life of Christian discipleship can we consider an adequate answer to the question "Can I disagree with church teaching and remain a Catholic in good standing?"

But consider it we must, if only because our generation has seen an unprecedented expansion of the exercise of the magisterium. The fifty-plus years since the council have witnessed an unprecedented proliferation of catechisms, directories, encyclicals, episcopal letters, and curial instructions. "Church teaching" no longer means simply the creed; it has expanded to include questions on the morality of *in vitro* fertilization, capital punishment, federal funding for abortions, and the willful destruction of our planet, as well as such things as the approved recipes for eucharistic bread. Catholics today require considerable guidance if they are to discern the appropriate response due to such a wide range of church pronouncements.

DISCERNING THE APPROPRIATE RESPONSE TO CHURCH TEACHING

In chapter 9 we considered four basic gradations in the authority of church teaching. It follows that, if the centrality and authoritative status of church teaching differs, the response of believers to these various teachings will also differ.

The Appropriate Response to Church Dogma

Catholicism holds that dogmas are the most authoritative of church teachings for the simple reason that they mediate divine revelation, the substance of God's saving offer to humankind. Since dogmas mediate God's revelation to humankind, the appropriate response of a believer to church dogma is what Vatican II called an "assent of faith" (LG 25), for faith is our most basic response to the revelation of God's love to us.

So how do we address the situation in which a Catholic finds they are unable to offer an assent of faith to a particular dogmatic teaching? Roman Catholicism has traditionally held that, due to the central role that dogma plays in communicating God's saving Word, membership in the church of Jesus Christ would be called into question by the obstinate and public denial of dogma. This kind of formal rejection is called "heresy." Formal heresy, however, is quite rare. The actual stance of most Roman Catholics to certain dogmatic teachings will often fall somewhere between explicit affirmation and explicit rejection.

Most of the church's central dogmatic teachings are found in the creeds or are concerned with the liturgical and sacramental life of the church. Beyond these central teachings, a student of the history of dogma might offer other dogmatic pronouncements defined by popes or councils to deal with important historical threats to the integrity of the church's faith. At one point in history these dogmatic statements may have been vital to the church's life, yet many have now faded from view, not because they are not true but rather because they were addressing questions that nobody is asking today and within philosophical and cultural frameworks that few employ today.

Many Catholic Christians, secure in their fundamental profession of faith in Jesus Christ and with a firm hope of salvation, will never find reason to consider many teachings that have dogmatic status. There is a difference between what Karl Rahner called "the inner knowledge" of the Christian faith and an explicit grasp of particular dogmatic teachings.[4] Questions regarding the existence of angels, the belief in purgatory, the question of whether Christ has one or two wills—these matters may never trouble a good many believers, nor need they. To say that they have given these teachings an explicit assent of faith would be misleading, as would the claim that they were rejecting them simply because their faith life has not demanded that they take them up at all. Although we should never diminish the value of being a well-catechized believer, the fact remains that there are and always have been countless believers with little grasp of church doctrine who still possess a deep religious faith. In this situation, the stance of the believer can hardly be characterized as obstinate and public rejection.

We must also point out that within the life of faith there must be ample room for doubt and struggle. A person who suffers the tragic loss of a child and struggles to retain their faith in a gracious and providential God is not a heretic; she is simply a human. A person who has intellectual questions regarding the immaculate conception, presuming they remain open to new insight in the midst of their struggle, does not commit heresy. Many a spiritual writer has reminded us that the opposite of faith is not doubt: it is certitude. Pope Francis himself once observed: "If one has the answers to all the questions—that is the proof that God is not with him. It means that he is a false prophet using religion for

---

[4] Karl Rahner, "The Faith of the Christian and the Doctrine of the Church," in *Theological Investigations*, vol. 14 (London: Darton, Longman & Todd, 1976), 24–46.

himself. The great leaders of the people of God, like Moses, have always left room for doubt."[5]

Given all of these necessary qualifications, we need to acknowledge that while a Catholic may never formally give a specific assent of faith to any number of dogmatic teachings, once they have engaged them, those teachings still lay a particular claim on the faith of church members. Explicit rejection of a dogma of the Catholic Church would not place one outside the sphere of God's saving grace, but, at some point, such a denial might place one outside the Roman Catholic communion.

The Appropriate Response to Definitive Doctrine

The second category of church teaching that we have considered, definitive doctrine, includes teachings that do not themselves mediate divine revelation but are necessary to safeguard and expound revelation. Since definitive doctrine does not mediate divine revelation, there can be no question of a response of faith. Official church documents teach that the believer is bound to "firmly accept and hold as true" those teachings proposed as definitive doctrines. I find no evidence in tradition that the denial of definitive doctrine has ever been viewed as heresy in the modern sense of the word. Consequently, the rejection of a definitive doctrine would not seem to demand the same consequences as the denial of a dogma of the church. Provided that one's rejection were well informed and in keeping with a firm desire to be united with the faith of the church, the withholding of an internal assent from such a teaching, although potentially a serious error against the teaching of the church, would not necessarily place one outside the Roman Catholic communion.

The Appropriate Response to Authoritative Doctrine

Many of the church's teachings, particularly regarding the moral life, fall into the third category of church teaching, which we have called simply authoritative doctrine. Making sense of the appropriate response to these teachings is complicated by the fact that, in the case of authoritative doctrine, there is an implicit admission of the possibility of error, however remote. The response of believers to such teaching may have to take that possibility into account. According to Vatican II, Catholics are expected to give "a religious docility [*obsequium*] of the will and intellect" (LG 25) to the many teachings that fall in the third category

---

[5] Pope Francis, "A Big Heart Open to God," *America* (September 30, 2013), available at http://americamagazine.org/pope-interview.

of authoritative doctrine. The precise meaning of this phrase has been a matter of great debate. The key Latin word, *obsequium*, is variously translated as "obedience," "submission," "docility," "due respect," or "assent." In truth, the Latin term can embrace all of these different senses. Although there are sharp disagreements on this question, I would propose that the appropriate response to authoritative doctrine requires the believer to make a genuine effort to assimilate the given teaching into his or her personal religious convictions. In so doing, the believer is attempting to give an "internal assent" to the teaching. In the vast majority of cases, a believer will do so naturally and without any difficulty. Most Catholic Christians readily assent to church teaching even where infallibility is not invoked. In most cases, they do not go through any explicit process of analyzing the arguments underlying a particular teaching. They accept the teaching because they sense its intuitive "rightness" or because they trust in the general authority of the magisterium that has authoritatively proposed it. Sometimes, however, this ready acceptance of authoritative doctrine does not happen. On occasion, a believer may face a particular teaching that, at least at first glance, seems problematic. This was the situation of Michael and Marie that we discussed above. Now what happens? In the language of Vatican II, what does "religious docility" demand in such a situation? I would propose three things.[6]

First, if I possess a religiously docile attitude to a problematic teaching I will be willing to engage in further study of the issue. Perhaps my questions are the consequence of poor or inadequate catechesis and can easily be resolved with further study. Second, if the teaching in question regards matters of morality (e.g., cohabitation before marriage, the church's condemnation of capital punishment, recourse to artificial contraception) I ought to engage in an examination of conscience. This means asking myself some difficult questions regarding the nature of the difficulties I am having with a given teaching. Am I struggling with this teaching because I cannot discover in it the will of God, or is it because this teaching, if true, would demand some real conversion from me? Perhaps some basic aspect of my present lifestyle, or certain political convictions, would have to change. Third, I must consider whether my difficulties lie not with a particular teaching but with a general rejection

[6] In what follows I am adapting Francis Sullivan's helpful treatment of the dynamics of internal assent in *Magisterium: Teaching Authority in the Church* (New York: Paulist Press, 1983), 162–66.

of the very idea of a formal doctrinal teaching authority. To be a faithful Catholic is to accept the basic legitimacy of the church's magisterium, even if one may have some objections about how that office is structured and/or exercised in practice.

This is a fairly demanding regimen, as it ought to be if I am going to take issue with accepted church teaching. If I have had difficulties with a particular teaching and I have fulfilled these three steps and still cannot give an internal assent to that teaching, however, I have done all the church authorities can fairly ask of me, and my inability to give an internal assent to this teaching should not in any way separate me from the Roman Catholic communion.

The Appropriate Response to Concrete Applications of Church Teaching, Prudential Admonitions, and Church Discipline

Finally, the particular response that a believer owes to concrete applications of church teaching, prudential admonitions, and church discipline could vary considerably. The American bishops recognized that, at the level of concrete applications of church teaching, it was possible for a Catholic to disagree with such applications in good conscience. Although the opinion of the bishops on such matters must be taken seriously, a Catholic does not have to agree, for example, with the bishops' specific policy proposals for improving the plight of the poor or with Pope Francis's specific policy proposals for how best to respond to global climate change. The Catholic *does* have to accept the church's teaching that every baptized Christian bears responsibility for the welfare of the poor and every Catholic does need to accept what Pope Francis has taught about our fundamental obligation to care for "our common home."

When matters turn to church discipline, usually enshrined in both the universal and particular laws of the church, we are called to accept the discipline of the church as the here-and-now way in which our community of faith seeks to organize its concrete life. One can do so even while questioning some of these disciplinary practices. To take an example from the civil order, I can think the speed limit for the streets in my neighborhood is too low but still obey the law. In the life of the church, I can disagree with the laws of fasting and abstinence or the determination of the number of holy days of obligation established in my country and still obey them for the sake of preserving the unity of the church.

There are times, however, when matters are not quite so simple. First, we can never follow a law when doing so would lead us to sin. Second, we must remember that church law does not exist for its own sake. Sometimes one is called to exercise the virtue of *epikeia*, that virtue that seeks what might be called "the spirit of the law." The practice of *epikeia* suggests that a law need not be obeyed if "its observance would be detrimental to the common good or the good of individuals."[7] It is worth remembering that church law exists to maintain church order, assist individual members in the call to holiness, and further the mission of the church. When the application of the law in a given instance does not demonstrably further these goals, it may yield to alternative actions that do further these goals.

To conclude this section, it may be helpful to line up the various responses demanded toward church teaching in the following chart:

LEVELS OF CHURCH TEACHING	RESPONSE OF THE BELIEVER
Dogma	Assent of Faith [The believer makes an act of faith, trusting that this teaching is revealed by God]
Definitive Doctrine	Firm Acceptance [The believer "accepts and holds" these teachings to be true]
Authoritative Doctrine	A Religious Docility of Will and Intellect [The believer strives to assimilate a teaching of the church into their religious stance while recognizing the remote possibility of church error]
Provisional Applications of Church Doctrine, Church Discipline, and Prudential Admonitions	Conscientious Obedience [The believer obeys (the spirit of) any church law or disciplinary action that does not lead to sin, even when questioning the ultimate value or wisdom of the law or action]

[7] *HarperCollins Encyclopedia of Catholicism* (San Francisco: HarperCollins, 1995), s.v. "epikeia."

Our faith in Jesus Christ is always greater than the sum total of the individual propositions and teachings to which we can give an assent. It is natural that our individual convictions will vary in the intensity of our commitment. We stake our life on the fundamentals of our faith, on our belief in God's saving love for us, a love that was incarnate in Jesus of Nazareth. At the same time, we acknowledge that as Christians we may be called on—in humble reliance on the guidance of the Spirit— to stake out formal positions on the implications of the Gospel and the life of discipleship about which we cannot be absolutely certain. To remain silent might be an abdication of our responsibility to explore the specific demands of discipleship. To ignore the provisionality of some of these church positions, to act as if every formal teaching of the church is equally central and lays the same claim on believers, is to be guilty of ecclesiastical hubris, a presumption to a kind of answer-book view of the church's doctrinal teaching authority. This viewpoint is far removed from the approach of Vatican II, which admitted that the church "did not have a ready answer" to every question posed today (GS 33).

Up to this point we have considered the obligations of ordinary believers to respond appropriately to formal church teaching. But the issue becomes a bit more complicated for those who are called to public leadership and ministry in the church. Surely they are not exempt from any of the struggles and demands for discernment that we have discussed above. The questions remain, however: In what way do their own personal struggles impact their pastoral ministry? What are their responsibilities to those to whom they minister, when people may pose to them the question with which we began this chapter, "Can I disagree with church teaching and still remain a Catholic in good standing?"

THE RESPONSIBILITIES OF THE PASTORAL MINISTER IN ASSISTING THOSE WHO STRUGGLE WITH CHURCH TEACHING

Pastoral ministers are often put in very difficult situations as they try to respond to individual Catholics who struggle with one or another of the church's teachings. As *public* ministers, they must be conscious of their responsibility to present faithfully the teaching of the church. Although every pastoral minister ought to be doctrinally and theologically well formed, their role is not identical with that of the professional theologian whose work is often more speculative and exploratory in its methodology and tentative in its conclusions. As *pastoral* ministers, however, they also need to honor the real struggles of those to whom they minister. They know well that they are often ministering to adults with a deep and rich life of faith, many of whom are highly educated and accustomed to forming their own views—views that they expect to be taken seriously. In order to help pastoral ministers navigate this minefield successfully, I propose three basic responsibilities incumbent on every pastoral minister in the presentation of church teaching.

The Responsibility to Present the Official Teaching of the Catholic Church Comprehensively and Sympathetically

Every pastoral minister, ordained or lay, has the responsibility to present the official teaching of the Roman Catholic Church. This should be so obvious as to require no further comment. Nevertheless, there may be some misunderstanding regarding what this responsibility actually entails. No church minister has the authority to offer an expurgated version of the Catholic faith. There is often the temptation to ignore those church teachings that may present difficulties, either for the minister or for those whom the minister is addressing. This temptation is understandable. There are many faithful church ministers who will not be equally comfortable with every teaching of the Catholic faith. In this situation, there is a tendency to avoid the topic altogether for fear of being in the position of questioning church teaching in public, defending church teaching without conviction, or presenting church teaching in a superficial or haphazard fashion. I once had a conversation with a priest ordained over thirty years who said, with pride, that he had never publicly addressed the issue of artificial contraception in his priestly ministry. It was obvious from his comments that he had serious difficulties with current Catholic teaching on this issue. He is certainly not alone. But is there not a latent paternalism here that assumes the minister knows better than the one being ministered to which official positions of the church merit serious consideration and which do not? The minister must remember that not everyone will share his or her personal difficulties and that everyone has a right to a clear, comprehensive, and sympathetic presentation of church teaching. For any minister to edit the church's teaching because of personal difficulties is to let their own judgment replace that of those they are teaching. To be clear, there is another form of paternalism that goes in the opposite direction by demanding unwavering and unthinking obedience to that teaching. Every adult Catholic deserves to have the teaching presented to them *as adults*, that is, in a manner that honors their own responsibility to wrestle with the teaching of the church. The minister cannot do that wrestling for them.

Besides this latent paternalism, there are other factors that contribute to a selective presentation of the Catholic faith. One factor is the poor theological formation of some church ministers, including many clergy. Too often a minister will struggle with an official teaching of the church because of inadequate theological formation. Teachings on Mary, eschatology, original sin, eucharistic real presence, sexual morality, etc., are often ignored because the minister finds popular/traditional treatments of the subject less than persuasive. Proper theological formation and ongoing education for ministry is absolutely essential for the minister to be able to present adequately the church teaching in language and concepts intelligible to the modern Catholic.

The responsibility to present the church doctrine *comprehensively* risks being misunderstood if it is conceived as simply going through a checklist of doctrinal propositions. Rote memorization and repetition of formal doctrinal propositions is not catechesis. Formal dogmas and doctrines are summary statements, bottom-line summations of a rich theological tradition. The church's ministers require formal theological training precisely so that they can go beyond the mere repetition of doctrinal propositions. For example, contemporary models of catechesis in the catechumenate rightly begin, not with doctrinal propositions, but with the liturgy, liturgical calendar, creeds, and Lectionary. This leads us to the second responsibility of the public minister.

The Responsibility to Make Explicit, When Appropriate, the Binding Character of a Particular Teaching

In chapter 9 and again in this chapter we have highlighted an elementary gradation in the authoritative character of church doctrine. Similar distinctions (once referred to as "theological notes") have long been part of the Catholic theological tradition. Unfortunately, these distinctions were often considered of mere academic value, of use only to clergy and theologians. Even today one can find voices in the church who insist that the ordinary Christian faithful need not be informed of the authoritative status of a teaching, largely for fear of encouraging a "cafeteria Catholicism" where Catholics feel free to reject any doctrine that has not been proposed infallibly. Too often in contemporary preaching and catechesis there is scant consideration of the important gradations of authoritative church teaching. Here we encounter yet another form of ecclesiastical paternalism. These distinctions have developed within the Catholic tradition for a reason: not everything taught authoritatively by the magisterium is divinely revealed. Consequently, with regard to the church's authoritative but nondefined teaching, there is at least a remote possibility of error. One can imagine pastoral situations in which it would be appropriate to inform an individual struggling with a given teaching of the relatively binding status of the teaching at issue.

How does the minister determine the authoritative status of a church teaching? This responsibility has traditionally been given to the community of theologians. Sometimes the theologian can assess the form in which a teaching had been proposed (for example, solemn definitions might introduce a dogmatic statement with "I/we solemnly define and declare"), the authoritative status of the document within which a teaching was proposed (e.g., a constitution, encyclical, apostolic letter), the historical context out of which the teaching emerged, the frequency with which it had been taught, and how the document grounds its teaching in Scripture and relates it to revealed truth.[8] The theologians would then offer their judgment regarding the authoritative status of that teaching, and that judgment would be included in theological manuals and catechisms. This tradition of assigning a particular "note" to a teaching has fallen into disuse. The lack of any alternative system creates special difficulties for the public minister. One can only hope that in the future official catechetical materials will draw on the careful study of theologians and do a better job of explicitly stating the authoritative status of a given teaching.

The Responsibility to Offer Pastoral Guidance to Those Who Struggle with Church Teaching

When accompanying someone struggling with a difficult teaching the pastoral minister will often take on a role not unlike that of a spiritual director. The task of the good spiritual director is to help the directee recognize the signposts on his or her particular journey of faith:

---

[8] Francis A. Sullivan, *Creative Fidelity: Weighing and Interpreting Documents of the Magisterium* (New York: Paulist Press, 1996), 109–10.

it is not to chart a spiritual path for him or her. When individuals come to a public minister of the church with questions or difficulties regarding a church teaching, it is the task of the minister to guide them in the process of arriving at internal assent. This guidance would certainly include a fair presentation of the official teaching of the church, including the theological arguments that have been proposed in support of this teaching. It may also be helpful to acknowledge opposing arguments while stressing that these arguments do not possess the same official or authoritative character. Second, the minister must clarify the authoritative status of the particular teaching. Are we dealing with a central dogma of the faith (e.g., the bodily resurrection of Jesus) or with a particular teaching of the church that, while authoritative, would have a significantly different status (e.g., the church's position on tubal ligation when a woman is medically unable to bring a pregnancy to term)? Obviously, difficulties regarding the first example would be much more significant than those related to the second. Third, the minister can invite the individual to an examination of conscience in order to ascertain whether the difficulties lie in a fear of the conversion that assent to a particular teaching (particularly in the area of morality) might demand. Finally, the minister can ask the individual to assess his or her attitude toward the authority of the ecclesiastical magisterium. In our society, particularly in this country, it is easy to fall prey to an attitude that sees any exercise of church authority as archaic or out of step with the times.

Having completed this process, the minister has fulfilled his or her responsibility to assist the individual in the proper formation and examination of conscience. The decision to give or withhold assent is placed where it rightly belongs, with the person who has the difficulties with the given teaching. In daily Christian living each believer must engage his or her conscience in concrete decisions for which he or she alone will be responsible before God. Of course, he or she must also take responsibility to see that the conscience is properly formed. In the Declaration on Religious Liberty, *Dignitatis Humanae*, Vatican II taught that, in the formation of conscience, the Christian faithful "*must pay careful attention* to the holy and certain teaching of the church" (DH 14). At the time this text was being debated, a number of bishops proposed an amendment in which the phrase "must pay careful attention to" would be replaced by "ought to form their consciences according to." The theological commission responded that "the proposed formula seems excessively restrictive. The obligation binding upon the faithful is sufficiently expressed in the text as it stands."[9] The public minister must be mindful of the fact that he or she is presenting church teaching to responsible moral agents who alone will have to give or not give an assent to a particular teaching and engage their consciences on that basis.

It is possible that those with whom the minister is dealing will not want to assume their proper responsibility. On the one hand, they may want the minister to give them permission to reject a certain teaching. But this "permission" is not the minister's to give. On the other hand, neither is it the place of the minister to pronounce judgment on the ultimate spiritual consequences of a failure to arrive at internal assent (e.g., "if you do not agree with church doctrine on this matter you stand in peril of your salvation"). No minister of the church, from the pope to the parish catechist, is empowered either *to command* assent to church teaching or *to dispense* from that assent, and no minister is empowered to pass formal judgment on the ultimate spiritual consequences of a particular stance toward church teaching.

Finally, the permissibility of withholding assent as a matter of conscience, in these carefully defined circumstances, must not be viewed by the minister as a mere act of condescension to human weakness and error. Because the magisterium itself grants the possibility of error in the proclamation of authoritative doctrine, the difficulties raised by believers may positively assist the church in recognizing its error and moving forward in pursuit of the "plenitude of truth."

In the end, the ultimate responsibility of the public minister as a teacher within the Catholic Church is to proclaim the Gospel of Jesus Christ as it finds expression in the Roman Catholic tradition. The minister proclaims church teaching comprehensively, sympathetically, and in a pastorally sensitive manner. At the same time the minister must always remember that responsibility for responding to that teaching lies with another. Every minister prays that he or she might be an instrument of the Holy Spirit. But that same Spirit works through those who seek to make the teaching of the church their own, and *their* struggles, their often courageous attempts to wrestle with the demands of church teaching, also constitute a valuable contribution to the life of the church.

---

[9] *Acta Synodalia*, IV/6, 769.

DISPUTED QUESTIONS

(1) The category of definitive doctrine is a new one in the current taxonomy of church teaching. Many questions remain, not only regarding the scope of this category of church teaching, but also regarding the consequences for not giving such teachings an internal assent. This remains an open question. In a commentary on the Profession of Faith, then-Cardinal Ratzinger and Archbishop Bertone claimed that those who fail to give an internal assent to a definitive doctrine are not "in full communion." The language employed is ambiguous at best. For example, it is not clear whether those who do not give an internal assent to these teachings would be excluded from the sacraments.

(2) In this chapter we have generally discussed the situation in which a believer cannot give an internal assent to a particular teaching. One sometimes comes across the language of "dissent" to describe this situation. I generally prefer to reserve the term "dissent" for public statements of disagreement with church teaching. The processes for arriving at or withholding an internal assent to a given teaching are central to the life of discipleship and often cannot be avoided. When one dissents from a teaching one is making one's disagreement public. Current ecclesiastical documents tend to give more leeway to the possibility of privately withholding assent than they do to the legitimacy of public dissent.

In the pontificates of John Paul II and Benedict XVI church officials emphasized that public dissent was always inappropriate. Pope Francis has generally avoided the question of dissent. Many theologians would argue that the legitimacy of public dissent depends in large part on the underlying motive. If the dissent is motivated by a desire simply to discredit the magisterium, then such actions would not be in keeping with authentic church membership. If, however, such public dissent is engaged in with proper respect for church tradition and the magisterium, it is conceivable that such public action might become an instrument of the Spirit in effecting necessary reform and renewal in the church, particularly as regards church teaching. The question of dissent among theologians will be handled in the next chapter.

FOR FURTHER READING

Congregation for the Doctrine of the Faith. "Profession of Faith and Oath of Fidelity." *Origins* 18 (March 16, 1989): 661, 663.

Curran, Charles E., and Richard A. McCormick, eds. *Readings in Moral Theology*. Vol. 6: *Dissent in the Church*. New York: Paulist Press, 1988.

Dulles, Cardinal Avery. *Magisterium: Teacher and Guardian of the Faith*. Naples, FL: Ave Maria Press, 2007.

Gaillardetz, Richard R. Chapter 5 in *Teaching with Authority: A Theology of the Magisterium in the Church*, 255–73. Collegeville, MN: Liturgical Press, 1997.

Ratzinger, Cardinal Joseph, and Archbishop Tarcisio Bertone. "Commentary on Profession of Faith's Concluding Paragraphs." *Origins* 28 (July 16, 1998): 116–19.

Sullivan, Francis A. *Creative Fidelity: Weighing and Interpreting Documents of the Magisterium*. New York: Paulist Press, 1996.

———. *Magisterium: Teaching Office in the Catholic Church*. New York: Paulist Press, 1983.

TWELVE

WHAT IS THE PROPER RELATIONSHIP BETWEEN THE MAGISTERIUM, THEOLOGIANS, AND THE SENSE OF THE FAITHFUL?

The popular view of the relationship between the magisterium and theologians has not been positive in the decades since Vatican II. Particularly during the pontificates of John Paul II and Benedict XVI, one read regularly in newspapers and on blogs of "dissenting" theologians and doctrinal "witch hunts" conducted by church officials. The overall sense communicated to the public was of a relationship characterized by suspicion and animosity. Yet this perception did not take into account the many bishops who held theologians in high regard and consulted them regularly. It did not consider the many theologians who assisted the various committees and subcommittees of the bishops' conference or served as delegates on the many ecumenical dialogues sponsored by a bishops' conference or the Vatican. The public was generally not aware of the serious attempts of the various professional societies in theology, canon law, and biblical studies to work collaboratively with the bishops on projects of mutual concern. These things do not appear in the modern media largely because they are not provocative. Nevertheless, one must admit that in the decades since the council the church has struggled to arrive at an adequate theological framework for considering the proper relationship between the magisterium, theologians, and the faith of the entire people of God. Here again, as with so many other topics, the church is still struggling to realize the full implications of the teaching of Vatican II. To better appreciate the challenges that remain, it might be good to consider the dominant conception of the magisterium–theologian relationship on the eve of the council.

THE PRECONCILIAR VIEW OF THE MAGISTERIUM–THEOLOGIAN–SENSE OF THE FAITHFUL RELATIONSHIP

Before the Second Vatican Council many ecclesiastical documents viewed theology as an auxiliary service to the magisterium. In this view, St. Peter and the apostles were sent forth by Christ with a unique teaching mission and were promised the assistance of the Holy Spirit. The pope and bishops were the unique successors to this teaching mission and also shared in the assistance of the Holy Spirit such that they, and they alone, were the authoritative teachers of the church. Theologians might have an official teaching role, but only by way of a kind of deputation from the magisterium that prohibited the theologian from ever departing from church teaching. The pope and bishops belonged to the teaching church, and everyone else, including theologians, belonged to the learning church. This view of teaching authority fit well with the strictly propositional view of revelation dominant in the decades prior to the council. Divine revelation was construed as a set of fixed propositional truths that quantitatively comprised the deposit of faith. The pope and bishops were the sole custodians and authoritative transmitters of that deposit.

Within this framework, the role of theologians was often reduced to explicating the meaning of these propositional truths. Their scholarship was required and valued, but largely as a way of defending church teaching. They were expected to submit their work to the authoritative scrutiny and potential censorship of the magisterium. Dissent, understood as the rejection or even questioning of any authoritative teaching of the magisterium, was viewed with suspicion as a negative attack on the authority of the magisterium itself. Of course, this was not absolute. The dogmatic manuals popular before the council acknowledged the legitimacy of limited speculative discussion that was critical of certain doctrinal formulations. Nevertheless, the assumption was that if theologians discovered a significant difficulty with a doctrinal formulation, presuming it had not been proposed infallibly, they were to bring the difficulty to the attention of their bishop in private and to refrain from any public speech or writing that was contrary to received church teaching. In his 1950 encyclical *Humani Generis*, Pope Pius XII taught that "if the Supreme Pontiffs in their official documents purposely pass judgment on a matter up to that time under dispute, it is obvious that that matter, according to the mind and will of the Pontiffs, cannot be any longer considered a question open to discussion among theologians."[1]

In sum, the basic dynamic of the magisterium–theologian relationship moved uni-directionally from the pope and bishops to the theologians and, through their explication of magisterial teaching, to the people of God (see figure below).

Preconciliar View of the Magisterium–Theologian–Sense of the Faithful Relationship

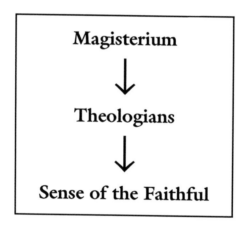

Even prior to the opening of Vatican II, important elements of this conception of the magisterium–theologian relationship were beginning to be questioned. New developments in the theology of revelation challenged the somewhat simplistic conception of the transmission of church teaching as the handing on of a collection of individual truths. Moreover, there did not seem to be a sufficient acknowledgment of the role

---

[1] Pope Pius XII, *Humani Generis* (1950), art. 20. This document may be accessed online at: http://w2.vatican.va/content/pius-xii/en/encyclicals/documents /hf_p-xii_enc_12081950_humani-generis.html.

of the Holy Spirit in the life of the whole church. The dominant conception of the church itself was excessively pyramidal and consequently was prone to conceive of revelation as "trickling down" from the hierarchy, through the theologians to the laity.

VATICAN II'S NEW FRAMEWORK FOR CONSIDERING THE MAGISTERIUM–THEOLOGIAN–SENSE OF THE FAITHFUL RELATIONSHIP

The inadequacies of this understanding of the magisterium–theologian relationship were brought to light, at least indirectly, in the teaching of Vatican II. In some ways, this relationship was changed in the very conduct of the council, as bishops and theologians worked side by side in the crafting of key texts. The council presented divine revelation as the living Word of God communicated in its fullness by the power of the Holy Spirit in the person of Jesus Christ. This Word was addressed not exclusively to St. Peter and the apostles or to the pope and bishops but to the whole church and, indeed, to all humankind. The magisterium was to be a servant to this Word as its authoritative interpreter. In this regard, the vocation of bishops and theologians shared a common foundation, service to the Word of God.

At the council the bishops envisioned a church wholly animated by the Spirit, a recipient of both "hierarchic and charismatic" gifts. The introduction of the biblical concept of "charism" opened up the possibility that theologians might exercise their work, not by way of delegation, but by the direct exercise of a theological charism vital to the building up of the church in faith. Finally, the council's teaching that the church did not have all truth as its possession but rather moved toward the "fullness of truth" suggested a prominent role for theologians in the ecclesial work of reflection and discovery as the church journeyed toward the "fullness of truth."

The council did not reflect explicitly on the role of the theologian in any depth. Nevertheless, several passages are worth considering. The bishops insisted that the work of biblical exegesis and theology must be done under the guidance of the magisterium:

> Catholic exegetes . . . and other students of sacred theology, working diligently together and using appropriate means, should devote their energies, under the watchful care of the sacred teaching office of the Church, to an exploration and exposition of the divine writings. (DV 23)

They reiterated that it was the responsibility of theologians to interpret and explicate church teaching faithfully. These tasks did not, however, exhaust the work of theologians. Theologians must also consider new questions:

> Recent research and discoveries in the sciences, in history and philosophy bring up new problems which have an important bearing on life itself and demand new scrutiny by theologians. Furthermore, theologians are now being asked, within the methods and limits of theological science, to develop more efficient ways of communicating doctrine to the people of today. (GS 64)

Though the council texts did not develop this, the work of the theologian was presented as a mediation between insights gained from a study of the contemporary situation and the ongoing reinterpretation of the received church tradition. The bishops encouraged theologians to explore unresolved doctrinal questions (LG 54) and reminded them of the importance of keeping in mind the ecumenical dimensions of their work (UR 10).

Although not dealing explicitly with the vocation of the theologian, one of the most significant contributions of the council was its treatment of the prophetic office of the church. As we saw in the last chapter, the council borrowed from the work of Yves Congar, adopting the scheme of the three offices of Christ (priest, prophet, and king) and the functions that correlate to them (sanctifying, teaching, governing) as a framework for reflecting on the life and mission of the church. Of particular interest is the claim that all the baptized participate in the prophetic office of the church. This represented a shift away from the assumption that the prophetic office of the church and the teaching ministry of the magisterium were one and the same ecclesial reality. Vatican II explicitly expanded its understanding of the prophetic office, affirming that all the baptized share as well in that prophetic office. In its treatment of the exercise of their *sensus fidei* the council also nodded to the necessary contributions of theologians. *Dei Verbum* taught that tradition grows and develops by "the spiritual experience" of believers, their "contemplation and study," and the preaching and teaching of the bishops (DV 8). The reference to "study" here was added explicitly in reference to the contributions of theology.

Ormond Rush has offered a compelling systematic treatment of the council's teaching on the prophetic office of the church. Implicit in the council's teaching, he contends, is the assumption that there are in fact three complementary authorities active within the one prophetic teaching office of the church: the magisterium, the work of theologians, and the *sensus fidelium*.[2] We shall return to the interrelationship between these three authorities below.

Postconciliar Reflection

In the years after the close of Vatican II, the International Theological Commission (ITC), newly created by Pope Paul VI, explored in a much more systematic manner many of the themes tentatively touched on in the council. In 1975, they issued a document titled *Theses on the Relationship between the Ecclesiastical Magisterium and Theology*,[3] which sought to apply the teachings of the council specifically to the question of the proper relationship between the magisterium and theologians. The ITC presented the work of theologians as a two-way mediation between the magisterium and the people of God.[4] With reference to the magisterium, the theological community tries to ensure that the authoritative teaching of the church is communicated as clearly and effectively as possible. With respect to the people of God, the theological community discerns the unique insights of all the baptized and provides them with a more systematic theological articulation. What was most striking about this document was the way the commission further developed the council's tentative shift from the descending, preconciliar model of the magisterium–theologian–people of God relationship. The document offered in its place a much more cooperative and dialogical view of the relationship between the theologians and the bishops.

Since the publication of the ITC document, two other ecclesiastical documents have appeared that address the relationship between the theological community and the magisterium. In 1989 the American

---

[2] Ormond Rush, "The Prophetic Office in the Church: Pneumatological Perspectives on the *Sensus Fidelium*-Theology-Magisterium Relationship," in *When the Magisterium Intervenes: The Magisterium and Theologians in Today's Church*, ed. Richard R. Gaillardetz (Collegeville, MN: Liturgical Press, 2012), 89–112. See also *The Eyes of Faith: The Sense of the Faithful and the Church's Reception of Revelation* (Washington, DC: Catholic University of America Press, 2009), 175–214.

[3] The English translation of this document can be found in *Readings in Moral Theology*, vol. 3, ed. Charles E. Curran and Richard A. McCormick (New York: Paulist Press, 1982), 151–70.

[4] For an analysis of this document, see Francis A. Sullivan, *Magisterium: Teaching Authority in the Catholic Church* (New York: Paulist Press, 1983), 192–93.

bishops, in collaboration with the Catholic Theological Society of America and the Canon Law Society of America, promulgated *Doctrinal Responsibilities: Approaches to Promoting Cooperation and Resolving Misunderstandings between Bishops and Theologians.*[5] This document drew heavily on the earlier ITC document as it sought to provide guidelines for resolving disputes between the bishops and theologians. Although the document was widely praised, since its promulgation its guidelines have never actually been employed to resolve a dispute between a bishop or bishops and a theologian.

In 1990, the CDF issued its own document, "Instruction on the Ecclesial Vocation of the Theologian."[6] The document offered some helpful considerations but overall was dominated by a defensive tone that emphasized the prerogatives of the magisterium and the need for theologians to simply conform their work entirely in accord with official church teaching.

Though they are not equally successful in this regard, all three documents do share, to a certain extent, the new ecclesiological foundation established by Vatican II. The CDF describes the role of the theologian in this way:

> His role is to pursue in a particular way an ever deeper understanding of the word of God found in the inspired Scriptures and handed on by the living tradition of the church. He does this in communion with the magisterium, which has been charged with the responsibility of preserving the deposit of faith.[7]

The theological community seeks this "deeper understanding" of God's Word by employing the appropriate scholarly tools along two axes. The first axis is historical and entails critical reflection on the key elements within the great tradition (e.g., the Scriptures, doctrinal statements, theological treatises, ritual actions and symbols). The proper application of the scientific tools for historical study will be critical to the successful retrieval of the apostolic faith as it is encountered in its many and diverse

---

[5] NCCB, *Doctrinal Responsibilities: Approaches to Promoting Cooperation and Resolving Misunderstandings between Bishops and Theologians* (Washington, DC: USCC, 1989).

[6] Congregation for the Doctrine of the Faith, "Instruction on the Ecclesial Vocation of the Theologian," *Origins* 20 (July 5, 1990): 117–26.

[7] Ibid., art. 6.

historical expressions. At this point specialists in biblical and historical studies will have a particularly important contribution to make.

The second axis considers the diverse testimonies of communities of faith at the present moment, each striving to address the pressing concerns and insights of their particular communities. Theologians must be in critical conversation with these communities, assisting them in interpreting the signs of the times and helping to discover the unique insights that these communities offer regarding the Christian faith in the present moment. Among its many tasks and responsibilities, theology must help facilitate a critical conversation between the historical expressions of the Christian faith and the new insights and questions of the people of God today. Avery Dulles articulated well the distinctive role of the theologian vis-à-vis the magisterium:

> The theologian . . . cannot be rightly regarded as a mere agent of the hierarchical teaching authority. His task is not simply to repeat what the official magisterium has already said, or even to expound and defend what has already become official teaching, but even more importantly, to discover what has not yet been taught. . . . The theologian . . . is concerned with reflectively analyzing the present situation of the church and of the faith, with a view to deepening the Church's understanding of revelation and in this way opening up new and fruitful channels of pastoral initiative. To be faithful to his vocation, the theologian often has to wrestle with unanswered questions and to construct tentative working hypotheses which he submits to the criticism of his colleagues.[8]

Theology is, at its best, always a fragile enterprise. It moves forward tentatively, often exploring certain questions while leaving others behind. As Cardinal Newman once noted, truth "is the daughter of time."[9] The temptation to rush to doctrinal judgment with every new theological exploration forgets Newman's important insight: divine truth emerges only slowly, patiently, and always with a certain tentativeness. The work of theology is akin to the ministrations of a midwife; it is the work of theology to assist patiently in the birthing of God's Word in our time. By contrast, the rush to doctrinal judgment is not unlike the frantic father wishing to hasten the birthing process even if it places mother and child at risk.

---

[8] Avery Dulles, *The Survival of Dogma* (New York: Crossroad, 1982), 98, 101.
[9] John Henry Newman, *An Essay on the Development of Christian Doctrine*, 6th ed. (Notre Dame, IN: University of Notre Dame Press, 1989), 47.

The three postconciliar documents also affirmed, again in differing degrees, the critical dimension of the theological enterprise. The International Theological Commission wrote:

> [T]he theologian's task of interpreting the statements of the past and present magisterium, of putting them into the context of the whole of revealed truth, and of seeking a better understanding of them with the aid of the science of hermeneutics, brings with it a function that is in some sense critical. This criticism, of course, must be of the positive, not the destructive kind.[10]

It is the recognition of this critical task, more than anything else, that differentiates this view of the theological vocation from that dominant immediately before Vatican II. Constructive theological criticism need not be a sign of disloyalty but a genuine service to the church.[11]

Finally, we should note that all three documents situate the ministries of both the magisterium and the theological community within the larger context of the people of God.[12] The Word of God is the private possession of neither the magisterium nor the theologians but resides in the whole church. Cardinal Ratzinger, in his commentary on the CDF instruction, drew attention to this fact:

> Looking at the articulation of the document, one is almost struck by the fact that we have not introduced it by speaking first about the magisterium, but rather about the topic of truth as a gift from God to his people. The truth of faith is not given to isolated individuals; rather through it God wanted to give life to a history and to a people. The truth is located in the communitarian subject of the People of God.[13]

Ratzinger sees in the CDF instruction a shift from a " 'magisterium-theology' dualism" to a "triangular relationship: the People of God, as the bearer of the sense of faith and as the place common to all in the ensemble of faith, Magisterium and theology."[14] This triangular relationship (see figure below) better reflects the proper role of the community of theologians in the process of ecclesial reception.

---

[10] *Theses*, 8.2. See also CDF, "Instruction on the Ecclesial Vocation of the Theologian," art. 9; NCCB, *Doctrinal Responsibilities*, 7.

[11] CDF, "Instruction on the Ecclesial Vocation of the Theologian," art. 30.

[12] See *Theses*, 2 and 3; CDF "Instruction on the Ecclesial Vocation of the Theologian," arts. 4 and 5; NCCB, *Doctrinal Responsibilities*, 3.

[13] Cardinal Joseph Ratzinger, "Theology Is not Private Idea of Theologian," *L'Osservatore Romano* 27, English ed. (July 2, 1990): 5.

[14] Ibid.

DIALOGICAL MODEL OF
MAGISTERIUM–THEOLOGIAN–SENSE
OF THE FAITHFUL RELATIONSHIP

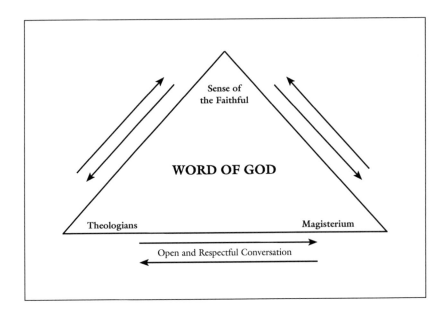

This diagram conforms well to Rush's assertion that there are three authorities within the one prophetic office of the church. According to him, each authority draws from diverse sources. The proper authority of the *sensus fidelium* is grounded in baptism and the supernatural instinct for the faith (*sensus fidei*) offered to each believer and the believing community by the Holy Spirit. The theologian's authority presupposes her own exercise of the *sensus fidei* but draws additionally on both academic competency and a charism for theological reflection. The teaching authority of the bishops draws on both the exercise of the *sensus fidei* and the charism for pastoral leadership that presumably led to his episcopal ordination. That ordination, in turn, provides the special grace of the sacrament that can assist the bishop in his distinctive responsibility to preserve the integrity of the apostolic faith. Each of these authorities has a role to play in the exercise of the church's prophetic office and no one authority can properly fulfill its responsibilities apart from the others.

DEALING WITH CONFLICTS

The ministry of theologians shares with the ministry of the bishops a common commitment to the Word of God, but the principal responsibility of the bishops is to safeguard the integrity of the apostolic faith. This means that the magisterium is, by definition, conservative. I do not use the word "conservative" here in its ideological sense (conservative as opposed to liberal) but in its most fundamental meaning. As Francis Sullivan has observed, "Its [the magisterium's] primary function is not to penetrate into the depths of the mysteries of faith (the task of theology) but rather to safeguard the priceless treasure of the word of God and to defend the purity of the faith of the Christian community."[15]

The work of the theological community is, by its nature, more tentative and experimental than that of the bishops. It is oriented toward deepening the church's apprehension and assimilation of that faith. Frequently, when a theologian publishes a work, the assumption is not that she is offering the final word on a topic but that she is offering an approach or insight to the theological community for its assessment. Anyone who has attended a serious theological conference knows that the community of theologians takes this responsibility very seriously. Major theological contributions are invariably subject to intense academic scrutiny. The best theologians welcome the critical conversation that ensues on publication of their views, for they view each publication not as a definitive pronouncement but as the contribution toward a larger work in progress. Those who argue that the magisterium has an obligation to take an aggressive, interventionist stance in policing the work of theologians overlook the effective way in which the theological community assesses its own productions.

Frequently, when a theologian makes a new contribution to her field, the critical give and take among her fellow scholars revolves around the fruitfulness of the particular line of inquiry taken in the work. Scholars might criticize the interpretation of historical data or the methodology employed. Occasionally theologians will find it necessary to make their own judgments regarding the coherence of a particular theological work with the received teaching of the church. They do so with the humble recognition that all theological reflection falls short in some decisive way before the incomprehensible mystery of God.

---

[15] Francis A. Sullivan, "Magisterium," in *Dictionary of Fundamental Theology*, ed. René Latourelle and Rino Fisichella (New York: Crossroad, 1994), 616.

Even granting the work that theologians do to assess their colleagues' work, Catholic teaching holds that the pope and bishops bear ultimate responsibility for determining whether a theological work is congruent with the received teaching of the church. But how ought that judgment be exercised?

History suggests that the most effective exercise of doctrinal judgment must be undertaken judiciously and with great prudence. Some of the saddest episodes in the history of the church have occurred when overzealous holders of church office entered into premature and/or ill-informed judgment of a theologian's work. Consequently, one of the most significant exercises of doctrinal judgment by the magisterium may be the *refusal* to offer a doctrinal judgment at all! As we have already seen, in the sixteenth and seventeenth centuries there was a notorious dispute between the Jesuits and the Dominicans regarding the relationship between divine initiative and human freedom. After considerable theological debate and a series of ecclesiastical investigations, Pope Paul V's exercise of doctrinal judgment consisted in prohibiting either side from condemning the views of the other! This papal act implicitly acknowledged the difficult and speculative theological issues being considered and the need for theologians to have some freedom in probing the mysterious interplay of divine initiative and human freedom. Of course, formal condemnations are occasionally necessary, but they ought to be the instrument of last resort in the fulfillment of the magisterium's unique responsibility for safeguarding the faith.

One sometimes hears the complaint that Catholic theologians today present themselves as a "competing magisterium" to that of the college of bishops. This appears to be something of a straw man that has gained credence more by its widespread repetition than by any objective analysis of the situation in the church today. There are few if any Catholic theologians who hold that they possess the same authority as that of the college of bishops. The vast majority of Catholic theologians recognize the unique role the bishops play in the life of the church. They acknowledge a legitimate accountability to the ecclesiastical magisterium even as they may disagree with the concrete manner in which ecclesiastical oversight, in particular instances, is exercised. Indeed, one could argue that if there is an alternative magisterium at play in our church today, it is evident on countless right-wing "Catholic" websites that have usurped the role of the bishops as self-appointed watchdogs for the orthodoxy of the faith.

The dangers posed by "dissenting" theologians appear to be much exaggerated. Credentialed Catholic theologians are readily identified and, to the extent that they speak in public or publish their views, are easily held accountable for their fidelity to the great tradition of the church. If a particular theologian proposes a position clearly at variance with church teaching, the appropriate church authority may find it opportune to make a straightforward statement to the effect that position *x* proposed by theologian *y* does not, at present, represent the accepted teaching of the church. This it does in order to assist those who, lacking scholarly expertise, might be misled regarding the status of a given theological perspective. It is quite another thing, however, to brand a scholar indiscriminately as a "dissenting theologian." A theologian might, in the course of her work, offer a viewpoint that in the judgment of the magisterium is not in accord with church teaching. That hardly means that everything that theologian writes or says must be held suspect. It goes without saying that in a Christian community committed to the principles of justice and charity, rigorous standards of due process and the determination to read a theologian's work in the best possible light will govern any necessary doctrinal investigation.

In this volume, the question of authority has been consistently situated within a theological vision of the church as a spiritual communion and a school of Christian discipleship bound together by a common faith and a common love of God that sends us forth in mission. A church that dares to call itself a community of disciples of Jesus of Nazareth must make charitable and respectful dialogue and a willingness to both give and receive fraternal correction the hallmarks of its communal existence.

DISPUTED QUESTIONS

(1) In the decades since the council, important questions have been raised in the church today regarding the role of dissent in the work of the theologian. The CDF document "Instruction on the Ecclesial Vocation of the Theologian" allowed for the possibility that a theologian might not be able to give an internal assent to an authoritative teaching of the magisterium. It assumed, however, that in such cases the theologian must communicate his or her concerns

to the appropriate church authorities and then, if necessary, "suffer in silence." The CDF condemned the practice of "public dissent." If theologians were allowed to dissent publicly from church teaching, they would undermine the authority of the magisterium and cause confusion among the faithful regarding the reliability of church teaching.

Many consider this blanket rejection of public dissent inadequate. First, there is the question of what constitutes public dissent. Is the publication of a scholarly article critical of an authoritative teaching of the church "public dissent" or does "public dissent" mean organized and antagonistic resistance to the magisterium? The CDF appeared to have had in mind the latter more than the former, but it was not as clear on this question as one would like. More important, if one recognizes that there is a possibility of error, however remote, in the exercise of the ordinary magisterium, then might not the respectful "public dissent" of theologians be an instrument of the Spirit for necessary change?

(2) In 2001, at the urging of the Vatican, the American bishops passed juridical norms for the implementation of Pope John Paul II's *Ex Corde Ecclesiae*, an apostolic constitution on Catholic higher education. Those norms required that Catholic theologians teaching the "sacred sciences" at a Catholic institution must request a *mandatum* from their local bishop declaring that they teach Catholic doctrine as the authoritative position of the church. This requirement has been a matter of no small controversy. Defenders of this policy see it as nothing more than "truth in advertising." Students and parents of students have a right to know whether faculty members at a Catholic institution are teaching the official doctrine of the Catholic Church. The *mandatum* does not impinge on academic freedom; it merely ensures that Catholic theologians will not teach speculative opinions as the official teaching of the church.

Critics of this policy see it as a return to the kind of ecclesiastical McCarthyism that followed the condemnations of modernism at the beginning of the twentieth century. They fear that the procedures for granting or withholding the *mandatum* will not be conducted uniformly and that what constitutes "full communion" with the church will be interpreted quite differently from bishop to bishop. Many fear that the decision not to seek a *mandatum* may unfairly brand some theologians as heterodox.

(3) In chapter 9, during our discussion of the four categories of church teaching, we considered within the fourth category prudential admonitions offered by the magisterium regarding the work of some theologians. Such a "prudential admonition" appeared in 2011 when the USCCB Committee on Doctrine issued a notification on a book by the noted theologian Elizabeth Johnson, *Quest for the Living God.* Their notification warned of doctrinal deficiencies in the book.[16] Most theologians agree that offering such notifications is a legitimate exercise of the bishops' teaching ministry. Indeed, the committee justified their actions by noting the popularity of Prof. Johnson's book and expressed a concern that its doctrinal deficiencies might "confuse the faithful."

Nevertheless, the notification created some controversy as several professional Catholic theological societies protested what they saw as a lack of due process granted to Prof. Johnson. Beyond this there was a more pressing question. Although it certainly belongs to the duties of the bishops to preserve the integrity of the faith by ensuring theology's congruence with fundamental church doctrine, this is not the same as assessing the helpfulness or even adequacy of certain theological trajectories or schools of thought. The issue here is the proper scope of these kinds of magisterial prudential admonitions. Perhaps an analogy will help.

In the midst of this controversy, the chairperson for the USCCB Committee on Doctrine, Cardinal Donald Wuerl, proposed that the committee, in offering its notification regarding Prof. Johnson's book, served a role not unlike an umpire or referee in sports. The umpire or referee is charged with ensuring the players play by the rules. The analogy presumes a distinction between doctrine (the rules of the game) and theology (the game itself) and establishes the fundamentally different responsibilities of the bishops (umpires in this analogy) and the theologians (the players). This analogy may illuminate a controverted feature of the dispute in the Johnson case. Consider the respective roles of umpires and players in the game of baseball. Imagine that a batter has decided to lay down a bunt at a crucial point in the game. An umpire can legitimately rule whether,

---

[16] For the full documentation and commentary on this case, see Richard R. Gaillardetz, ed., *When the Magisterium Intervenes: The Magisterium and Theologians in Today's Church* (Collegeville, MN: Liturgical Press, 2012).

in the process of laying down the bunt, the batter prematurely stepped out of the batter's box (a violation of the rules), but he cannot challenge the batter's decision to bunt in that situation. The batter's decision can be legitimately challenged by his teammates, coaches, and even fans, but such criticism is *not* the prerogative of the umpire. In the Johnson case, some might argue that many of the committee's "prudential admonitions" were really nothing more than negative judgments of Johnson's theological treatment of topics like the meaning of divine impassibility and, consequently, were more akin to debates regarding the decision to lay down a bunt rather than a ruling on whether a bunt was legal.

FOR FURTHER READING

Boyle, John P. *Church Teaching Authority: Historical and Theological Studies*, 142–60, 171–75. Notre Dame, IN: University of Notre Dame Press, 1995.

Congregation for the Doctrine of the Faith. "Instruction on the Ecclesial Vocation of the Theologian." *Origins* 20 (July 5, 1990): 117–26.

Dulles, Avery. *Magisterium: Teacher and Guardian of the Faith*. Naples, FL: Ave Maria Press, 2007.

———. "The Two Magisteria: An Interim Reflection." *Catholic Theological Society of America Proceedings* 34 (1980): 155–69.

Figueiredo, Anthony J. *The Magisterium–Theology Relationship: Contemporary Theological Conceptions in the Light of Universal Church Teaching Since 1835 and the Pronouncements of the Bishops of the United States*. Rome: Gregorian, 2001.

Gaillardetz, Richard R., ed. *When the Magisterium Intervenes: The Magisterium and Theologians in Today's Church*. Collegeville, MN: Liturgical Press, 2012.

International Theological Commission. "Theses on the Relationship between the Ecclesiastical Magisterium and Theology." In *Readings in Moral Theology*. Vol. 3. Edited by Charles E. Curran and Richard A. McCormick, 151–70. New York: Paulist Press, 1982.

Komonchak, Joseph. "The Magisterium and Theologians." *Chicago Studies* 29 (November 1990): 307–29.

National Conference of Catholic Bishops. *Doctrinal Responsibilities: Approaches to Promoting Cooperation and Resolving Misunderstandings between Bishops and Theologians.* Washington, DC: USCC, 1989.

Sullivan, Francis A. "The Theologian's Ecclesial Vocation and the 1990 CDF Instruction." *Theological Studies* 52 (1991): 51–68.

EPILOGUE

Several themes have run throughout this volume. The first is a theology of revelation that is personalist and trinitarian and that sees the whole church as the recipient of God's revelatory self-gift in Jesus Christ by the power of the Holy Spirit. Although that revelation can and must be articulated in the form of propositional truth claims, it cannot be reduced to that. Throughout the volume, we have worked to maintain the delicate balanced involved in affirming that the whole church is both the recipient of this gift of revelation and the instrument through which the divine self-gift can continue to be made known to humankind. A second theme is closely related as it involves the recovery of a robust pneumatology essential for an adequate consideration of the role of power and authority in the life of the church. A third theme emphasizes the plurality of authorities in the church and the need to support an ecclesiology that allows for their dynamic interplay. A fourth and final theme, perhaps less obvious, is that church authority is only intelligible within a community that holds to the belief that ultimate authority lies in God alone. The authentic exercise of authority within the community of faith depends on this vital conviction that God is the only ultimate spiritual authority in our lives and that all other "church authorities" are only limited mediations of divine authority. Words like "inerrancy" and "infallibility," while having a proper meaning and place in the Catholic Christian community, can mislead when they are used to absolutize some created authority, whether it is the Bible or the pope.

As Catholic Christians, we acknowledge the authority of the Bible, the pope, and the many other authorities in the church, fully aware that they share in a limited and imperfect though altogether necessary way in the authority of God. We know that our present historical existence calls us to engage these many authorities, attentive to their inevitable inadequacies and even dysfunctions. We live in a world in which the Author of our lives comes to us in often unexpected ways and through broken ecclesial vessels of one kind or another. We might wish that it were otherwise. We might long to get divine truth straight from the horse's mouth, as it were. We might wistfully imagine a Bible where the fingerprints of flawed human authors were not so apparent. We might pine for church leaders who were always wise, prophetic, and comforting, all at the same time. We might expect that baptized followers of Christ would imitate him a bit more closely. For that matter, we might wish that salvation had come in some other way than through an unlettered craftsman who never traveled more than a hundred miles from his obscure hometown and ended his grand movement executed on a cross. We might wish for these things. But we will cling nevertheless to modest, human instruments of divine authority, because, though flawed, we recognize in them a precious and necessary connection to the one true Author of our lives.

INDEX